A HOME FOR ALL SEASONS

GAVIN PLUMLEY is a cultural historian. He appears frequently on BBC radio, has written for newspapers and magazines worldwide and gives talks at leading museums and galleries. He grew up in Wales, before moving to London, and studied music at Keble College, Oxford. He lives in Herefordshire.

A HOME FOR ALL SEASONS

GAVIN PLUMLEY

Atlantic Books
London

First published in Great Britain in 2022 by Atlantic Books,
an imprint of Atlantic Books Ltd.

This paperback edition first published in Great Britain in 2023 by
Atlantic Books, an imprint of Atlantic Books Ltd.

5   7   9   10   8   6   4

A CIP catalogue record for this book
is available from the British Library.

Paperback ISBN: 978 1 83895 480 2
E-book ISBN: 978 1 83895 479 6

Printed and bound by CPI Group (UK) Ltd, Croydon, CR0 4YY

Atlantic Books
An imprint of Atlantic Books Ltd
Ormond House
26–27 Boswell Street
London
WC1N 3JZ

www.atlantic-books.co.uk

to Alastair and Toby, my home

Often I had gone this way before:
But now it seemed I never could be
And never had been anywhere else;
'Twas home; one nationality
We had, I and the birds that sang,
One memory.

Edward Thomas

Contents

Prelude — Linenfold

THEY'RE THE FIRST THING I see in the morning. Waking on my side, I immediately notice the dark outlines of the wood. They stand against sagey green walls in the weak light of daybreak, with a deadened gleam, buffed by time. I'm snug under the duvet, though there's a bite in the bedroom air; last night, we had to close the windows for the first time in months. Beside me, behind me, my husband Alastair sleeps on – he's never been a morning person. His feet are warm against my legs and his hand is under the edge of my pillow. The mild rush of his breathing is the only sound in the room, though outside there is the gravelly caw of a crow.

Reaching out to the bedside chair for my glasses, I can see more, though I know the view well enough. It's dominated by a pair of wooden panels. I bought four in total, all taken from the same house – not our house, sadly – and sold to me at an antique shop close to home. I couldn't resist them. I can never resist the opportunity to touch a part of history and enjoy that moment when something so distant becomes so tangible and mine. I wish I weren't quite as greedy, as acquisitive and, once acquired, as possessive, but it's part of trying to make what I read and discover more real.

'They're local,' the shop owner told me. 'They were taken from a large farmhouse near the border. Charming, aren't they?'

I nodded in agreement and took out my credit card. I already knew where the four panels would hang: two upstairs, in our bedroom; and two where our friends and family sleep when they come to stay. They fitted perfectly into the spaces on the wall I'd chosen, though they were never intended for such a lowly house as ours, even if they are from the same period: the last decades of the tempestuous 16th century.

The panels are symmetrical, more or less. They were designed to hang side by side, placed within a framework to fill the walls of a room. As well as providing insulation, the purpose was protective and decorative, concealing wattle and daub or rendered stone, though the panels themselves are anything but robust. The style is called linenfold and was pretty ubiquitous in affluent houses at the end of the 1500s – and those that wanted to emulate them – not only in England but also throughout northern parts of mainland Europe. The Flemish were particularly good at it and created meticulous examples. The French and English followed suit, though the craftsman in question in our bedroom proved slightly less assured than some of his continental counterparts or the examples you find in National Trust houses, castles and the V&A. In our much more modest home on the edge of England, they nonetheless look ravishing. I love waking up to them at the start of the day.

Normally, I then turn to give Alastair a kiss, but not enough to wake him, before rolling back to my side of the bed to put on my slippers – essential in a house with floorboards and flagstones. I make my way downstairs to the kitchen, put the kettle on the gas hob to boil and take our bounding working cocker spaniel Toby out into the garden for a pee. His morning constitutional done among the fallen fruit at the bottom of the apple trees, Toby trots back to the house to wolf down his breakfast of kibble and a little bit of canned tuna, before leaping up the stairs to join Daddy Alastair in bed. I follow with the tea – Earl Grey for me and robust English Breakfast for him – placing my mug next to a jar of asters. Outside, the church bells ring the hour, as they've done for centuries, from the days of fervent Catholicism to those of fading Anglicanism. The eighth stroke sounds and I return to bed, with every intention of reading, but, again, I'm drawn to the panels on the wall.

3

Each piece is about two feet long, ten inches wide. The symmetrical design fans out from the middle. Carved from oak, it gives the impression of something much lighter, much more malleable, hence the name: linenfold. And it is as if a beautifully creased piece of linen has been placed on top of the wood and somehow changed its nature. After the first pleat in the equal, mirrored design, the material folds back on itself, only to rise to another crease and then give way to a rolled flourish. It would take me hours to iron such a pattern into a napkin, let alone carve it into English oak.

If I take the panels off the wall, they are as light as air, fit to break down the pleats like an Elizabethan KitKat. Over time, four centuries and a bit, the wood has become thinner and cracked in a few places, even fraying at the edge like fabric. A bit of masking tape has been stuck down the back of the one on the left to make sure it doesn't snap, while the corner of the one on the right is fixed to the wall with Blu Tack.

Yet for all the lie of the panels' features, there is a detail in the centre of one of them that gives the carver's hand away: it's just above a cruciform pattern cut into the design, one at the top of the central fold and one at the bottom. Looking closer, I can see for the first time that the carpenter didn't have quite as steady a hand as he might — perhaps, like me, he'd enjoyed too much wine the night before. There's a slip, but it's also a glorious mark of the object's humanity. Certainly, no machine would have made such a mistake. Though no machine could have created such delicacy either.

There's absolutely nothing industrialized about the view

from my pillow — well, apart from a radiator, and an Anglepoise lamp that makes bedtime reading easier. Around the two noble if somewhat imperfect panels are the marks of other pasts, some linked, some contrary. Instead of a polished oak frame, the linen-fold pieces hang on a cracked, bulbous wall between the joists of a rougher timber structure. A leaded light, with its view over to the 13th-century belfry and 14th-century church, is hidden behind linen curtains, which we bought at one of our favourite local shops. They feature a pattern that also looks back to the Elizabethans via William Morris. There's a Victorian elm chair too, two brass candlesticks from my maternal grandfather's farm-house, a glass carafe etched with stars and a matching drinking glass that rattles in the night, as well as a few thumbed books. Among them is a paperback of Virginia Woolf's *Orlando* and a heavy catalogue of Bruegel paintings from Vienna that's really awkward to read in bed, as well as various weekend supplements that will soon be used to light fires.

I love this bedroom and have always slept well here, which is not something I can rely upon. I've relished collecting the things within it, adding to them over time. And although many of the items reveal layers in which I had, and could have had, no place, I am afforded a quiet and belated opportunity to hold their histories in my hands.

It's like the house itself, placed on the edge of an ancient churchyard in an ancient market town in one of the remotest corners of England: the house at the heart of my story. Here, I encounter villagers past and present, as well as centuries of over-lapping seasons and traditions, to which we, Alastair and I, are adding our own. And all of them are reflected in poetry, prayers and paintings which deepen my attachment to the past, its customs, its objects and its characters, whether they're as aristocratic as Orlando or as rustic as a Bruegel.

I.

Never a Native

BEING A GAY HISTORIAN is a paradoxical experience. Dealing with periods long gone, I always feel an incurable sense of homelessness, an exile from the place and time I'm investigating – and daring to call my own. Because it's not my own, never was and never can be. It's not just a matter of seasons having slipped away, but also because almost every age brings the realization that I – or my equivalent – would have had only a limited role within it, lacking identity or agency. Yet the past, L. P. Hartley's 'foreign country', remains such a beguiling thing.

The obsession began in childhood. Most weekends, my parents would wield our family National Trust card and take my brother and me off in the Austin Montego to discover a new house, a new group of occupants, a new period in time. We even had passports and collected stamps at every property we visited. And there were the guidebooks too, to be pored over once we'd returned home, not least during the winter months, when the houses in question were shuttered, the tea rooms closed. As a result, I developed insufferably precocious levels of discernment. I knew good Chinese Chippendale when I saw it and would be able to note when a house's painting collection wasn't quite up to snuff. I delighted in the vestiges of past eras: the soda syphons, the bell pulls, the butter moulds. A budding musician,

I also managed to wangle my way into playing the pianos of various grand houses when the lids weren't locked, doubtless to the annoyance of other visitors. Generally, however, my interest was piqued by earlier (pre-piano) properties, with their moats and drawbridges and priest's holes: places with fantastical names like Baddesley Clinton and Ightham Mote.

As a blissful childhood gave way to the horrors of a dank, rugby-obsessed boarding school on the Welsh border — it was my choice to go, not my parents', before you blame them — I was forced to realize *just* how hard it was to find complements to the person I was becoming. Reading novels, watching costume dramas stolen from the English department or dutifully recorded by my parents at home, I at least found some paths of escape to supplement the National Trust trips. Similarly, my searches for the locations in which the tales of the Bennet sisters and the Honeychurch family had been filmed allowed me to indulge in other dreams, including finding my own Will Ladislaw or a suitably secluded boathouse.

I had been born with nostalgia in my veins. The ailment began as an acute case, but soon turned chronic. And it really is a kind of disease. I suffered, and continue to do so, from a strain that the late Svetlana Boym called reflective nostalgia, the primary symptoms of which are collecting and hoarding. Those who experience the illness know its other signs too, particularly of yearning for times gone by — 'a precious moment gone and we not there'. One of the healthier symptoms is self-awareness. After all, fellow reflectives and I don't suffer from that much more serious — and increasingly widespread — disease of restorative nostalgia, when the patient, normally a populist politician, assumes it's entirely reasonable to envisage rebuilding the past. Luckily, gay historians, knowing Edward II's death, the Wilde trial and Alan Turing's chemical castration by rote, are only ever likely to be reflectives. The gayness is key, for the nostalgic, as Svetlana Boym explains, 'is never a native but a displaced person who mediates between the local and the universal'. But it didn't stop me wanting to be a native or to find a home in that history.

Away from school and its boarding and bullying, my place was London. My mum and dad, living in the suburbs, were the warmest and kindest I could have wished for and the opportunities they gave me to explore the capital with a Travelcard during my teenage years provided exciting new chapters. I loved the thrill that London brought, not least the anonymity, as well as the layers of the city's past and the chance to learn its streets and stories. It was like a giant stately home and my innate sense of direction meant that I could traverse Westminster and the City efficiently but absorbingly – I still can. Over three decades, as curiosity gave way to knowledge and teenage dependency turned to adult freedom, as well as happiness in my own skin, I felt safe in the city's midst, drinking with friends in Soho or having a Saturday coffee at Louis in Hampstead (now sadly changed). I became thoroughly convinced I was an urban soul and no number of pretty pictures of the countryside could persuade me otherwise.

But Alastair did. At the height of my heady, hedonistic relationship with London, living in an attic room in Fulham, in a flat behind Olympia or at the top of a Victorian conversion above

Swiss Cottage, I began cheating on my first love with a defiantly rural being. He was kindness personified, with a long face and a lithe body, smiling quietly but cheekily behind his frameless specs. Inquisitive though never boastful, he perhaps seemed a little too meek for me, though the glint challenged the meekness.

We met in Yorkshire. Alastair, a countertenor, was singing in a choir that I conducted there one summer, thanks to the invitation of a mutual friend. I'll never forget the moment he walked, late, into my rehearsal. I couldn't be angry; I was smitten. But despite us both having been trained as church musicians, with a love of music stretching back to the Reformation, and both being Roman Catholics – our first proper date was among the ruins of Fountains Abbey – it was a potentially terrible match: Alastair was just about to return to a job at a leading boarding school in the East Midlands.

Leaving my own school at the age of eighteen, I had vowed never to set foot in such an institution again – the rising cost of therapy was cause enough for my decision. Yet Alastair somehow made it worthwhile, a healing in and of itself. When I had a panic attack crossing the threshold from his flat into an adjoining boarding house, he simply held my hand and promised that it would be OK. And I learned that, even in a short period of time, such institutions had largely moved on. Being gay was no longer an obstacle to being a member of the First XV; there was even a Stonewall poster on one of the noticeboards. And around the school, the flat, expansive countryside, with its spires peeking through fields, made for a surprisingly welcome escape from town.

One wet April evening, I took the familiar, and familiarly drab, journey from King's Cross to Peterborough, where Alastair was due to be waiting in his battered VW Golf. He was twenty minutes late, just like the day I met him, but I kept telling myself not to get irate, to remain calm, given that I was carrying a pair of silver cufflinks with which I was about to propose.

We arrived back at his flat and Alastair went to the kitchen. Standing just inside the bedroom door, where I'd put down my bag for the weekend, I breathed and silently rehearsed some sort of script, unsure as to whether I should kneel as tradition dictated. Finally determining to do just that, my plan was thwarted by Alastair bumping into me as I stepped onto the landing. He immediately saw the egg-blue box in my hand.

'What's that?'

'Oh, um, I was just wondering whether . . .'

But even before I could complete my sentence, Alastair was pulling at the white ribbon.

'You can't have what's inside without giving me an answer – and the right one!' I snapped, jokingly. So, I began again: 'I was just wondering whether you would like to spend the rest of your life with me.'

He was shocked at my timing, but, thankfully, said yes.

Living together full-time was going to be very different from what had effectively been a peripatetic weekend relationship. And although we were overjoyed at our news, I began to realize that anything resembling a permanent life in the countryside just wouldn't work for me – and now, as a result, for us. At the time, I was glued to a desk in an arts administration job, long before work-from-home policies had become the norm. I knew, however, that it was going to be difficult for Alastair to leave his school and the countryside, to merge with that modern trend of more of the world's population living in urban centres than outside them. But luckily – at least for him – it was only for four years, as Alastair's promotions through the ranks meant that I was then forced to abandon London.

My career had likewise altered. Instead of tending to the needs and deals of talented theatre practitioners, I had taken the decision to focus on my own artistic ambitions, to write, broadcast and give talks about aspects of history and culture that interested me most, from gin-soaked Hogarths to doom-directed Habsburgs, and various other points between. As a freelancer, I could no longer claim the need to be based in the city, whereas Alastair's career demanded new pastures, first in not-so-pastoral Bedford and then in the West Country, where he was set to become a headmaster.

Such a deeply rural location, three hours or more from London by road, and with no train station, made me nervous, despite the obvious pride I felt. And what of the natives? The only immediate bonus, as far as I could see, was that we would finally be able to put down roots and buy a house. Happily, Alastair had been given accommodation with the job, so we were in the privileged position of investing our savings exactly where we wanted them.

Together, we planned for the change and drew a large circle around Alastair's new place of work, covering two hours in each direction. Even if we had wanted to make the longer journey to

London, our budget didn't allow for anything much more than a studio, so rural it would have to be. Alastair was overjoyed, while I made one thing absolutely clear: the property needed to tap into history – my sense of nostalgia, the love of the National Trust, died hard. Devon, Dorset and the Cotswolds were all within our target area, but proved on the steep side financially and, for our taste, a little too gentrified. So we began further west, in Herefordshire, near the border with Wales, with every intention of travelling east until we found the right spot, at the right price.

SPARSELY POPULATED, essentially agrarian and almost totally lacking in motorways, Herefordshire is unashamedly sleepy, the third least populous English county after the Isle of Wight and Rutland. Post-war modernizers forgot the region almost entirely, with a position on the periphery guaranteeing its preservation. Ancient structures were left more or less intact and, as a result, to drive through Herefordshire is to encounter that history first-hand. Blink, ignore the car you're sitting in, and it could be the Middle Ages, given how little the settlements have changed. You can almost hear the stamp and bagpipes of peasants, with their white hose and scarlet tunics, accompanied by clattering empty pitchers. And it is such a beautiful county, the very picture of what 'England' is in the collective mind's eye, with villages of black-and-white houses nestled among rivers, farmland and hop gardens. As a local and suitably Falstaffian shop owner bragged, 'Civilization begins west of the A49, just don't tell anyone.'

HEREFORDSHIRE

FAIR LAND OF ENCHANTING BEAUTY

TRAVEL BY TRAIN

Two decades had passed since I'd spent any amount of time in the area. One of the few comforts of my years at school had been the ability to escape the boarding house and its bullies at the weekend. Come the longer days of spring and summer, I loved getting out into the landscape, taking my bike and crossing the Monmouthshire border into Herefordshire, 'where the sexy airs of summer, the bathing hours and the bare arms, the leisured drives through a land of farms are good to a newcomer', as another former resident, and one of my heroes, W. H. Auden, described. His relishing of Herefordshire and the entire Marches area, much as it was loved by Edward Thomas, Robert Frost and figures such as William Wordsworth, A. E. Housman and Edward Elgar, to begin an extensive list, told of the region's cultural richness, alongside its natural beauty.

Alastair and I drove over from Bedfordshire one Saturday afternoon in late winter, travelling cross-country into Buckinghamshire, Oxfordshire and Gloucestershire. We saw the bridge over Edward Thomas's famous railway at Adlestrop and passed through Stow-on-the-Wold, packed as ever with tourists and teashops, before descending Stanway Hill and working further west. As the deadest of seasons wended its own deliberate way, the countryside appeared much more bleached than I remembered from my springtime teens. But even without that chlorophyllous boost, it was impossible to deny the beauty.

The first property Alastair and I had landed upon during hours spent looking at Zoopla and Rightmove was situated in the shadow of the Black Mountains, in the south-west of Herefordshire. Perched on the side of a hill, it was an old woodman's cottage and felt romantic enough to rouse my interest. After three hours in the car, we pulled into the driveway, hopeful but quickly losing focus when we went inside. Sadly, despite the love and care the owners had taken over the house, their taste, a dogged tribute to Formica, was far from ours and the garden much too large for what would, effectively, become a bolthole.

They were confident and we tried to be as polite as possible when shown around, looking longingly at the views across the emptied fields to Hereford towards the Malverns, but as lovely as the vista was – and as even more glorious it would prove when filled with summer – the house was not for us. So we drove away, annoyed at having wasted our time and theirs, and wound through the back lanes, weary at the thought of a long search ahead.

The next property we were due to visit had languished on the market for over six months. It was hardly a recommendation, though the particulars had stuck in our minds and on our list of favourites. The main problem was that the house was situated at the edge of our two-hour circle, in the furthest corner of Herefordshire; I had thought of cancelling the viewing to make time for more practicable places. Travelling through the Golden Valley, past Arthur's Stone and over the Wye at Bredwardine, where the diary-keeping priest Francis Kilvert had once ministered, Alastair and I made our way north.

The destination was Pembridge, a village I knew by name and briefly by experience. It was where the first gay couple I'd ever met had lived. One of them still does, though sadly without his husband, the man who, as my chaplain at school, had effectively saved my education and, it's no exaggeration to say, my life. Together, John and John had turned a hamlet outside Pembridge into a haven of happiness, until a debilitating disease claimed the first of them. But despite such a sad ending, John's memory had always been a cheerful one, as were the few trips we'd made to their 16th-century timber-framed cottage, latterly in John's quiet sickness and, before that, in his raucously laughing health.

Alastair turned towards the village, dodging potholes and skidding through a half-frozen ford, as I looked again at the Pembridge house on my phone and tried to make sense of its mix of architectural styles and levels, as well as its perplexing position next to what looked like a small hotel. It was definitely a historic property, but neither the estate agent's details nor the attached pictures yielded clues.

'Is that a bedroom in the basement?' I said, waving my phone in front of the steering wheel.

'I don't know, darling. Just let me drive. It'll become clear soon,' Alastair responded, patiently.

'I hope it's not damp down there.'

'Is this us?' he ignored, wiggling by a bland village hall and a series of 1960s bungalows. I wasn't impressed. There followed some older barns and the entrance to a school, before a much more pleasing view down a gentle incline to the centre of Pembridge. We parked in the Market Square, a slightly rough gathering of

timber-framed buildings, of which two stood out. There was an open-sided Market Hall in the middle, no more than a steeply-pitched roof on eight wooden pillars, but somehow redolent of ancient status. And beyond, there was the pub, The New Inn, an imposing black-and-white structure that was sadly no longer a hotel. The whole square was well kept, though there was a dustiness about the place, the colours mute with age and woodsmoke. I felt a sense of reality rather than museum reverence.

Across the way, Stepps House, the property in question, stood three storeys tall, opposite the front door to the pub and a little gangly in the context. We'd arrived half an hour early for our appointment, which the Leominster estate agent had underlined they wouldn't normally take on a Saturday afternoon. So I'd exaggerated our situation, said we were in a terrible rush and very likely to make an offer. None of which was true.

'Pint?' Alastair asked, hoping to shield from the dank of the day.

'Pint,' I confirmed. A much better option than sitting in the car for thirty minutes. Plus, I needed to pee.

We made our way up the cobbles to the front door of The New Inn and I looked over at the house again. From this angle, the whole square somehow fitted together; everything was in proportion. Inside the pub, a couple was paying up after lunch, but otherwise, on a winter's afternoon at 2 p.m., it was, to say the least, quiet. Behind the bar was a calmly unimpressed publican, who melted with a bit of flirtation. Her colleague, a cook emerging from the kitchen behind the public rooms, was contagiously effervescent and the two went into something of a double act, asking where we had come from and where we were going.

Alastair found a seat beyond the first bar, next to a large open fire, as I asked for two pints of ale and explained that we were looking for a home and about to have a tour of Stepps House. Their faces lit up immediately.

'It's lovely inside,' the publican gleamed, handing over the first pint. 'The current owner's done such a nice job. He's spent lots of time and money on the place over the years, hasn't he, Rose?' as the other one began to chip in.

'You'd be very happy there. It's a super house and *such* a nice village, isn't it, Jane?'

'I've been here thirty-four years. Can't complain.'

'Thank you,' I responded, taking the second pint. 'Pembridge does seem nice. We like the look of the house, from what we've seen. I've just got to persuade him next door.'

'Good luck,' they said, as the conversation continued and I made my way through to what is known as the back bar to join Alastair. I sat down and he smiled, showing that he'd heard my plotting with the ladies of The New Inn, as well as registering his quiet delight. Watching a criss-cross of apple wood smoulder in the hearth, I began sipping my pint and slid further into the settle that filled the room.

'This place can't have changed for years,' Alastair remarked.

'Look at that shelf,' I giggled, pointing to a structure that would have made Escher blush.

We sat contentedly for twenty minutes; the fire hissed and the chat continued next door. By the time we finished our beers and left, waving to the ladies who owned the pub while placing our glasses on the bar, the front door of Stepps House was open, with a dour estate agent on the threshold, keys in hand.

'I've opened up. You can help yourself. Just let me know when you're done,' she said, more cheerily, but without a hello, an introduction or the offer of a tour. Instead, she sat under the Market Hall in the centre of the square.

We reached the door and took a breath, looking cautiously at each other before walking into the house. I was the first to step out of the mute sunlight, under a lowish lintel, holding the door back for Alastair. The house had a placid glow. In front of us there were stone steps, which broke at a landing. Rooms went off left and right, as well as further upstairs. The flagstones cooled the welcome, though this was countered by the afternoon light, which threw our shadows on the steps in front of us. Outside, I'd been unsure if intrigued, but inside, I knew immediately that this was a happy place.

There were quite a few rooms to take in – three bedrooms, I think. Odd choices of furniture too, including bits of Ikea and a collection of strange bespoke items. They didn't fit at all. We walked around in silence. There were exposed timbers in the sitting and dining rooms, but the age of the house was rather concealed. Other buildings in the village were in that picture-book black-and-white style, like the pub, but I couldn't place Stepps House in such a heritage, though it was surely old. In fact, the whole structure was just as difficult to piece together as it had been online. The outside space Alastair had remembered from the particulars was absolutely charming, with lots of box hedging, like a knot garden, though it was more or less empty that afternoon, bar a few serrated hellebores. And when I think back, I can't really remember any of the specifics – nor, rarely for me, did I care – I was just happy to follow an impulse. This was going to be our home.

'It's nice,' Alastair said, non-committally, moving towards the front door.

'Isn't it?' I replied, eagerly, trying to slow his retreat. Nonetheless, we made to go and thanked the estate agent for her time, as Alastair remained utterly sphinx-like. I pulled myself into the passenger seat and sat in silence, furious at how oblique he could be. He pressed the ignition, still giving absolutely nothing away. We hadn't even passed the village limits before I blurted, 'Come on, you had to feel it!'

'Feel what?'

'We're going to *have* to make an offer.'

'But the road! It'll be really annoying come the summer. We'll be sitting in the sun and the lorries will drown out our conversations.'

'The *house* is gorgeous. Perfect. *And* that garden.'

'I wanted hills.'

'There *are* hills,' I said; 'you can see them from our bedroom' – already claiming it.

'That's a lovely room,' he paused. 'But we ought to check out a few more.'

Ever cautious, never one to let his emotions run away, let alone express them. Which is why he's perfect – in many ways – and why he's so bloody annoying. Alastair had nonetheless learned over fourteen years that any resistance was futile. So, turning to look out of the window, I pouted, 'It always falls to me, the research, the enquiries. And now we see a house that is lovely and you're dithering. Yet again.' •

'I'm not dithering; I just want to be sure.'

'*I'm* sure!'

'I know you are. And,' pausing again, 'you do tend to have the right instincts about these things.'

'Stepps House will be a gorgeous place to live, to escape to, to get back to us.'

I wittered endlessly as Alastair returned to silence, a familiar tack. We were driving eastwards to the Malvern Hills and from there we would go back to Bedfordshire. Malvern would, thankfully, give us a moment of reflection. It was a favourite spot and our cocker spaniel Toby had been waiting uncomplainingly in the boot for his much-mentioned, much-delayed walk. I knew *he* would approve of the house, even if he hadn't been able to see inside. If in doubt, I could always invoke him as another way of conquering Alastair's reticence; my husband would never say no to the dog. A walk in the hills would cement the decision, I thought.

WE RETRIEVED Toby from the back of the car and, knowing the way from previous trips, he shot ahead, first climbing up Summer Hill and over towards Worcestershire Beacon. I lagged behind, as Alastair stepped past a drift of snowdrops. In time, they would give way to daffodils and bluebells and vaulting summer foxgloves. Above us, the sky grimaced with rain. Clouds were skirting where we walked, so we decided not to risk a caper to the summit. Instead, we stood on a plateau before the final pull to the top and gazed out over the county I was hoping would become ours. I'd been here before too, a dejected teenager, dreaming of the very moment when I might find a home with a man I loved.

The fading winter light was glorious. Amidst the scudding rainclouds, crepuscular rays pierced the grey, low on the horizon. The gleams picked out details with follow-spot clarity: farms and fields, and the odd grander house. The contrast between shadow and filtered sun rendered the landscape almost two-dimensional, taking on the quality of one of those interwar railway posters advocating FRESH AIR FOR HEALTH or some other such wholesome message, from a time when Elgar, Housman or Auden might have seen it too.

Elgar was a particular favourite among this crowd and he had certainly walked here, cycled as well and, in Ken Russell's 1962 documentary for the BBC, cantered over the hills on a pony. We could also see into Housman's country if we peered through a rain-streaked ray that was lighting the path to Wenlock Edge and the Long Mynd. And it was on this very 'fathom of earth' that Auden had stood 'alive in air' with an illicit beloved in the 1930s, with England (and the prep school where he taught) below him. And yet the sky looked as if it came from another time, perhaps like a Constable, the painter my mum loved best, with hibernal fog rising up in marshmallow clumps, only to plummet in a downpour of pewter. But unlike Constable's scenes of Essex, Suffolk and Salisbury, we were not in the field; we were perched high above, as in something much older, an oil or tempera on wooden panels, seen by the eyes of an ancient deity or an artist presuming such a role.

It was like those wide views that reach beyond the virgins and the virtuous of a medieval polyptych, including the Van Eyck Ghent Altarpiece that we'd seen the previous summer, with its minutely detailed cityscape of the New Jerusalem, or the so-called World Landscapes of the 16th century by Joachim Patinir, Cornelis Massys and, most famously, Pieter Bruegel the Elder. As I stood there that afternoon, the images flicked through my mind like a medieval zoetrope, with dusty villages and lusty peasants, seasonal feasts and yearly famines, as well as scenes of religious observance and fun-loving secularism, cradled within a countryside that was both fertile and fierce. With the icy Welsh winds rising to the edge on which we stood, it was thrilling to be afforded that kind of Olympian view, condensed into a single mind's eye.

'Let's do it,' Alastair said. Toby paused on the path, as if he too were surprised.

'Are you sure?'

'You're sure.'

'I am,' I said slowly, guiltily. 'But just look at it.'

'You're right. It's a beautiful place. And it is a beautiful house. Not too far from work.'

I wrapped my arms around the back of my husband, leaning my chin on his shoulder. We took it all in, bracing ourselves against the chill.

Alastair knew I had a sharper sense of direction and asked where Pembridge was within this shifting, Bruegel-like spread. But the sun's late beams and his sudden change in attitude had dulled my senses too, and as much as there are major hills *around* Herefordshire, there are few defining features in the heart of the county. Dinedor Hill, where my sister-in-law had grown up, marks the southerly edge of the suburbs of Hereford and I could just about spot it behind another wintry squall. Dinmore, subdued and more of a gentle crest than a clear incline, separates the cathedral city from Leominster. And beyond Dinmore, but far outweighed by the distant heft of the Black Mountains, is Wormsley Hill and the twin cones of Robin Hood's Butts, which helped me work out where Pembridge might be. Like most of Herefordshire, the village was burrowed within a jumble, shunning announcement.

But it was impossible not to be impressed by the county's boundaries, defined by an almost unbroken ridge. We were standing on a major part, the Malverns, the eastern limit, with their Tuscan contours emerging from the Severn Plain. To the south was Monmouthshire, the site of my teenage unhappiness, with Gloucestershire's May Hill and the Forest of Dean at its edge. Most impressive, however, bar the Malverns, were the darkling Celtic frontiers, from the Skirrid and the Sugar Loaf to the vertiginous drop of Hay Bluff and further into Wales. Also straddling the border, a little north, was Hergest Ridge, with its ancient trails, and Radnorshire and mid-Wales beyond. Then our eyes moved along the base of the Shropshire Hills, through Housman's landscape of lovelorn lads, and closer into view via the Bromyard Downs to Malvern itself. Words such as punch-bowl and crucible were often invoked in these instances, and they would have been fitting for Herefordshire were it not for the scale: this wasn't one feature, it was an entire county.

I stood there and realized that the hills and the places between them provided another analogue, at least to my mind. *Between* the hills. It was the name of the farm where my mother had been born and raised in Wales: Bwlch-y-rhiw — sometimes spelled as one word, sometimes hyphenated. It was far in the distance, due west in fact, in the Cambrian Mountains. But the flattening afternoon light made its presence quite palpable. The farmhouse, long since sold, sat beneath my late grandfather's 'mountain' of Mynydd Mallaen, though it was only a little taller than the hill on which I was now standing and made in part of the same Llandovery sandstone, the earliest Silurian rock, that also rises to the Malverns. My uncle still owns the land, and just as my grand-dad's traditional hill-farming life has continued, so too has our family's attachment to the place. It is where my mum's parents are buried and where we go every year to hear the cuckoos sing.

'It would be lovely to feel a connection,' I said, breaking the silence.

'Like in London?'

'Yes. No. Not just that . . . with you. It would be nice to have a geography for our marriage. To be rooted.'

'Isn't it odd that it's not the city, though?'

I asked Alastair whether he would have preferred London after all.

'No, I don't mean that. It's strange that you're being so gung-ho about the countryside,' he responded. 'You were always a city boy.'

'I suppose I was.'

For the first time ever, I thought my urban life could have been an aberration, the real connection being with the countryside: the family farm in South Wales and the mountains of Snowdonia, where I'd lived until the age of seven. But I didn't have a home as such. Even Oxford, a giddy place, was only ever going to be for a three-year stint, and my happy early adult life in London was again punctuated by various moves between flats and friends. Maybe the locus of feeling settled was irrelevant. The most important thing was the association itself, the ability to know a place, inhabit its past and present and witness the turning of another year.

II.

The Unanswered Question

A FEW DAYS LATER, OUR offer on Stepps House was accepted and everything was put in train. But after the initial hurry came the tedium of phone calls to mortgage companies, as well as providing proof of income and engaging solicitors. Spring came and spring went; weeks went by. It blinded you to the potential joy of the situation and the thrill of new discoveries, to say nothing of the realization that we were getting much more than we had ever bargained for. Choosing Stepps House, I had followed my feelings – and persuaded Alastair to do likewise – but we really hadn't thought about what the property meant: a house in the middle of a village that, as in that view from the Malverns, looked like it had come straight out of a medieval or Renaissance painting.

Quickly, however, we had to start grappling with that history, even before we had completed the purchase and could call the property our own. We were asked the question by our insurance company. The solicitor reminded me that the responsibility for insuring the building was ours from the day that we exchanged contracts. I'd just finished giving a history of art talk to a group of pensioners in a village hall in Oxfordshire when the message arrived. The voice on the other end told me that all the outstanding issues with the purchase were resolved and exchange had taken place. Sitting in a stuffy car outside a pub, I had to phone the insurers.

'What's the number or name of the property?'

'Stepps House. Two p's.'

'And how many bedrooms does the property have, sir?'

'Three.'

'Is the roof made of tile or slate?'

'Tile.'

'Walls. Brick or stone?'

'Both,' I said, 'though it's also partly timber-framed.'

'Tim-ber fray-m-ed,' I heard, as my answers were typed into the database.

'Partly,' I added.

'And what is the age of the house?'

'I don't know.'

'What do you mean, you don't know?'

'I don't know.'

'OK. Could you have a guess?'

'Well, it's old! I know that. I've asked the estate agent for more detail, because I was curious, and they've now checked with the current owner. Supposedly, it's 1800, but that can't be right, given the timber frame.'

'OK . . .' the response came, with a further pause. 'What we could do, sir, is take the 1800 date now and when you've got a more accurate answer, come back to us. As soon as possible, preferably.'

I concurred, but felt uncertain – and I feared uninsured, when push came to shove. Suddenly, I was regretting that we hadn't established any of the specifics before agreeing the purchase. I'd also turned down the mortgage company's offer of a full structural survey. But I was certainly excited by the prospect of having to find the right date. I knew that there must be records, of course, something in the house itself, but had no idea what or where. As it was, we had little choice but to return to the challenge of dating Stepps House when we collected the keys, though completion was still weeks away and my curiosity now fully piqued.

I could see that there were more contradictions than clues. The building was piecemeal – the source of our confusion and memory lapses after the initial and only viewing – with elements of what might be Tudor, even older, like many other properties in Pembridge, attached to 19th-century bits, with less impressive, less well-built sections from more recent decades thrown in for good measure. From the Market Square, it almost looked like two houses, one on two storeys and the other on three.

It was faced with brick and the whole edifice was mounted on a kind of stone plinth, roughly hewn. To the left of the house was the garden, stretching down to the main road, and to the right were the steps that rose from the square to a large churchyard. Partway up that public stairway was a door, though it must have been superseded by the entrance from the Market Square at some point in time. The old front door was set into the timber-framed section, the entire structure of which was clearly visible from the churchyard. From there, slightly raised above the rest of the village, it was also possible to view other, obviously more impressive buildings and I had already learned that their provenance was pretty well documented. Unable to access the house, I could at least begin to look for information elsewhere.

Pembridge forms part of a trail of black-and-white villages in the north-west corner of Herefordshire, including places like Dilwyn, Eardisland, Eardisley, Kingsland, Lyonshall, Weobley, Wigmore and Yarpole. Timber-framed houses fill each of these villages. Limewash or paint covers the former – or, in some cases, still extant – wattle and daub panels, while tar or linseed oil has, more often than not, been applied to the exposed oak beams, thereby turning them black. Many examples of the style, however, are neither white nor black, including a delightful pink and brown structure on the edge of Pembridge – just one of many houses in the area I'd come to covet. Such was the concentration of these buildings that the county was a natural point of focus for the Royal Commission on the Historical Monuments of England during the early part of the 20th century. Having begun a comprehensive study in Hertfordshire in 1910, the commission made its way to Buckinghamshire, Essex, London and Hunting-donshire, before arriving in Herefordshire in the early 1930s.

Reviewing what was standing, the survey prompted three volumes filled with the finest and most important buildings in the county, though the inventory did not include our home-to-be. In any event, although finely published, with charming maps of the villages and their glories, the commission's findings had since proved inaccurate. It made the bold claim that most of the buildings in the black-and-white villages, specifically those with cruck trusses – an overarching timber structure visible at the ends of the houses – dated from the 14th century. This proved overly generous, however, when, later in the 20th century, huge advances in dendrochronological science, focusing on the signature patterns of the tree rings in the beams, made it possible to establish a more accurate time of felling for the timbers used in the construction. Once that database was established, it confirmed that there were, in fact, very few extant buildings in Herefordshire that contained wood from anything before the 15th century.

Instead, Pembridge's Market Hall, just outside our new home, was from the early 16th century. Beyond it, with more recent tiling advertising BUTTER EGGS OATMEAL, was The Old Stores, with a 19th-century front concealing elements of the 17th and even 15th centuries behind. And then there was The New Inn, announcing itself as 14th-century on the signage on the outskirts of the village, but more likely to be from the beginning of the 17th century (perhaps embracing or, at least, replacing parts of an earlier structure, which may or may not have been a farmhouse).

The square was – and had long been – the village's hub, yet Pembridge can trace its history much further back than any of these construction dates. Built at a crossing on the River Arrow (which rises in Powys and flows into the Lugg and, eventually, the Wye), the village, once considered more of a town, was listed in the Domesday Book, the invading Normans' catalogue of land and property ownership, and had begun to thrive following Henry III's granting of a weekly market and annual fair to Henry de Pembrugge (Pembridge) in 1239. The village's heyday lasted well into the 16th century, the time the current Market Hall was constructed (on two storeys), though its subsequent survival as a one-storey edifice is as much a narrative of failure and disinterest in costly demolition or reconstruction as it was of earlier success.

Come the 17th century, the rot had really set in. Pembridge adopted a staunchly royalist stance during the Civil War and supposedly entered the fray as a town of two thousand souls. The place was then overrun by Cromwell's troops, who pillaged property, destroyed monuments and medieval glass in the church and left the marks of their musket balls in its west door. Many farm lads were killed and families who had previously dominated the village's history were wiped out or forced to flee. While the county records cite only one badly wounded villager, David Prosser, who was granted a pension of £1 6s at the Herefordshire Quarter Sessions in 1673, other injuries and losses simply weren't logged. The parish records had been abandoned at the outbreak of hostilities and were only properly resumed in 1649. Nonetheless, there can be no doubt that village life changed, never to recover.

The Industrial Revolution only added insult to injury. The advent of the railway to the north of the village, complete with a small station, resulted in the centre being bypassed by livestock, formerly taken to market by the drovers, who had been frequent visitors in these parts. And the immediate access of the Welsh coal seams took away those villagers without permanent employment in the fields, which proved problematic come harvest time, with a lack of seasonal workers. After further losses during the two world wars, as well as a steady stream of rural to urban migration right across the 19th, 20th and early 21st centuries, the census in 2011 recorded a parish population of 1,056, just over half what it had been during the early 17th century.

Fragments of Pembridge's rich past nonetheless remain. As you walk down its main east–west axis, from what was once called London Street to West Street, you see the names of various former businesses and amenities. The Malt House was doubtless home to a brewer. Opposite sits Mender's Cottage, while further down the street, towards The New Inn, is the Pump House, one of many such sites in the village before mains water arrived. There's an Old Forge (one of at least two that used to operate in Pembridge), the Old Wheelwrights, conveniently just a few doors down, and a Cobbler's House too. Judging by a collection of photographs by John Bulmer from the 1960s, much of this life, including a butcher's, a bread oven and a tobacconist selling Woodbines and Senior Service, was still operative. All have since gone.

As I began searching for the former chapters of our house and the village, I also discovered suitably evocative surnames, such as Roger Vicaredge alias Carpinter and his son Thomas who had, unsurprisingly, been carpenters and lived in the former vicarage. There was also a Roger Tanner and a Thomas Baker in the annals, whose professions were just as easy to guess. And likewise, Court House Farm, a stone's throw from our new home, spoke of its wider role in the village and the authority it held in both name and size.

How did we fit into this history and our immediate and, in some cases, much grander neighbours? Were we, and our house, an aberration? And to get to the thought that was irking me most, would our insurance be somehow invalidated were our home to burn down before I could find an accurate construction date? Sadly, an unlisted property, with no mention in the most significant surveys of buildings in the area, including a recently revised edition of Nikolaus Pevsner's architectural guide to the county, wasn't providing much of a clue. It sat on the margin of importance, if not outside the ring entirely. It was a bit like the village, at least according to our removal men.

'Bloody miles away from anywhere,' one of them said as we arrived, after waiting hours for the release of the keys. A disgruntled removal man was always a headache.

'Beautiful, though,' the other piped up, as a swoop of swifts screamed above. It was a glorious summer's day.

'And the villagers are very welcoming,' Jim, the first one, softened, telling us how coffee and cake had been brought to them while they were waiting under the Market Hall.

'Good to know the locals are friendly,' I said, fearing quite the opposite.

'It's a fascinating place. Did you know about the belfry? And there are gunshot marks from the Civil War in the church door.'

'You've done the rounds, then,' I responded.

'We're glad to hear you've been looked after,' Alastair added.

Their wait for us was much longer than it took them to unpack the van. Within forty-five minutes, all the boxes, furniture and pictures were in, most of our stuff having gone to the school accommodation. Instead, we had bought some bedroom furniture from the previous owner of Stepps House, avoiding the cost of moving it, both for him and for us. Given the heat, it was also a welcome relief not to have to hump and dump thousands of items up and down the stairs. We were, however, able to spend hours trawling nearby Leominster's many antique shops, finding side tables, a Jacobean chest, a kilim and an old hayfork, which seemed to fit right in.

The welcome given to the two chaps who moved us was replicated over the next few days and evenings as we unpacked and gave the place a sense of order, finally taking a hold on the structure of the house. One of us was usually halfway up a ladder when there was a knock or ring at the front door and rarely did an hour go by without interruption. Offers of welcome drinks, pints left behind the bar at The New Inn – the currency of social exchange in the village – and a generally high level of questioning, sometimes with a slightly aggressive edge, came with frequency. We were no longer anonymous, but there was no denying the warmth.

'Our friends feared for us when we moved here,' our new neighbour Jean informed us, after doorstep introductions had been made.

'Coffee?' I asked.

'I don't want to disturb,' she responded politely and returned to her anecdote. 'One of them, in Worcester of all bloody places, said, "I can't imagine why you'd want to be out in the boondocks. It must be like *The Archers*." I told her it was more like *Tales of the City*.'

We laughed at mention of one of our favourite series of novels; we were clearly going to get on well with Jean. She had been in Pembridge for over three decades, where she and her late husband Simon, a film-maker, had raised their children with such happy results that all of them still live within striking distance. They'd often escaped to a place in France that she was now trying to sell, as well as travelling extensively with Simon's work, but Pembridge was Jean's anchor. I did begin to wonder, however, whether her suggestion of Armistead Maupin's bohemian existence in late-1970s San Francisco would be entirely replicated in the Market Square. Alastair and I had thought we were, at least, going to bring some colour to the proceedings, though the village already had its own Mrs Madrigal – Maupin's cherished landlady – in the transgender resident of one of the houses opposite, who had swapped life in the States for rural Herefordshire. Two gay men were clearly old hat in terms of arrivals.

Indeed, I soon learned from the churchwardens that it wasn't so much our sexuality that was troubling them – or anyone else in Pembridge – but the placement of our bins, which was upsetting the aesthetics of the Market Square. Nobody else had theirs out all week, I was told by Gill, a forthright but forbearing figure; nobody else, I responded, lacked storage space on street level. Slighted though I was by the attack on my (newly absorbed) recycling processes – why does each council employ an entirely different yet equally impenetrable approach to the issue? – I was intrigued to be told in the same conversation that we were occupying the old saddler's house.

'My grandfather had many a horse saddled here,' Gill offered.

'What was his name? The saddler?' I asked.

'Rowlands. Buried in the churchyard, along with most of my family and many hereabouts.' This last comment sounded just a little threatening. But what had started somewhat frostily turned into a very happy natter, even if I'd refused to brook compromise on our rubbish disposal.

It was during this baroque arrival choreography that Alastair uncovered a pile of documents in one of the kitchen drawers. I became excited, though most of the papers were infinitely dull:

vesting deeds, probate and valuation certificates from the 1970s and 1980s. Others, from the 1930s, were written with great calligraphic panache. And an indenture from 1871, when the house was known as Church Stile Cottage, was more like a piece of art on translucent paper, marked with a fifteen-shilling stamp and the date and place of *Hereford 3.2.71*. It detailed the ownership of the house, including mention of George Rowlands's Saddler's Shop. There was also a heavily folded leaflet for an auction at The New Inn on 12 May 1904 at 4 p.m. 'to the minute', with particulars and conditions of sale. One of the lots being sold by Rowlands was our home and its garden, itemized as Lot 5: 'all that messuage or tenement known as "The Steps" or "Church Yard Cottage"' – messuage, as I learned, was a Norman French term, indicating a house with land or an adjacent building. The individual rooms in the property were listed as 'kitchen, parlour, pantry, shop, back kitchen, cellar, two bedrooms and linen closet'. But as much as these papers helped to form a family tree of recent owners and residents, they were useless for the insurers, presenting only 150 years between them.

'Are *these* any good?' Alastair said, handing over two more spiral-bound publications.

The first was the Parish Plan, published over twenty years ago, with pictures of our home on the cover. (Opposite the main pub, our house, even just a corner of it, is often found in photographs and paintings of Pembridge.) It contained a brief village history, though little detail about the individual buildings. But another brochure, produced by the village's Amenity Trust three years later and again featuring a cover picture of Stepps House, proved more comprehensive and included a name I had already encountered in my Pevsner: Duncan James, listed as the survey's architectural consultant.

There was a blow-by-blow account of what he perceived as the most crucial buildings in the history of the village – again, not including our home – accompanied by 'additional notes concerning tree-ring dating'. It was from this, as well as other books, that I began to learn an entirely new vocabulary; not only was there a vernacular architecture but also a strange patois pertaining to the style of construction. Mentions of notched spurs, crucks, pegs, trusses, bays, jetties, yokes and purlins spoke of Duncan James's extraordinary grasp of the dialect, as well as his knowledge of the various methods and dates. It was, fair to say, a life's work, using what was hidden within these rather humble domestic buildings to re-create a narrative that had once been absolutely plain to see in Pembridge's streets and squares.

Houses on the main road betrayed evidence of 15th-century felling dates, according to the seemingly dark art of tree-ring dating, including two houses from as far back as the 1420s. There was also the suggestion, 'without any evidence in history', that Owain Glyndŵr, the great defender of the Welsh, had been the cause for this building spree in the so-called modern life of Pembridge, after Glyndŵr and his followers wreaked havoc throughout the Marches and destroyed much of what they found. Supposedly positioning his troops on a hill above Pembridge – the one we had seen from our bedroom window when we first visited Stepps House – Glyndŵr descended into the village in 1401 and burned it to the ground. But just as Pembridge suffered from its proximity to the border, so it flourished, with English wool merchants being able to meet their Welsh counterparts in relative safety in a small but significant trading centre, ensuring that the construction of residences and other buildings continued for up to two centuries. When Henry VIII brought Wales under English jurisdiction, however, Pembridge's power and leverage began to fade, eventually resulting in the establishment of two sets of almshouses for the village's poor. And it was doubtless because of consequent poverty rather than any lasting attachment to earlier methods that most of the houses survived.

It all sounded very *Boy's Own*, with marauding Taffs and houses built like medieval Meccano, but it was a wild goose chase as far as the insurance company's question was concerned, for no further information related to Stepps House itself.

Standing in the garden, I looked up at our new home, armed with some of these details. Noting joists and mortises, I tried to interpret the framing on the eastern side of the building and compare it with other properties listed within the surveys. I also tried to imagine our home within this history of gabled wings and hipped roofs and parallel ranges, but there was too much to take in and I had none of the expertise. Clearly, our lowlier or, at least, later residence had not warranted the same level of study, but there it stood, amidst the hollyhocks, right in the heart of everything.

DURING THOSE first August weeks in the house, I realized that there were very few dog days, even on the edge of England, generations after the village's prime. Pembridge was a hive of activity as the season marched on. In part, it was due to tourists making their way west to the Cardiganshire coast, though not before stopping for an hour or two in the pub or going for a wander around the churchyard. But the real and most lasting activity came from the residents. A baking summer had followed a prolonged, wet winter and there would be a bountiful harvest. Deep into the night, contractors worked up and down the fields to gather in the wheat and oats, forming patterns as meticulous as the furrows that had been ploughed the previous autumn, winter and spring. Tractor lights scanned the ground where we walked Toby and once the job was done, the exhausted farmers sloped off to The New Inn to grab a pint before returning to the land.

Given that the reception rooms in our house occupied the first floor, we were offered a perfect view of the commotion. We were central to the drama. So central, in fact, that just days after we moved in, with the last pictures still to be put up, I found myself embroiled in an argument with one of the farmers. I had been watching that day's round of harvesting unfold as a procession of different contracting teams, along with sons and daughters, helped bring in the crop. A pause would ensue, dust hanging in the still-hot air, before the next team began. Sometimes, they would overlap and the roads became crowded. The machinery was enormous and completely unsuited to a village built on a medieval scale – like cruise ships passing through Venice. But no sooner had I slipped away from my position at the window, leaving the real-life equivalents of my old Britains toys to go to and fro, than the doorbell was ringing, not once but incessantly. Alastair continued to work in the garden – always his domain, while the kitchen is mine – as I ran back into the house and down to the front door, where I found a red-faced farmer standing in the shadow of an enormous combine harvester.

'Move your car!' he shouted.

'Sorry, is there a problem?' I responded, a little taken aback by the volume.

'Move your car! I've gotta get on.'

'There are ways of asking,' I sputtered.

'MOVE YOUR BLOODY CAR!'

'I'm sorry, I'm not quite sure why there's an issue,' I continued, calmly but clearly. 'For days, your colleagues have been driving through with combines and tractors and they've managed to get by perfectly.'

'And all this bloody foliage is gonna have to come down,' he said, pointing to where our vines and shrubs were hanging

48

attractively over the road. The farmer's Herefordshire vowels were now becoming much stronger.

'No, it's not, actually.'

'It's gonna scratch the new combine. Do you have any idea how much these cost?'

'I can't imagine they're cheap, but I'm not just going to shin up a wall and cut down trees and bushes on demand. Frankly, given your tone, I'm not going to move my car either. You'll just have to cope.'

'Then I'll have no option but to trash it.'

'Which would be criminal damage,' I said, slamming the door and leaving the farmer to move on to Jean's house and remonstrate with her, where she stood fresh from her early-evening bath in a towelling robe. Given that Jean had been in the village for years, I was heartened to see that the farmer's opprobrium wasn't only limited to the two poofs who had just moved into the square. There was clearly nothing more important in Pembridge than farming and everyone had to step aside when the harvest began.

Once my ire had abated, the event reminded me of one of the other bits of reading I had managed to do about the village, thanks to a copy given to us by Jane and Rosie at The New Inn. A 1960s journalist called Martin Page, with something of an eye for division, had written about the then parish priest's indignation that farming was above everything, including God. Accompanied by the John Bulmer photographs I had already found online, the article was published in the *Sunday Times* magazine, one of the earliest colour supplements:

Pembridge first decided that it did not like the Rev. Eric K. Andrews — and has not subsequently changed its mind — soon after he came there just over ten years ago. The weather during his first months in the parish had been bad, but the skies suddenly cleared in time for a late harvest. All available help was mobilised on the farms, during all the hours of daylight, to gather in the crops before the rains returned. Mr Andrews, facing a depleted congregation in church that Sunday, gave a stern sermon on keeping the Sabbath holy and named prominent local farmers whom he considered were violating it.

Nothing had changed. And very little I imagined had changed in the half a millennium since most of the village had been built — except that the machinery was different. I suddenly felt ashamed at having challenged the farmer's request, even if I loathed his tone. Mum's dad, Dadcu, would have been one to approve of my new home having agriculture at its heart — though he was definitely less belligerent about it — so I quietly slipped out of the house, bowed to tradition and moved the car. Slowly, the bucolic beast squeezed by — a visitor's four-by-four parked opposite was the real culprit — and the contractor nodded a gesture of thanks.

In a village conceived prior to the advent of motorized vehicles, such instances were to be frequent occurrences. Even more invasive were the teams who came to dig up our ancient roads just a few months after they had been resurfaced to weave fibre-optic cables through for rural broadband. And it must have been the same when electrification and the supply of mains water came to Pembridge rather late in the day, at the beginning of the 1960s, shortly before the *Sunday Times* article was published. Before then, the houses were lit by oil lamps, while the village's water was drawn from a series of pumps and wells, including one that used to stand on the Market Square, diagonally opposite our front door.

Our predecessors would have witnessed every visit to that pump. And when harvesting crowds gathered at The New Inn, they would have known about it too, just as we knew about it now. Behind us was the church and its eccentric separate belfry, the site of so many festivals, fetes and funerals. And the Market Hall itself spoke of the centrality of our position, with The Old Stores, since converted into a home, also crucial to the lives of Pembridge folk, like the old school two doors up. Frustratingly, however, there was still absolutely nothing to tell us when our building had taken its place within the story. The only option was to ask the experts to visit the house.

III.

Between Bark and Heart

D UNCAN JAMES WAS NOT at all what we expected. He may have had the predictable beard of an archaeologist, but his arrival on motorbike, buzzing into the Market Square, was rather more surprising. When we opened the door, he was quietly spoken, almost monkish in demeanour. I put the kettle on, but he quickly gestured to the kitchen door as if to say, 'Do you mind?' We nodded and he made his way into the stairwell and, eventually, the sitting room. Slowly, silently, he began analysing our home. It was the closest I'd been to a seance or a tea-leaf reading – even a post-mortem – all the time ignorant of the processes but captivated by the idea that an answer to our query might emerge.

Duncan's hands worked along the beams in the sitting room, diving into notches, noting the timbers from different angles. Occasionally, there was a slight sigh or an audible pause. He realized, of course, that we were waiting for his blow-by-blow observations, but simply turned and smiled, sometimes with a chuckle, and then moved into the dining room. Immediately, he came back into the sitting room, before swinging around the divide once more, lingering there. The 'ground' level duly noted, he made his way up the staircase that bisects the two main rooms. Above, there was our bedroom, as well as one of the spare rooms and a tiny space for a shower and loo between them. Climbing up, he looked at the wooden frame marking the walls. I made to follow, but Alastair waved his arm, so I did as I was told and remained downstairs, with our fortune teller creaking on the floorboards above.

When, finally, Duncan returned to the sitting room and we sipped our coffee, screeds of that inimitable and impenetrable language I had only just begun to learn came forth. He knew our main question, of course, that of the date of the house, but it was one that would be arrived at by much longer means. The answer needed demonstrating.

Duncan thought the house had been much altered over the course of time. Marks in the beams showed removed sections of lath and plaster, probably from the 19th century. The nail holes for the lath strips were still visible in the oak, a wood that, as we learned, continued to show its bruises and stigmata long after the damage had been done. There were also numerous other nicks in the timbers, betraying the even rougher plastering techniques of

the 18th century. But there was no doubt that the main section of the house was much older.

He showed us where posts had formerly been mortised into one of the principal beams spanning the sitting room, with peg marks too. Between these, which were six inches wide, there were holes of one inch in groups of odd numbers, marking where hazel stakes would have been jammed for the wattle and daub panels. Once you had seen these holes, they were everywhere, as were other dents and divots. One of the beams, on what was once an external wall, betrayed a much larger mortise and Duncan suggested it had been appropriated from an earlier building. He explained that the 16th century witnessed a revolution in sawing techniques which meant that posts could be much slenderer than before. It was a lot to take in, though I had noted the century that had already been mentioned and I was getting excited that our lovely if mysterious house was having flesh put on its bones.

'This,' Duncan said, pointing at a timber down the middle of the sitting room, with evidence of modest but attractive moulding, 'this isn't primary.' Another word we were having to get used to: 'primary', original to the building.

'Why's that?' I asked.

'Because . . . it wasn't built as a residence.'

This was absolutely news to us – it was all news to us – though the subsequent explanation of the building's purpose was entirely understandable, given the position. Neither of the chimneys, one in the sitting room and the other in the dining room, formed part of the original structure, which had, effectively, been just two spaces with a loft above. When you went outside – and this was repeated elsewhere in Pembridge – the chimneybreasts looked rather crude, more like stacks appended to the house rather than occupying the original footprint. Previously, fireplaces had been in the middle of the medieval 'hall' structure, with a single opening in the roof above. But where other chimneys in Pembridge were built from rough stone, at least at the base, ours was entirely made of brick, and therefore much later. Originally, our home had no fire.

'The building was probably used for mercantile purposes,' Duncan said.

'What do you mean?' Alastair asked.

'Commercial. Relating to the market and the Market Hall.'

'Do you mean trade, Duncan?' I asked, wryly. 'Because when it comes to two gay men, you don't have to shy away from the use of the word "trade". In fact, it's positively encouraged!'

'Well,' he laughed, 'trade it certainly is.'

Looking at the timbers, Duncan had noted the presence of a lot of sapwood, the softer, more recently formed outer layers of a tree trunk, between the heartwood and the bark. In some places, there was even evidence of the bark itself – left for centuries, since the timber was first felled. For a higher-grade domestic building, the strongest part of the oak, the heartwood, would normally have been used, yet there was little evidence of it in our home, apart from that single moulded beam – an anomaly, added later.

'This is a well-constructed building,' he reassured us, 'but the cruder materials show that it was not originally intended as a residence.'

At some point in its history, Duncan explained, the purpose

had changed or, certainly, changed in part. It was then that the floor above the reception rooms was adapted from a loft into a level of its own, by raising the upper part of the structure – you could see the change in the outline from the churchyard – though Duncan confirmed that the primary purlins, the timbers going down the length of the roof, had been similarly repurposed at the time. With a second floor added for sleeping quarters, chimneys were also needed and the, no doubt, draughty wattle and daub panels were replaced with brick – more technically, Flemish bond nogging – between the posts and rails of the outer structure. The Flemish bond, mixing the long sides and the short ends of the bricks in an even pattern, could indicate a date of change at some point in the 17th century, when the fashion for this (erroneously named) patterning was at its height, though something as modest as our home would probably only have caught up with the trend during the 18th century. It was around that time that the thatched roof was also replaced with tiles – eminently practical but infinitely less beautiful.

Admiring though we were of Duncan's ability to summon such a forensic hold on our home – and in such a short space of time – time itself was of the essence.

'Ah, yes,' he said, 'your question,' reading our minds.

Both of us looked on, waiting for the seer to speak.

'We'd only really get an accurate date through "dendro".' Duncan again referred to the process of dendrochronology, in which samples bored from the timbers in a building are compared to a database in order to establish a felling date for the trees in question.

'Is it worth us pursuing that?'

'Maybe. It depends how accurate you want to be.'

'I'm intrigued.'

'Well, it's an intriguing building, Gavin.'

'Indeed. So what do you think it was? Originally, I mean,' taking another tack.

'The position is fascinating, between the church and the market. It could even have been on church land. It was probably a storehouse, maybe a shop, trading out of here,' he said, pointing to where the steps ran up from the Market Square to the graveyard.

'When from?' I asked, annoying even myself with my insistence. He paused further.

'Early 17th century – no, somewhat earlier, towards the end of Elizabeth's reign. This timber-framed range is probably from the later part of the 16th century.' He waited and looked around again. 'It's quite robust.' A euphemism for unsophisticated, I thought. 'I base the date on looking at a lot of frames over the years.'

'So any time between, say, 1580 and Elizabeth's death?' I asked, one last time.

'Thank you for the coffee,' he said, not really answering.

And with that, Duncan bowed, kannushi-like, and left on his motorbike.

'Late 16th century?' Alastair pondered. 'I thought it might have been earlier. You said there were much older houses in the village.'

'I did. There are. And it could be; he didn't entirely rule it out!'

'But Elizabethan is pretty cool. Is that what you thought?'

'It's certainly what I hoped for.'

Finally, we had some kind of figure for the insurers, certainly more accurate than the date that had been left out of the particulars and then summarily plucked from the air by the estate agent. The insurance company blanched at the suggestion, of course, indicating that it wasn't in the business of covering buildings from before 1800. But when I intimated that we would have to take our money elsewhere, the underwriters were magically able to 'accommodate our needs' and the policy continued, 'albeit subject to a potentially higher premium come the point of renewal'. In that last regard, the company proved entirely true to its word.

I was in awe at Duncan's ability to 'read' a building and piece together its history. Yet I couldn't help but feel disappointed by the lack of absolute certainty. Soon, what had started simply enough began to dominate my thoughts and I decided to ignore Alastair's pleas to let sleeping dogs lie. Instead, I commissioned a dendrochronological survey to establish the felling date of the trees that had created our home.

Duncan had explained that our type of building was thrown up quickly. The oak was chopped and cut, 'wet', in late winter or early spring, with the timbers prepared at a saw pit and yard off-site. According to deeds relating to a house built in the 18th century behind The New Inn, a neighbouring village saw pit continued to operate until at least the 1700s; another was situated in the nearby hamlet of Weston. The wood was then brought to the relevant plot and the structure assembled at speed, as established

by various studies tallying tree-ring dating and other documentary evidence. In situ, the timbers were joined together according
to a system of carpenters' marks, normally low-grade numerals,
many of which were still visible inside our home. They were the
keys to the building's construction.

Our nameless carpenter's markings were largely Roman in style,
at least on the timbers that had originally constituted the outside
of the house to the north, though he had followed the tradition of
nine being given as VIIII, to avoid any confusion of IX being read
upside down as XI. Other markings inside the main structure
looked almost runic. Some, with overlapping Vs, may have been
intended as Marian marks, 'Virgo Virginum', though these might

have been added later, perhaps by recusant Catholics. As the practice of timber-framed buildings developed, so did the markings to aid their construction, from early medieval times to the Victorian era and beyond, pretty much whenever wooden trusses were employed in a roof structure (even if the main frame was made of stone or brick). The earliest ciphers were sweeping and confident, made with a race knife or timber scribe. By the 17th century, however, the system had changed and carpenters tended to score their wood with a gouge and a knife or chisel, becoming neater and deeper by the 18th and 19th centuries. The markings in Stepps House were of the oldest, crudest variety, which made me wonder whether even the late 16th century was too conservative a date. They were all slightly haphazard and, like the carvings of ancient Norse tribes, promised to bring the dead back to life.

That is currently the case in Paris, as carpenters, architects, historians and scientists work to reconstruct Notre-Dame after the fire of 2019. Although most famed for its stone carving, windows, bells and organ, the cathedral also contains one of the most complex wooden structures of the medieval period. Dating to the late 12th century, the so-called forest is a network of 1,300 oak trees that underpins the lead roof of France's most famous edifice. When flames ripped through the cathedral on the evening of 15 April 2019, the tinder-dry timbers burned with alarming rapidity and fell into the choir and nave below. But despite being charred, they still bore the original carpenters' marks. Studying them, it has become possible to propose a forensic reconstruction of this crucial part of one of the medieval wonders of the world.

When it comes to a much smaller timber-framed building in Herefordshire, the puzzle is a little less complex, though the principle remains. Each scheme of construction had an individual plan. Following this, the carpenters assembled the main structure, whether it was intended to be a house or barn or part of a church, which was then left to dry over the spring. Wattle and daub panels were added in late summer or early autumn, along with the thatch, so that the property was watertight and ready to be occupied as the nights drew in and the harvest came to an end. Such a hasty but efficient system meant that dating the construction of these buildings has proved relatively accurate. Instead of wood being stockpiled, the timber was cut as needed — oak is much more malleable when it's wet — so a felling date was, effectively, a construction date, give or take. It was so tantalizing to think that, just by enduring a day of drilling, we would be able to find our way to an accurate answer, armed with the detail of Duncan's specialist observations.

IN CAME the dendrochronologists, Robert and Alison. Over many years, they had studied hundreds of samples of oak trees and felled timbers, using the criterion of the tree's growth rings, which are added every calendar year, as any primary-school botanist knows. The width of the ring is mainly, though not exclusively, determined by weather conditions, from spring to autumn. The pattern revealed over time, with rings of varying widths, establishes a calendar of climatic circumstances that, when expanded to decades rather than years — thereby avoiding small-scale repetitions – and compared with dozens of other samples, correlates to a specific date.

Robert and Alison had undertaken the coring and comparing of samples from numerous timber-framed structures across England and, driving all the way from Nottingham, were clearly game for the same job in a village as famous as Pembridge, at least within their line of work. That was until we chose a day dogged by appalling rain, which caused long delays on the M42 and M5 and an even slower slog from Worcester – a tedious road at the best of times. The whole visit was to be much more frustrating, however, and significantly briefer than Duncan's seance.

They arrived and Toby fussed as I put the kettle on and left the pair of them to look around the house, just as we had done with Duncan. But by the time the water had boiled, they were sitting at the top of the stairs looking rather deflated.

'I'm afraid, Gavin, that we're not going to be able to help you,' Robert said.

I felt a twinge of annoyance, which I did my best to swallow, as he explained that to get a proper sample they needed rings of fifty-five years or so, avoiding those minor repetitions. Sadly, the majority of the oak in our house had grown so quickly, with widely spaced rings, that they wouldn't be able to get a model to compare with their databases. Many of the timbers also showed only the outer rings, having been cut from the sapwood and the bark – we had already learned this from Duncan's visit – whereas heartwood, from the centre of the trunk, is more immediately decipherable. Herefordshire is so lush, Alison added to try and soothe my disappointment, that oak absolutely thrives. While there's no difference in strength when the timbers are used for construction, their height-leaping youth doesn't help with the dendro process; in fact, Robert and Alison reassured me, one in three site visits proves abortive. So they had their coffee and biscuits and went on their way.

Dendrochronology has been hugely helpful in establishing a history of vernacular architecture – and had been particularly effective, though not exclusively so, in determining the dates of a number of buildings originally built for domestic use in Pembridge – but it has also revealed limitations. There is a general problem with dating trees in the British Isles, given the lack of what is termed climatic stress, or major weather incidents. So it can take up to a hundred years of growth, rarely found in most timber-framed buildings, for the patterns to be revealed and the process to work.

New methods under development at Swansea University involving the study of isotope deposits would be prohibitive for us, though the process had been markedly successful in a farmhouse over the border into Wales called Llwyn Celyn, owned by the Landmark Trust. There, after tree-ring samples had likewise failed to provide a date for the property, the isotope method indicated that one of the timbers had been taken from a tree felled in 1418. But as tempting as it was to call in the same experts, I had to resist – I'd already tested Alastair's patience enough – and rely instead on the corroborative dates of surrounding buildings in Pembridge, including the 1590s barn at Court House Farm, just up the road, and the late-16th-century cottages on the other side of The New Inn, as well as the pub itself.

Duncan's suggested date of the last decades of Elizabeth's court was absolutely of a piece.

As well as appeasing the insurers, his suggestion finally allowed us to sit within the timber-framed walls of our new home and begin imagining the trappings of the history that played out here, a history of trade, connected to the market outside, which may also have operated in the churchyard beyond our garden hedge. Or both. And the house had clearly been built to last. The 'common' or 'English' oak, prevalent in the deeper, water-retentive soils of this part of the world, hence the rapidity with which it grew, has as its Latin name *Quercus robur*, from the same root as robust. These were the oaks that, although cut wet, toughened quickly. And even though half of the homes in the county were made from the material, felled intensively over the course of the early modern period, there are still three hundred trees in Herefordshire that are more than four hundred years old.

'Do you have any ancient oaks on your land?' I asked Tony, one of Pembridge's most established patriarchs and owner of one of the largest farms.

'Some. Ash and field maple too,' he replied, enthusiastically, swigging his pint. Tony, rare among the village elders, drank from a straight glass rather than a dimple mug.

Jane, the publican, was being absolutely meticulous in ensuring that Alastair and I were introduced to all her regulars.

'These are the boys who have just bought Stepps House,' she said.

'How are you getting on over there? Lovely house,' he responded.

'Thank you. I'm trying to discover a bit more about it,' I ventured, hoping he would be able to help.

'It was the Saddler's House.'

'Yes, we heard that. I've been going back a bit further. Duncan James thinks the core is from the late 16th century, judging by the timbers and the construction.'

Tony told me that the Elizabethan era was not only evident in the village itself but also in the woods and fields surrounding Pembridge. Nature hadn't moved on. Despite the concentrated chopping of oaks and hazels for the construction of the timber-framed houses, including his own farm, to say nothing of on-going clearances for arable land and pasture, there were still fragments of ancient woodland where time had not trod. The human inhabitants may have long gone, or their descendants had changed the use of the acreage, but the coppices adjoining the farmland were often filled with the same flora and fauna that had been there during the 16th century.

Notably, Tony didn't tell me where to go to find these spots, though it was, surely, best not to disturb, simply to imagine. And, in any event, I didn't have to go rooting around in the undergrowth to find the tallest and broadest survivors of the era. Smack bang in the middle of a footpath through another farmer's field, recently divested of rapeseed, there were three enormous oaks that had survived, remarkably so, given what a hindrance they must have been to ploughing, sowing and harvesting, requiring the farmer to sweep great circles around their extensive root stocks. I decided to wrap my arms around the middle one of the three, knowing from the Vitruvian Man that my arms were as wide as I was tall: six foot one, or 185 centimetres. It took three of me to hug the tree entire: 555 centimetres in total. According to the Woodland Trust's reckoner for estimating the age of oak, this one probably dated to just after the end of the Civil War, a time of marked despair in Pembridge. But I also found a veteran oak at the entrance to the village campsite that measured between six and seven metres. I loved it best of all; its cousins and contemporaries would have provided the material for our home.

Tony and Jane smiled at my tree-hugging escapades. So did my old friend John, who told me that oak returns the favour: 'Wood is very embracing.' But however warm the timbers in Stepps House were, they constantly reminded us of the world beyond. Just like the trees from which it had been formed, the house was a living, breathing thing. I could hire as many experts as possible to tell us about the details of its construction, including pinning down the date of the timbers, but with the insurance company's question answered, at least as far as was necessary, it was now more about my curiosity, to establish a sense of what Pembridge was like around the time our home was erected. Only then would we get a proper sense of why – and perhaps when – it was placed here.

ARMED WITH Duncan's information, I went to the archives in Hereford. I was determined to continue the family tree of the ownership of Stepps House that had been started by the conveyancing agreements left by our predecessor. With each contract, new characters, new inhabitants of our bedroom, new figures who had cooked meals, drunk wine, mowed lawns and planted bulbs in Stepps House appeared from the documents, computer-generated, typed and handwritten in turn. These were the branches I took with me, noting the different names for the property: Stepps House, as it's known now, through Steps House (with one p), The Steps, Churchyard Cottage, Church Stile Cottage and several other variations on a theme, which made my searches rather more convoluted. The archivists listened patiently and then led me through what was considered the first port of call for anyone who had got as far back as the 19th century.

The benchmark was the Tithe Maps of 1840, a collection of charts detailing the size, ownership and value of all portions of land in Britain, a kind of Victorian Domesday Book. Drawn with the finest of hands, they were the result of the Tithe Commutation Act of 1836. It referred to the old system of parish tithes, originally one tenth of all produce from an individual's land, paid to the rector as compensation for his services, but which were then converted into monetary sums by the Act. Previously, physical tithes had been stored in a barn attached to the parish, and maybe Stepps House, though small, had served such a purpose, given its position on – or neighbouring – church land. Tithes were also sometimes paid to private landlords, in places where they hadn't been abolished entirely. The Commutation Act sought to reorganize this hotchpotch system.

Scrolling through the microfilm of the parish map for Pembridge, I was able to find our home relatively quickly, with its garden plot stretching to the north. Tiny apple trees indicated it may have been an orchard at the time. The house was listed as No. 4, which tallied with a separate apportionment list written in beautiful copperplate to match the confident lines of the map. Unfortunately, it had been photographed upside down, so required a little more dexterity with the machine, but once I'd scrolled, inverted and read the list, the owner of No. 4 was recorded as George Ruddle in 1840. His ancestors were registered with the ownership of lots of other property in the village. Our house, simply named 'cottage and garden' – none of the various monikers was mentioned – was occupied by William Harris, whose family was also listed in the 1841 census, including his wife Sarah and their three children.

Once I'd found the tithe map and apportionment for the plot, I was told that I had to make a leap of faith and return to the land tax registry of 1830. The critical decade divide between these sources meant that most people researching the history of their homes failed to draw the requisite link. And with none of the properties named – only inhabitants are detailed – it can be a tricky task to match values between the years, before going further back, all the time repeating the process with older and older land tax registers, until the full historical ownership of the house becomes clear. Sadly, the path came to an abrupt halt at the first hurdle, somewhere between 1840 and 1830, thereby falling far short of the 16th-century date that was my aim. It may have been that the house only changed from mercantile to domestic use in the 1830s, though the crude 18th-century plastering techniques, which were then replaced by lath and plaster, as well as the brickwork of the chimneys, said otherwise.

I could, however, begin to look around Duncan's hypothesis that our home was part of the market in the village. It certainly proposed another line of enquiry and there were many more documents relating to the commercial life of Pembridge — though sadly little of 'trade'. Jacobean and subsequent rent rolls itemized the income and rent from each fair (two a year) and market (two per week) that were held in the village, though these likewise showed that Pembridge's fortunes were tied in part to the Lord of the Borough, Thomas Coningsby.

He was a major landowner in the borderlands, with extensive property in Herefordshire and neighbouring Shropshire and Worcestershire during the Elizabethan and Stuart eras. A friend of the poet Philip Sidney, his wealth had largely been inherited from his father and elder brother, though he galvanized his position by means of an association with Robert Devereux, the Earl of Essex and steward of Leominster, with whom he fought at the Siege of Rouen in 1591, where he was promptly knighted on the Queen's behalf. It was to the Essex dynasty that rent from the lands surrounding Pembridge (rather than the village itself), and listed as 'Pembridge Foreign', was sent, tying up further swathes of local income. Such a system was ratified again in 1610, when James I gave the manor and borough to the Earl of Essex and his tenant.

Eventually, the moneys returned to Pembridge, again largely to its rectors, whose receipt of market tolls is detailed in documents as late as 1802. But the church had long controlled those parts of the village not under Coningsby or Essex. Inventories of its property were keenly guarded, not only by the parish itself, but also by the monarch, given the decisive shift in land ownership during the English Reformation. By 1636, the rectors of Pembridge were still receiving income from various orchards, fields and pastures in the parish. A list or 'terrier' of these 'glebes' on 16 January that year, detailing the parcels of land owned by the church or rented for its benefit, shows that 'the Churchyard and one . . . building built on the Churchyardland out the Northgate of the Churchyard' were the rector's property, as were 'the Parsonage house and one Croft adjoining to it . . . on the Lords land and Harklints Croft'. I wondered, just for a moment, whether Harklints Croft was the original name for our house, given its proximity to the old parsonage (now the village shop on the other churchyard steps). Or whether the 'building built on the Churchyardland' referred to Stepps House.

As the glebe terrier continued, all documented by William Sherborne, Pembridge's parish priest at the time, and signed off by the Bishop of Hereford, there were further lists of what were locally termed burgages—enclosed fields—as well as half acres, acres and other plots of meadowland and pasture. The largest of these constituted eight acres of arable land in the common field north of what was called the Longmeadow down by the River Arrow. Each parcel would have had rent levied against it, which would have been paid to Sherborne in coinage or kind, with the latter stored in a tithe barn (which may or may not have been our home).

All of this was imposed on top of the cost of the individual stallage at the village's twice-weekly market. I had assumed that these payments were collected at the Market Hall or perhaps at The Old Stores, with its commanding view over the square, which Duncan James had suggested was central to the operation of trade, given its position. But when I looked at maps, up to and including a detailed Ordnance Survey chart attached to the planning permission for the most recent extension to our house, I found the name 'Market House', which didn't seem to apply to either the open-sided Hall or The Old Stores (both of which were marked) but hovered at the bottom of our garden around the footprint of a former outhouse. You could still see the foundations. Perhaps that or an adjacent building had acted as a booth for those trading at the market or even those passing along what was now the A44. But it was just as likely, I thought, to have been a mistake in the drawing of the map.

As I pulled more documents out of the archive, dirtying the white gloves I was required to wear while cracking open 400-year-old parchment, I also encountered a series of strange and badly spelled references to landmarks long since gone and the ancient names of the village's fields. While Longmeadow, Manley and Nutfield were still in use, most of the Elizabethan (and later) sobriquets had been neglected. But legibility was the main problem I encountered, not least in the era's court rolls, with their customary mixture of cod Latin and English, scrawled in the poorest of hands and the cheapest of ink. An academic friend said that it was comparatively easy to read what was called 'secretary hand', the script of almost all educated people at the time – it was only from the 18th century onwards, she informed me, that things went awry with the advent of idiosyncratic handwriting – though she hadn't experienced rural Herefordshire record-keeping. Other documents were much clearer.

I found that wills and probate documents generally provided a sharper picture, not least of the value of the fields and burgages, as well as attached houses, tenements and messuages. While most of these papers related to the wealthier members of Pembridge society and the manor houses that still surrounded the village, including Tony's farm at The Leen (or Lene), there was also a handful of final testaments from various other walks of life.

An innkeeper called Solomon Wellington, 'being weak in body but of a sound and perfect mind and memory blessed be Almighty God for the same', may have been largely without property, but still had enough value among his 'goods, chattels and personal effects' to spread the interest from money arising to several members of his family in nearby Kington, Lyonshall and Pembridge. Similarly, while a shoemaker called Thomas Davis had no house of his own, his effects 'within doores and without doores', at least according to his will of 1652, were to be given to his wife Anne 'for the duration of her widowhood' and thereafter divided between their three children. Judging by the records, however, Anne didn't benefit for long, as her own last will and testament was recorded in the same spidery hand later that same year. The bequests of cordwainers, widows and butchers largely followed a pattern, being brief and poorly logged, while those of yeomen and land-owning farmers demanded a finer hand, like that of William Hoetts of 1582. In the first instance, money and the cost of bread for the village poor was to be taken from his estate and only then was his 'housse and burgage in Pembridge' itemized. Virtue signalling was clearly big business.

Among the farming wills, set out with lavish calligraphy for the initial letter and a bold and meticulous script, there was one dated 1581 on behalf of Harrye Stede that proved particularly telling as to what was most important and valuable among his estate. It specified that his 'bodye [was] to be buried in the Church yarde of Pembridge aforesaid' – just outside our bedroom window, in fact – before stipulating which of his 'beste oxen' were to be given to his 'eldest sonne', and which 'lambes' to his siblings. Agriculture, as ever, was forefront and centre. Property in nearby Marston and Lyonshall was registered and bequeathed, followed by the gift to his wife of the 'housse, Messuage and Tennemente' in Pembridge itself. And I wondered, given the date and the list of Harrye Stede's properties, by no means brief, whether it might have included our home. Or whether this was still in the ownership of the church. Or whether Stepps House – or whatever it was called, if it actually had a name – had even been built. As ever, no names for the properties were given. But, slowly, a picture of early modern life in Pembridge was beginning to clarify, with each and every house and burgage, ox and lamb.

IIII.

Picturing Arcadia

IT WAS one day of August, and the harvest was

IT WAS THE LAST day of August and the harvest was pressing on. After the wheat, barley and oats had been gathered in, the farmers' focus turned to the hops and, eventually, the apples. The latter had begun to ready in our garden too. First came the desserts, a seeming hybrid of the native Bloody Ploughman, named after a Victorian field hand who was shot for scrumping, and a less romantic British Colombian variety called Spartan that turned purple as the skins became more tannic. And then came the Bramleys, with their girlish blush of red. Over the coming weeks, if he wasn't careful, Toby could find himself near concussed while going for his early-morning pee, though the plump thud of the fruit on the path was a pleasing soundtrack to the change in season. The Japanese anemones likewise announced the shift by dropping their petals, while the yew at the bottom of our plot speckled the ground with berries that stained the flagstones.

We tried to stave off the return to work by taking another weekend, leaving the unpacking at school until the very last minute, just before the start of term. We deadheaded the listing blooms in Pembridge and decorated the house with hops, hanging them from the beams that were just beginning to yield their secrets. The girls at the pub had told us where to go for the bines, giving details of a farm a few miles south of the village named The Haven (also, incidentally, the go-to place for semen from prized Herefordshire cattle). In exchange for a few pints of beer, Jane and Rosie had beautiful garlands above the bar.

'You've just caught me,' Carole, the farmer's wife, said through the car window, as we drove into the yard. 'These were only picked this morning.'

Jane had told us that the hops would be available from the first day of September, so we were chancing our luck.

'Sorry, we've come rather early,' I apologized.

'Not to worry. Autumn's on its way,' Carole said, pointing to a coil of swallows above the kiln chimney. 'They love it up there. It's the wasps. That's the second hatch fattening now. It won't be long till they're gone.'

Two of the birds swooped down into the yard as the barn door was pushed back on its runners. Inside, more of the migrants were whirling around, readying for the journey south. The hops were slung over the cow stalls and the smell was intense, familiar from our place in Bedfordshire, where we used to suspend hops from an ugly box concealing a rolled steel joist. Now, we'd be able to hang them alongside Elizabethan beams.

Carole began sifting through the bines, selecting the plumpest she could find.

'Better give you good ones if you've been sent up by Jane.'

'We're going to wrap them into each other,' I said, awaiting approval.

'Oh, that's a good idea. Big beam, is it?'

'Well, in the kitchen, yes.'

'How about this one?' she said, handing over a prickly rope of leaves, specked with the most delicate flowers. She had gloves on.

'Perfect. Three more like that, please.'

Holding the hops, I sniffed them up close and got a grassy rush. But they were a bore to handle and were already making my skin itch. Having handed over the money, we then laid the bines carefully in the boot of the car and drove back to the village, spending the afternoon making botanical plaits on the lawn, before draping them over nails, which once again wounded the oak.

THE HOP perfume lingered in the car long after we'd returned to term. Alastair wasn't sleeping well and I was customarily fidgety. There had been too much change in such a short space of time and it was impossible to settle into the new routine. I also had work to do, a normally pleasant combination of an article on Strauss's opera *Salome* and a documentary script about the Weimar Republic. But instead of researching and amassing material, I kept being drawn back to Pembridge and the 1500s. It was a kind of homesickness, the like of which I hadn't experienced since first going off to school. I constantly found myself looking for paintings, posters and photographs of the village, which I decided we were going to put up in the school house as a reminder of our own haven at the end of a two-hour journey.

There were plenty of 20th-century images. One, which I kept for Alastair's Christmas present, was a 1960s poster encouraging its viewers to DRIVE BRITAIN, with an image of The New Inn and a beautiful red Austin Healey, somewhat incongruous but unashamedly glamorous. Railway posters, both real and reproduced, extolled the beauties of Herefordshire, with capriccios of the Malverns and timber-framed villages, much like our own. And there were similarly idealized views from the 19th century and the brush of the Birmingham-born watercolourist David Cox and his namesake son.

But I was struggling to find anything from the actual period in which our home was built. Like much of the parchment in the archive, the 16th-century paintings that survived in national collections revolved around the upper echelons of society, including portraits of Pembridge's tax-collecting squire, Thomas Coningsby, and the members of the Devereux family, kept in the National Portrait Gallery. Few if any pictures remain, if they were ever created, of those involved in trade in a dank Marches village. There were the clichéd, mind's-eye notions of codpieces and ruffs, but little that was concrete or specific.

I managed to find a woodcut of a street scene from a collection of broadside ballads. It included exaggerated details of contemporary village life, with a young girl defecating and a wild boar eating her shit. There were raving drunks too, a jug of piss being tipped out of the upper windows of an inn and a bishop seemingly shovelling horse manure. Most notable was how widely this kind of bawdy imagery was distributed, largely in chapbooks, a cheaply produced, folded pamphlet, where they were seen alongside vulgar songs, stories, news items and folk tales. Another from 1607 told of appalling floods south of Pembridge, with an image showing the tragedy in primitive and, unfortunately, rather comic terms. A church spire is just about visible through the flood waters, as peasants and livestock are forced to go for an unexpected swim. Others are sitting on the roofs of their homes, while a child in a cradle floats by. It's hardly documentary stuff, though it says much about the way in which things were presented and interpreted: symbolically, rather than with any sense of verisimilitude. Only in court portraiture was there the illusion of authenticity, though I remembered from both my school history lessons and recent period dramas (when I wasn't distracted by Henry VIII's pecs and abs) that Hans Holbein's representation of Anne of Cleves was far from precise.

Woodcuts were, for better or worse, the only imagery to spread far and wide, including to market towns and villages. The illustrations were reused frequently and circulated among various printers or were distributed by a single publisher for multiple platforms. They were the stock libraries of their day. Artists were rarely, if ever, given credit – there was no copyright

— and the work was often considerably cruder than the woodcuts of continental counterparts like Albrecht Dürer and Holbein, as well as the latter's brother Ambrosius. Simplicity nonetheless guaranteed adaptability. One illustration featuring a religious procession for the Feast of Corpus Christi from a devotional text of 1516, complete with vestments and a monstrance, could be easily repurposed as an image to mock such rituals in an Edwardian Reformation text of 1548.

Moving between the ribald and the religious, the creators of these woodcuts became responsible for a pictorial vernacular. As well as encompassing feast days and ecclesiastical contempt, the images demonstrated methods of animal slaughter, food preparation, fashions of the day and the services of nightwatchmen. Indeed, all walks of life were recorded, from peasants to well-dressed aristocrats, and there were entertainments from ballad singers, as well as games for adults and children alike. And when the pictures were grouped together, regardless of their subject, it was plain to see that this was an imagery, a visual language, that was absolutely obsessed with time and its passing, especially when focused on the traditions of the rural world.

A particularly widely disseminated collection accompanied poems by Edmund Spenser (though some or all of the images may have been used elsewhere). Now more famed for extolling the virtues of Elizabeth I in *The Faerie Queene* of 1590, which also featured a poetic portrait of the Herefordshire noble and jousting champion James Scudamore, Spenser's most popular work during the era was *The Shepheardes Calender*. It was published in 1579 and dedicated to Philip Sidney. Taking its model from Sidney's earlier pastoral romance *The Countess of Pembroke's Arcadia*, Spenser's *The Shepheardes Calender* is a strange work. On the surface, it follows the course of a rustic year, telling of the shepherd Colin Clout and his beloved 'countrie lassie' Rosalind, though it likewise comments on contemporary politics, not least the divisive subject of the Reformation, as well as providing paeans to the monarch.

The poem is split into twelve parts for the twelve months of the year and each of these sections begins with a woodcut and an eclogue, following the classical pastoral customs of Virgil and other Roman poets (much as Sidney had done). The woodcut illustrations in Spenser's response to this tradition were an integral part of the book, interpreting and complementing the text. They also provided those who couldn't read the verse with a set of pictorial clues and, for me now, some indication of representations (if not the actuality) of life in the countryside around the time our house was built.

Each of the woodcuts has similarities with the illustrations in the period's almanacs, all informed by the names of the months and their meaning, as well as basic astrological details and symbols of the changing seasons. They are defiantly secular and, in many ways, may be a pointed refutation of a publication from the 1490s with almost exactly the same title: *The Kalender of Shepherdes*. Reprinted throughout the 1500s, this originally French almanac featured a similarly bizarre mix – in its case, of astrology and religion. Spenser's response satirized its Catholic fervour. For January, at the beginning of the poet's *Shepheardes Calender*, a fat Aquarius hovers in a cloud, as does Pisces, my own sign, above the drear month of February. The appearance of noblewomen during April, in which Spenser praises Elizabeth I, is an exception to the predominantly peasant setting of the pictures and poems. May, however, returns to a much older tradition and features lovers in a carriage coming from church or going there to be married. There's an extensive harvest that covers June to August, with haystacks and hunting horns. And by September, the migrant birds are swarming overhead, leading us into the darker months, including November, with its barren trees and scrub, and December, with a low-lying sun.

But for all the suggestion of humankind within the landscape and the type of activities that would have been undertaken by villagers in Pembridge around the time that Spenser wrote and published his earliest success – the time our home was built – there is little that was specific about these woodcuts. Like the majority of images created in the 1500s, they are generic, riffing on established tropes from prayer books, calendars and yearbooks. And like many contemporary English illustrations, they probably aren't even native, Elizabeth's springtime portrait aside. The local visual arts tradition was poor, to say the least, and significantly lagging behind continental Europe. The large majority of paintings and prints during the 16th century was either imported or created by outsiders.

There simply wasn't a national appreciation of the countryside in and of itself during the era. The towns and cities of England were its markers of pride; locally, that would have meant Hereford, of course, and the biggest of the market towns, Leominster, Bromyard and Kington, followed by Ledbury, Ross-on-Wye and Weobley, as well as Pembridge too. Although the countryside provided the readiest sources of food, it was also a source of trouble, of theft and uncertainty when travelling between regions. The undulations that today make Herefordshire so attractive would simply have been a hindrance, as would the rivers. The timber-framed cottages, albeit lovingly constructed, were so ubiquitous as to have been considered the equivalent of a drab two-up-two-down. Working in such an environment was a struggle, so why fetishize it?

After all, Britons didn't even have a word for landscape – first appearing in print in English in 1603, it had derived from the Dutch – let alone a vernacular practice to celebrate it. That too would come from the Continent, principally from the same Northern European centres who loaned the word, with pictures of life and work within the English landscape reflecting their traditions. Even images of court were often by Flemish, Dutch and German artists, such as another exponent of early modern printing techniques: Marcus Gheeraerts the Elder. As with many arrivals in England during the 16th century, Gheeraerts had fled Protestant persecution in a homeland controlled by the Catholic Habsburgs. Reaching London, he discovered a brand-new market for his imagery and, given the locus of much of England's wealth and influence, decided to remain close to the capital. One of Gheeraerts's panels, featuring a fair in Bermondsey, nonetheless strikes an almost rural note (the presence of the City of London notwithstanding). The crowd is aristocratic, bar a few servants, yet the painting, filled with the kind of timber-framed houses found in Pembridge, didn't only remind me of our Herefordshire home but also of scenes created by one of Gheeraerts's predecessors, Pieter Bruegel the Elder, with his wonderfully energetic depictions of peasant life. These were the very images I had remembered while standing on the Malvern Hills the day we found Stepps House.

Like the illustrations for Spenser's *The Shepheardes Calender*, probably created by (anonymous) Flemish hands, the Breda-born Bruegel had relied on established iconography for his famous depictions of the passing of the year. And it was a set of images, times and customs that, as I pondered Pembridge and its chronicling over time, I was seeing every day in preparation for a lecturing trip to Vienna. As well as the city's usual repertoire of Klimts and Schieles and all the headachy brilliance of the *fin de siècle*, my tour included a major new Bruegel show at the Kunsthistorisches Museum. It was built around Vienna's main gallery's own impressive hoard of Bruegels, though other significant loans had been added to the list. One of the promised coups was the display of four out of the surviving five Bruegel paintings of the seasons. Created in 1565, these were perhaps the clearest, most detailed and most vivid evocations of rural life during the 16th century, regardless of their origins.

Three of the paintings came from the Kunsthistorisches Museum's own collection, while a fourth was to be brought from Prague. Sadly, the other surviving painting, kept in the Metropolitan Museum of Art in New York, was not going to make the long journey over the Atlantic. But it was that painting in particular that caught my attention. I knew its luxurious Manhattan home well: up the stairs from the Met's terminus-style foyer, to the left and into the third of a series of rooms above Central Park, where it hangs surrounded by Dutch Madonnas and other saints and sinners.

Now known as *The Harvesters*, though Bruegel probably never called it that, the painting shows a late-summer scene. In the foreground, under the laden branches of a pear tree, a group of agricultural labourers, men and women, rest from backbreaking work in the field. Others continue to gather in the wheat, scything the crop on the left, while sheaves are dutifully placed in the field beyond the picnic. The job isn't even half done. Down a great divide in the field, another workhand brings pitchers of refreshments for lunch, where Bruegel's foreshortening reveals just how much more has to be reaped, before the weather turns, the rain comes and the crop is lost. And that threat is present in the glowering, eclipsed sun – there was, indeed, a total solar eclipse on 29 May 1565, though it would not have been visible from Bruegel's homeland. Despite the obvious warmth, there are other foreboding signs too, with one of the scythes about to strike another refreshment jug. Nonetheless, it is a busy scene, the end of a bountiful season, with the heat captured in wavering, hazy light. A haywain is piled high in the distance, further highlighting the abundance. And while work continues in the fields, other villagers bathe in the ponds or play on the village green.

As I looked further into the details of the painting – an endless pursuit in Bruegel's richly loaded images – I could find within that distance a presumably Netherlandish village, filled with half-timbered houses. Thatched, in the main, they were present in each of Bruegel's season paintings. Sadly, spring was missing – and had been for centuries – though it too would have featured this kind of vernacular architecture. Yet, in truth, there was no vernacular to these paintings. Although, in other instances, Bruegel replicated scenes and towns he had witnessed in the Duchy of Brabant, with territory containing Brussels and the surrounding area, as well as Antwerp and north into the southern central part of the modern-day Netherlands, there were mountains in these paintings, glaciers too.

The physical geography of Bruegel's art defied the area in which he lived until 1569. The images were as much a result of the artist's memory as they were of his homeland. He had travelled extensively across the Continent. Like many artists in Northern Europe during the Renaissance, Bruegel's principal destination was Italy, though the journey there afforded him other vistas too, including life in Switzerland and the Alps. He then returned to Antwerp, where he was able to build a significant career as a painter and printmaker, benefiting from the wealth of an extraordinary trading post within Europe.

Britain exported wool in great bolts to Antwerp, with eighty thousand cloths constituting two thirds of all its trade in 1500, including from centres like Pembridge that had built their wealth on wool. Primarily, the material was compensated in the form of silks, damasks and fine linens – as opposed to the rough variety worn by British labourers – while English, Scottish and Welsh wool was then dyed, finessed and exported onwards from Antwerp, both further north and down into the Habsburg lands at the heart of the Continent. Important household objects such as pins, wax and starch were also traded in Bruegel's adopted hometown for wool, as were paper and luxury foodstuffs – wine, spices, dried fruit, sugar and oil – the hallmarks of the

16th-century dishes that still adorn today's cuisine. And it was also a city that directly benefited artists, who could find the finest pigments among its shops and stalls: from crushed roots, minerals and charred bones. Bruegel's home was the transhipment hub for it all, sourced locally and far, far afield. Through its Habsburg rulership, the port had direct access to the Mediterranean and the dynasty's possessions in Spain, which granted ill-gotten riches from the New World. Antwerp was therefore the perfect place for Bruegel to live, to profit from the wealth that trade brought, but also to reflect an increasingly globalized world within his art, which could be distributed through trade routes by the very ships that often throng the harbours of his paintings.

The season images of 1565 had been commissioned for an Antwerp merchant banker called Nicolaes Jonghelinck. He was exactly the kind of person you'd find in contemporary portraits in any major collection. Go to London's National Portrait Gallery, visit the Mauritshuis in The Hague or the Rijksmuseum in Amsterdam, and you'll find several Jonghelinck types: merchants, seafarers, people of court – executed or otherwise – and their seemingly endless wives. Significantly and rather atypically, however, Jonghelinck's brother was a sculptor called Jacques, with whom Bruegel had journeyed around Italy. Nicolaes shared his sibling's love of art – voraciously so – and his knowledge of the profession would doubtless have allowed Bruegel greater freedom than he would have found with other patrons of the period, most of whom saw an artist as a facilitator of their own image and ego. By the time Jonghelinck acquired the season paintings, he already had two Bruegels in his collection: *The Tower of Babel* and *The Procession to Calvary*. He decided not to display these in Antwerp itself, but in an elegant villa just outside the city walls. It was called Ter Beke, a house long since destroyed in an area now subsumed by the city, and it was for the villa's presumably capacious dining room that Bruegel was hired to paint his stirring images of the pageant of a changing year.

Rather than creating twelve panels, one for every calendar month, as in the poems and woodcuts of Spenser's *The Shepheardes Calender*, Bruegel divided the year into six, with the paintings representing two months each. The reason for six images rather than twelve months or a customary four seasons – like the somewhat copycat paintings of Joos de Momper the Younger that my parents bought in print form from their book club in the 1970s and which used to hang on our sitting-room wall when I was a child – may well have been boringly practical, reflecting six empty panels within the design of the dining room. But it also suggested a prevailing trend in Dutch art, in which autumn and winter are kept as separate seasons, but early spring is divided from late spring, and midsummer from late summer.

For Jonghelinck and the guests who came to his villa, Bruegel's images were intended to grant access to a world they could rarely see – and which was seldom witnessed in other paintings of the era, as I had discovered in my search for pictures of Pembridge. Looking around the room, Jonghelinck's diners would have been able to peer into lives they had not experienced, captured in infinite detail, perhaps placed between windows onto the outside world, yet offering their own windows into time and society and, moreover, a clear social order, with the viewers being near

93

or at the top of the pile, commanding the peasants below. But Bruegel's views were not replicated outside, with the flat horizons of the Low Countries. His season paintings weren't just a compendium of the year, they were a compendium of Europe as it was at the time – all of Europe, including far-flung villages like Pembridge. As there are timber-framed houses, so there are ships sailing for spices and the unknown, vertiginous snowy outcrops, herds of cows moving between highlands and lowlands, and glaciers and vineyards, all equally extraordinary to the eyes and minds of even the worldliest Antwerp merchant. Placed within nature, the characters of these seasons, geographies and vistas, including the agricultural labourers beneath the pear tree in *The Harvesters*, lunching on Gouda and bread and porridge studded with fruit, were part of the cycle itself.

Bruegel's vision represented both a philosophical and physical worldview. He was steeped in the humanism of his age. Instead of focusing on individualism and potential division, Bruegel concentrated on what is shared, what binds humanity together – regardless of class, role, nationality. That he could transpose elements of Italy or Switzerland to the Duchy of Brabant and grant the flattest part of Europe, saved from the sea in the 13th century, its own impressive massif, spoke of the 'everyman' nature of his world – and Europe's newly emerging tradition of landscape painting.

While Bruegel's concept was derived in part from his experiences of travelling across the Continent, it was also intended to be a visual atlas, an anthology of life, that could be appraised and understood as one. To survey the world in such a way was a moral–philosophical pursuit, the object being self-improvement. Perhaps that was to set the viewer apart from the peasants within, though Bruegel arguably pursues a more incisive quest, bidding the commissioner and his guests to understand better and more compassionately the people who work for them. It was the clearest and most accurate picture of rural life I was going to find.

THE SENSE of balance espoused by Bruegel was shared with many of his contemporaries and was derived from one of their best: Erasmus. Seeing humankind within the context of the cosmos, Erasmus of Rotterdam was a priest, philosopher and scholar who promoted a specifically Christian vision of Renaissance humanism. He felt that choice and free will, as both gifts and burdens, allowed humankind to rise or fall. God looks down but rarely interferes. A philosophical sceptic, steeped in the classics, Erasmus was a committed but rational believer who saw faults in both the management of his own Catholic Church and in the precepts of Lutheranism. *The Praise of Folly*, one of his most widely published texts, first issued in 1511, contained passages that ridiculed monks as being as obsessed with their rituals as they were with their wine and women, while the princes of the Church were upbraided for being even more arrogant than their secular counterparts. Erasmus's philosophies spoke of intellectual resilience. It is such a reasoning mind that sets humanity apart from the animals, though some of us can easily fall asleep during a picnic, snoring, mouth open, with a codpiece about to slip out of place, as Bruegel shows us in *The Harvesters*.

Observing his and Erasmus's view of the world and the philosophy it represents, we are also observing ourselves and apprehending our ability to transform and, thereby, self-transform. While Bruegel, like Erasmus, followed predominantly Christian tenets, his mind was clearly open to the realization that nature was not just a set of superstitions acting out a higher purpose, but something to be comprehended in and of itself in order that we might find a way to live within it. His ability to capture the differing light, visibility, air quality and humidity of the changing seasons also points to a proto-scientific level of observation. Pathos is ignored; instead, observation and understanding are key. We can stand on the hillside with Bruegel and, by extension, Erasmus, yet we are constantly invited to descend from our perch; not to take what we are viewing for granted, but to experience life directly and dive into the detail. History becomes tangible.

My own experience of the images Bruegel had created for Jonghelinck in Antwerp was somewhat different. I knew their provenance and inspiration, yet saw in those paintings a clear reminder of my new home, the village I had left behind at the peak of the harvest, filled with its own timber-framed buildings. In some ways, it was a leap, but there were clear links to be drawn between Bruegel's world and that of our home: the English word and tradition of landscape painting was borrowed from the Dutch; and so many of Bruegel's peers came to Britain to work at the time our house was built. But there were philosophical links too, not least as one of Erasmus's closest friends was the lawyer, philosopher, royal secretary, under treasurer and chancellor in Henry VIII's court: the later martyr and 'man for all seasons' Thomas More.

His saintly reputation has recently taken a bashing, thanks to the novels of Hilary Mantel and Diarmaid MacCulloch's biography of Henry's subsequent favourite Thomas Cromwell. All part of an arguably just rebalancing act, Mantel's fictional account can, however, be guilty of doubting one Thomas in order to celebrate the other: the self-made ruffian at the heart of her *Wolf Hall* trilogy. But I couldn't help but see beyond More's zealous clinging to an old faith in the face of a faithless court and admire the righteous and cherished figure whose philosophy echoed the works of Erasmus and the paintings of Bruegel. Certainly, More's seminal text *Utopia* (published in Latin in 1516 and, posthumously, in English in 1551) provided an anthology of viewpoints, a vision of an idealized society, reflecting the cosmos entire, in which he wrestles with what is wrong with his own world and what might be corrected – though history, or rather Henry, would steal the opportunity from him.

Perhaps it was all a bit highfalutin for little old Pembridge and our home. But just as I was about to turn away from this echo chamber of imagery and philosophy, two Herefordshire friends provided me with a resolutely local link. Ben is a farmer, the spit of Tom Selleck in *Magnum, P.I.*, and his husband Stevie is a GP, who looks like a hunky Tintin. They live about ten miles from Pembridge and had helped us in contacting Duncan James. They too were uncovering fascinating truths about their home, though Ben and Stevie's investigations quickly put ours in the shade, as they began to realize that their farmhouse was not entirely what it seemed.

Having decided to take down a stud wall in an upper bedroom, Ben and Stevie discovered a whole series of wall paintings. Unknowingly, until they knocked a hole in the partition, they had been occupying part of a medieval hall house; specifically, in the case of the bedroom, its private quarters or solar wing. The paintings had been hidden for many years, perhaps even centuries, but they dated from the late 1500s. Together, the scheme comprised angels, acanthus leaves, roses, fleurs-de-lis, breasted lions and all sorts of other heraldic and religious symbols. Researching the sources for these strange figures, as well as the knots and curlicues of the frieze that was repeated around the timber-framed room, Stevie established that the strapwork at the top had in fact come from cartouches by a Florentine artist, Benedetto Battini, which had appeared in a publication from 1553.

These schemes were employed to signify the humanism of the homeowner, a member of the village gentry or well-read yeoman, not least his knowledge of the classics – Erasmus and More would have approved – though such paintings were also to highlight social status. The most intriguing detail for me, notwithstanding the wonder of seeing the paintings uncovered, was that Stevie told me the original publisher of the cartouches was not a compatriot of Battini's, but Hieronymus Cock from Antwerp – Battini may have been his own alias. And not only did he distribute these decorative schemes, which were employed at other sites in Gloucestershire and Devon, Cock was also Bruegel's chief agent. Just ten miles from the timber-framed village I could see reflected in Bruegel's season paintings was a house containing designs from a publication that was printed in his place of work and by one of his closest colleagues.

Globalization was nothing new, but then a global vision was exactly what Bruegel, Cock, Erasmus, More and a host of others had championed during the 16th century. It spoke of their expanding world. Traded out of Antwerp, these images, as well as various less refined woodcuts for chapbooks, arrived through London or, more likely in the case of the nearby farmhouse, Bristol, and joined various cultures and philosophies together. The cross-pollination of tropes, as well as individual artists, also fed into what became our national culture and Britons' particular way of observing their land.

Bruegel's own images for Cock, including a drawing of spring from 1565 – the same year as the painted seasons and perhaps providing a hint of what the missing panel might have contained

– as well as summer from 1568, could likewise have made their way here in printed form. But it wasn't only Bruegel who created these pictures of peasant life. Cock was also responsible for a 1559 series issued under the grand title, originally in Latin, of *Many and very beautiful places of diverse village dwellings, homesteads, files, streets, and such like, and furnished with all sorts of small animals. Altogether drawn from life and primarily located around Antwerp*, which is now more commonly known by the name of its unidentified artist: the Master of the Small Landscapes.

Within its fourteen plates, all representing villages and hamlets around Bruegel's hometown, the artist, variously cited as Cock himself, as well as Cornelis van Dalem, Hans Bol and Joos van Liere – even Bruegel – recorded life as it was lived. With further editions appearing into the 17th century, there was a quiet humility to such scenes, what became known as *sancta rusticitas* (holy rusticity), with scrub roads, thatched roofs and women bleaching linen, all to draw the admiration of a merchant class that had formerly patronized such a world. So while I had searched in vain for specifically British iconography of what life in Pembridge and the Market Square, as well as within our humble storehouse, might have looked like, the images from *The Shepheardes Calender* and their roots in almanacs, contemporary chapbooks and Bruegel and his colleagues' dazzling chronicling of the seasons provided more than a hint of the moment when our timber-framed structure was thrown up one spring.

It was even possible to see in the imagined 'everyvillage' of Bruegel's world where our home was placed. *The Harvesters*, most of all, provided a replica of the geography of Pembridge. In Bruegel's late-summer painting, the top of the hill is dominated by the farm workers and, beyond them, the church. The view then sweeps down, past houses hidden within the trees and through the fields to a lake or pond and a river crossing – waterways were crucial when nearby roads proved impassable – as well as another gathering of dwellings.

Pembridge occupies a similar position. It too is set above a river crossing, the somewhat diminutive River Arrow at that summery point of the year, but a veritable torrent of flood waters from the Radnorshire hills come winter. As you approach the village, the church is also readily apparent, as is its separate belfry, one of Pembridge's earliest structures. But it hadn't always been the most prominent. South of the church, on the highest point of the settlement, is what is presumed to have been a moated castle, built, no doubt, to defend this significant site so close to the border with Wales. Manorial control takes precedence, with the church following and then, just below that, the Market Square. Viewed from an undulating vantage point, as if in a Bruegel painting, the power, beliefs and commerce of Pembridge are all in their rightful place, a hierarchy of sorts, a cosmos within the cosmos. Below these structures are the dwellings and the river that guaranteed the settlement's geographical importance. And sitting between the Market Square and the churchyard, our home had its role too.

V.

Safely Gathered In

I HAD ALWAYS WANTED TO escape into history. But the more I looked back at the origins of Stepps House, the more I realized our home had emerged from an era with unnerving elements of our own. The late 16th century was, despite an obvious female role model, deeply patriarchal and hierarchical. The gap between rich and poor was also vast, aggravated by the centralization of power. It was a violent time, with public executions, burnings at the stake and, more familiarly, staggering levels of knife crime – almost all Elizabethans carried a knife, largely for innocuous fashionable purposes, though these were easily adapted. And the 16th century was a world pulling apart, with the continent of Europe breaking up along religious–political lines, while expansion into the New World brought treasures and tension in its wake.

As much as I could perceive negative parallels between then and now, it was impossible to ignore that the late 16th century was also typified by the world coming together. It was populated by people trying to understand themselves and their place, through art, poetry, music, science and religious thought – the humanist hallmarks of the Renaissance. The adoption of these ideas was further encouraged by the rapid expansion of print culture, not least in the Low Countries, though this could just as easily be tied to commercial, industrial and political interests, as well as the dissemination of a new, reformed religion based more on the written word than the ancient veneration of saints and ceremonies. Yet however fervent these aims, both cooperative and conflicting, even the briefest of precis of the 16th century revealed a world (and a nation) unsure of itself, wrestling to find a path to self-assurance and prompting many to ask even more profound questions about their place within such a system.

There was, however, also the unmistakable distance of four hundred years of technological, scientific and medical innovation, which could make our 16th-century forebears appear less advanced, less progressive. And it was similarly easy to imagine a population in a rural outpost like Pembridge who had little idea of the order of the universe, to say nothing of where they might find their place within it. Our home, after all, was built on resolutely basic terms. There were few of the comforts that we now take for granted, including readily available light and heat. Without the later chimneys that Duncan James had spotted, our home, perhaps beginning life as a market storehouse, would have been very cold indeed. But that was the point. To store food without refrigeration, buildings had to be dark and airy. Were there even windows when it was first constructed? Or just shutters and basic wooden mullions?

Returning to the house after a few weeks away, we got a hint of that initial use. It was late September. As we drove into Herefordshire, the evening light was already lacking its summer generosity, though we were rewarded with other sensory pleasures, including the smell of apples at their peak. The windows in the car were down and the solvent hit of the mature fruit made us lightheaded. Alastair drove and I wound down the back windows to let the apples' boozy perfume pervade the car. Even Toby sat up in the boot, his sense of smell working overtime. It was an incredible homecoming, but it also pointed to work unfinished, to a harvest still ongoing.

Apples have been a major part of the Herefordshire economy for centuries, back to the time of the construction of our house and long before. On the exhausting hot days of summer, as in Bruegel's painting, cider provided refreshment – and could serve as ready payment for agricultural workers. Water itself was of little use. All kinds of diseases were passed through streams, rivers, wells and butts, so had to be avoided. Beer would also have been drunk during the Elizabethan era, but it expended grain, which could be better used for bread. Cider and perry were cheaper; in the same water-retentive soils that gave the oak from which our home was built, fruit trees grew in abundance.

Such was the richness of the county's pomaceous heritage that it became the focus of the work of many horticulturists over the centuries, including Thomas Andrew Knight and his *Pomona Herefordiensis* at the beginning of the 19th century. Printed by W. Bulmer and Co. for the Agricultural Society of Herefordshire, this lavishly illustrated directory not only described and offered watercolours of the huge number of apple and pear varieties found in the area, but also provided a no less richly detailed account of the ancient principles of cider making. Reading through the litany of varieties that Knight studied and catalogued is to experience the bucolic equivalent of the Shipping Forecast: the Redstreak, the Golden Pippin, the Foxwhelp, the Red Must, the Hagloe Crab, the Loan Pearmain, the Grange Apple, the Orange Pippin, the Downton Pippin, the Woodcock, the Oldfield Pear, the Forest Stire, the Teinton Squash Pear, the Foxley Apple, the Pawsan, the Best Bache, the Yellow Elliott, the Longland Pear, the Old Quining, the Holmore Pear, the Bennett Apple, the Golden Harvey, the Siberian Harvey, the Huffcap Pear, Stead's Kernel Apple, the Garter Apple, the Barland Pear, the Cowarne Red, the Old Pearmain and the Friar. To these were added the even more playful varietal monikers of *The Herefordshire Pomona* later in the 19th century, with further suggestions of villages, woods and fields long since lost to time: the Cocc-a-gee, the

Monstrous Pippin, the Jolly Beggar, the Bess Pool, the Kentish Fill-basket, the Peasgood's Nonesuch, the Queen of Sauce, the Gipsy King, the Schoolmaster, the American Mother, the Hoary Morning and the Bastard Rough Coat.

Some of these varieties were still in the orchards, even if long since abandoned or little harvested, while others were resolutely up to date, the gnarled trees having been grubbed up and replaced by such prolific fruiters that the county's cider makers already had three years of juice to ferment on tap. Cider is no longer the necessity it once was. Where, in the 1600s, Herefordshire was described as 'one entire orchard' and would remain so until the late 19th century when, together with neighbouring Worcestershire and Gloucestershire, as well as Somerset and Devon, the area boasted nearly ninety thousand acres of orchards, profitability soon paled in comparison with other more intensive methods of farming, which were to be exacerbated by both local and Europe-wide agricultural policies. As a result, the role of cider and the area's historic attachment to apples (and pears) waned. But in the 16th century, the link with that source would have been utterly direct when, of an early-autumn evening, the people who built and owned our storehouse locked up and returned to their lodgings or, as we were doing, went off to the pub. Theirs would have been an intense connection to food and drink, especially when subsistence was more common than the market society represented by our building.

Arriving in Pembridge and parking in the Market Square outside the house, already drunk on the apple fumes and filled with Bruegel's images of the harvest, I was aware how luxurious, how profligate our life would have seemed to our Elizabethan counterparts. Many of our own apples had already rotted and it was generally a job catching them before they split on the ground and bruised. Leaping up into the branches, I managed to get a dozen of the desserts for our table and store some of the Bramleys for winter by wrapping them in newspaper and shoving them in cupboards and under furniture. I also took an Ikea bagful for juicing, making myself almost sick on fifteen bottles of the sweet cloudy liquid. The waste, however, was largely due to lack of pruning, which left the majority of the fruit out of reach. Our predecessors would never have been so lax.

While few if any households in Pembridge were entirely self-sufficient at the time, given economies of scale, almost everything they grew would have been needed for survival. And it wasn't just the adults of the household who would have been afield, working on whatever crops they sowed and harvested, largely arable, with the addition of root vegetables (though not the mistrusted potato) and minimal livestock. Children were very much part of the workforce, which continued through to the industrial era, before the establishment of compulsory (and free) primary education at the end of the 19th century.

In the 1841 census, one of the earliest complete and comprehensible documents relating to the entire population of Britain, each of the five members of the Harris family who lived at Stepps House, from mother and father, aged forty-eight, to the youngest child, aged fifteen, was at work. Contrary to any patriarchal narrative, the mother and daughters performed as key a role as the men, though whether that was celebrated is another matter entirely. The oldest daughter was an agricultural labourer, while the seventeen-year-old son, named William, like his father, was a mason; the fifteen-year-old daughter, on the other hand, was a dressmaker. These 19th-century trades show some diversity in comparison to the inhabitants or, rather, the operators of the building in the Elizabethan period, given the even more challenging circumstances of the economy and its carefully defined hierarchy. In the late 1500s, more or less everyone's attentions were focused on the land, whether they owned it or not.

THE DELINEATION of class, seemingly a product of later politics, was already well established in the 16th century. Even among what might be called the general echelons of society, outside the ruffs of Elizabeth's court, things were clearly segregated, chiefly through property and the ability to earn and eat. Gentlemen owned land, but let it to others to farm, including through copyhold of inheritance or for life, the tenure of land based on manorial records. Sometimes, the land would be leased. A yeoman might also own freehold land, but more often than not it was let from a gentleman or the manor, and the yeoman would in turn employ labourers to assist with his farming. And then, towards the bottom of the pile, was the barely subsisting husbandman, who didn't own any land and normally had to rent it.

While some lets decreased after the Dissolution of the Monasteries, the consequent seizure of acreage into private (gentry-based) ownership meant that around 20 per cent of all cultivated land in England, including some of its most fertile and valuable manors, was under aristocratic control, as detailed in the village rent rolls. Added to this was the continued policy of enclosing common land, sometimes by newly ennobled proprietors and rectors, and, more often than not, the sudden removal of access and grazing rights, thereby allowing those with least even less. And when these policies combined, the situation for a single village and, particularly, the poorest among its population could become parlous overnight.

The seizure of shared land into private ownership, and the consolidation of smallholdings into larger farms, had been happening since the 13th century, but gained significant pace during the 1500s and would continue well into the future, until a 19th-century Trier-born philosopher was able to lament that 'the very memory of the connection between the agricultural labourer and communal property had, of course, vanished'. The policy perpetuated impoverishment and thereby widened the wealth gap even further, triggering various outspoken critics, not least Thomas More, who railed against enclosure in his influential *Utopia*:

Wherever it is found that the sheep of any soil yield a softer and richer wool than ordinary, there the nobility and gentry, and even those holy men, the abbots! not contented with the old rents which their farms yielded, nor thinking it enough that they, living at their ease, do no good to the public, resolve to do it hurt instead of good. They stop the course of agriculture, destroying houses and towns, reserving only the churches, and enclose grounds that they may lodge their sheep in them. As if forests and parks had swallowed up too little of the land, those worthy countrymen turn the best inhabited places into solitudes; for when an insatiable wretch, who is a plague to his country, resolves to enclose many thousand acres of ground, the owners, as well as tenants, are turned out of their possessions by trick or by main force, or, being wearied out by ill usage, they are forced to sell them; by which means those miserable people, both men and women, married and unmarried, old and young, with their poor but numerous families (since country business requires many hands), are all forced to change their seats, not knowing whither to go; and they must sell, almost for nothing, their household stuff, which could not bring them much money, even though they might stay for a buyer.

Applying his humanist philosophies to everyday commerce, More, like his less principled contemporaries, Cardinal Wolsey and Thomas Cromwell, wrestled with the issue throughout his officialdom. Most crucially, he felt, the enclosure of land and the change of its use robbed labourers of an important occupation. 'One shepherd can look after a flock,' he continued in *Utopia*, 'which will stock an extent of ground that would require many hands if it were to be ploughed and reaped.'

In a rent roll from the early 1600s, it was clear just how many residents in the village were occupied with agriculture, on both a self-sufficient and semi-commercial basis. The listings of the land owned by Thomas Coningsby at Hampton Court on the other side of Leominster were divided into the four quarters of the village: twenty-one entries for West Street, leading from the Market Square out to Kington; eighteen for London Street, leading east to Leominster and beyond; twenty-four for Bridge Street, down to the River Arrow; and seventeen for Buthall (or Boothall) Hill, where our house is situated. The unit of measurement was a burgage plot or tenement, a local variant of the customary subdivisions of acres, rods and perches. Occasionally, a burgage was a plot adjoining the house, though the term also pertained to an enclosed field, established by Coningsby (and others) as Lord of the Manor, by dividing manorial land.

The size of the plots varied from jurisdiction to jurisdiction. The burgesses were the tenants of these lands and paid rent in cash or kind. Even the smallest plot was listed. Thomas Bougough rented two 'burgadges' and eleven smaller units and was consequently charged 2s 11d. His wife or relative Katherine Bougough rented six and a half and was charged 6s 6d, though there were others with the tiniest of plots, indicating that these related to the division of fields rather than land attached to houses, which were more or less built in the same size and style. Likewise, the villagers may well have rented from the church, as listed in a separate glebe terrier, or from outside the immediate confines of the village, when they would have had to pay the Devereux family, given that this would have related to the tenancies of 'Pembridge Foreign'. On one of the rent rolls, two capons are listed as annual payment, which doubtless tolled the knell of that year's Christmas dinner.

Wealth disparity was prevalent within the system and survival was key, yet even those considered comfortable could struggle. A relatively well-to-do farmer or yeoman, such as Harrye Stede, whose will detailed impressive numbers of cattle and sheep, would have had to sow and harvest a hundred acres on the basis of a 25 per cent yield-to-seed success rate in order to make his bread, feed his livestock, prepare for the following year and have £70 surplus to be sold at market. That was what might have made its way to our house, to be kept over winter or traded in the Market Hall and on stalls in the churchyard – or on the conspicuously broad West Street – twice weekly. But even a yeoman, who was doing pretty well in general, might have struggled to maintain and harvest a hundred acres. He would have had to employ other workers, like those in Bruegel's painting, and they in turn would have had to be paid, in kind or otherwise, when they weren't toiling their own land. They would also need cider to refresh them during the day, made from the apples of the yeoman's orchard, though these likewise demanded strenuous hours of harvesting, pressing and bottling.

A husbandman, a rung further down the ladder, might only have had ten acres of arable crop – a statute of 1589 stipulated just four acres per newly built home – which, considering his own needs and that of his family, would give him a couple of pounds to spend every year. Almost nothing to live on. When the harvest was bountiful, prices would collapse and the husbandman would lose out entirely. While some families were able to provide just what they required, with a few fruit trees, a flock of sheep kept on common land and a share of the village's fields on a rotation basis, they were few and far between. Many would also have to rely on the market for produce. And for those who lived outside the sphere of agriculture, but who nonetheless depended on farmers, such as cobblers, farriers and wheelwrights, the effects could be even graver. It was a world of struggle, but it also meant that, far from being uncivilized, 16th-century society was in direct contact with what it grew and eventually ate and, moreover, who had created the produce.

The modern-day replica of the farming class system was clear to see in The New Inn that September evening. It was here that the landowners mixed with their tenants, while, down at the village's other pub, The Red Lion, the labourers and the younger, rowdier farmers tended to drink together. In the past – a source of local legend – there were around ten such hostelries up and down West Street, London Street and Bridge Street. Our house sat between the two survivors, but as our front door was directly opposite The New Inn, it proved a more immediate home, like an extension of our sitting room – I often forget to change out of my slippers. Inside, on that September evening, the fire was lit, slowly smouldering its way through a rotten oak that had been pulled down in one of the lanes. Piles of wood had been placed outside the door and would fuel the hearth for months ahead. The main bar was absolutely full, with everyone forced inside for the first time in weeks; we were glad to be back.

The New Inn is a defiantly analogue pub and has been for years. The 'tight-trousered farm labourers' of the 1960s, at least according to the *Sunday Times*, 'spurn the fruit machine and play dominoes, shove-ha'penny, darts and quoits, and sing their own, obscene versions of folk songs'. The fruit machines have now gone entirely, as have the cigarette vending machines – the shove-ha'penny board nonetheless remains – while Jane still refuses to play recorded music, so it's usually conversation

that provides the soundtrack, sometimes at a rising volume, mixing with those occasional folk tunes, as well as the omnipresent obscenities.

On Saturday evenings, Harold, a farmer in his eighties, arrives from Llandrindod Wells to have a single glass of ginger wine and regale the Pembridge locals with his stories and observations. A keen amateur economist, he uses the penning of sheep in the apple orchards of the Marches as a prime example of spreading fixed costs, challenging even Thomas Piketty to come up with a better illustration. Merry one evening, I encouraged him to go to the World Economic Forum in Davos the following year. And fruit was also the topic of conversation between Tony, my Elizabethan coppice friend, and Ian, another farmer who had recently deposited a bucket of damsons on our doorstep, which were steeping in gin for Christmas. In the far corner of the back bar that September evening, he and Tony were engrossed in trying to identify an apple.

They had already looked through copies of *The Herefordshire Pomona* and the *Pomona Herefordiensis* that had been handed down by Tony's great-grandfather, one of the first subscribers. But it was proving hard to match the apple to the beautiful watercolours. Instead, Ian had brought with him a later volume, full of hybrids and imports, and they were reduced to silence as they flicked through the pages, now and again raising the fruit to the light. Next to them, chattier by far, was Barry, a jeweller from Birmingham, who had determinedly journeyed to his cottage in Pembridge every weekend for years, even during the highest of floods. From Barry, now retired, came an intense list of instructions on how and where we should buy the best gold, the only metal, the only investment, he felt, that would improve in value over the years. By the time he had ventured into the darker recesses of my knowledge of the periodic table, encouraging us to purchase palladium – or was it polonium? – the pints had well and truly kicked in.

We left the pub with a few 'good evening, headmaster' farewells and went back to the house to turn on the hot water and begin making a tardy supper. I walked through the rooms, checking that everything was OK after the weeks away, but also imagining, instead of books, rugs, pictures and silver, what might have been there on an autumn evening just over four hundred years ago. The building's different levels, with their varying temperatures, as we came to learn on winter nights, would have served distinct functions. At the bottom, underneath the main structure and set within the earth – like many timber-framed houses, there are no real foundations to Stepps House – was, by far, the coolest part, the perfect place for fats and meat (perhaps like the butcher's stall in another Antwerp artist Pieter Aertsen's 1551 painting *A Meat Stall with the Holy Family Giving Alms*). The 'ground' floor, raised above the market and quite dry, might have been used for stockpiling grain. And at the front of the house, when the wisteria dies back, you can still see the outline of an old loading hatch. There was also the side door, leading onto the steps to the churchyard, with, next to it, windows that might have been a stall. And there was doubtless a similar arrangement downstairs – even in the 1970s and 1980s, the undercroft had been used as a workshop.

Finally, above the main floor, in what is now our bedroom with its raised ceiling, was the loft space. Apples and pears, placed on straw – so as not to waste the stalks of the arable crop – would have been left there over winter and turned every now and then to keep them aired, dry and free from rot. In its infancy, Stepps House was a resolutely practical building, just as it had, according to the estate agents, become completely impractical for most purchasers. We didn't care, however, that it had neither a designated parking space nor a bath or that the stairs were too steep. Young and just about fit enough to bound up the steps, we loved our harvest home, just like the one in that gleefully blinkered Victorian hymn, where 'all is safely gathered in, ere the winter storms begin'.

·　·　·

AS I sat in bed that evening, I couldn't get 'Come, Ye Thankful People, Come' out of my head. I'd raised the 'song of harvest home' and it had promptly turned into a tedious earworm. Its idea that God had provided the harvest, ready for the onslaught of colder weather, struck me as ridiculous, clouded in 19th-century piety. While it was more or less a philosophy espoused and understood around the time of our home's establishment, it rankled, tipping everything towards the (absent) heavenly provider and consequently underestimating the hard graft of the agricultural labourer and the exhaustion that followed the end of harvest.

Around the village, nature did indeed look wrung out. The hop bines were cut – our own had already crinkled – and the apples were being shaken from their trees, first by wind and then by machine. The wheat, barley and oats were long gone, with the stubble left to rot in the rain, in the hope of preventing erosion. It hadn't always been the case. I remember well the September journeys back to school across the Cotswolds during my early teens, when the escarpments were blazing with fire, until the Crop Residues (Burning) Regulations of 1993 changed all that. Now, the stubble is often ploughed back into the earth to boost organic matter, though, sometimes, the fields aren't tilled at all.

The following morning, as I took Toby for a soggy walk on an already darker day, I stood at the edge of one of the wheat fields that was about to be turned over to rapeseed, all part of a rotation process that dates back centuries. Although similarly ancient, rape has become more present in recent years. It provides greater advantages within the alternation of cereals and the yield can improve up to 10 per cent in the two years following a rape harvest.

It can also be planted with companions such as buckwheat and clover, to encourage beneficial predators and pollinators, suppress weeds and enrich the soil. But there was still something brutal about that word rape and something equally ruthless about the manner in which last year's crop was being wiped from the landscape. In the field beyond, the gold of summer was gone, replaced by a rich brown that proclaimed autumn even before the leaves began to fall and the sloes burst their bruise-coloured skins.

Seeing the fields sliced into ribbons by modern tractors and ploughs was nothing, however, compared to the brutality of another ploughman I had found in my search for images from the 16th century. Unlike Bruegel, who had left the process of ploughing out of his season paintings, Holbein didn't flinch at showing the sheer struggle of that work. In his woodcuts for *The Dance of Death* – created during the 1520s but first published in 1538 – a skeleton drives a sad quartet of emaciated, overworked horses, while the haggard ploughman dutifully follows behind. Around him, there are the familiar timber-framed cottages and farmsteads, a church too, rolling hills and the sun's late rays. A memento mori, the image, drawing on the older tradition of the *danse macabre* or *Totentanz*, is also a commentary on the hierarchy of the world, placed at the end of a sequence that begins with the Pope, the Emperor and the King before moving through the ranks to end with the Ploughman and the Child. Holbein's compassionate treatment of the ploughman underlines the exertion that was, and is, often forgotten yet essential to keep such a system and cycle going, to prop up those who wouldn't deign to dirty their fingernails, as George Sand, pondering the image, later described:

> The working man is too overwhelmed, too miserable, too afraid of the future, to enjoy the beauty of the countryside and the charms of rustic living. For him, the golden fields, the beautiful meadows, the noble animals, represent bags of coins from which he will take only a portion, insufficient for his needs, and yet those damned bags need to be filled every year to satisfy the master and pay for the right to live sparingly and miserably on his land.

Holbein's unshod ploughman, with threadbare clothes and a broken straw hat, had been replicated in part from an image for September from a 1524 spiritual almanac, albeit with the crucial figure of Death added, which in turn inspired the ploughman in Bruegel's famous 1558 painting (though his creation of it has long been in doubt): *Landscape with the Fall of Icarus*.

Standing afield outside the village that morning, however, with Shropshire's Titterstone Clee Hill peeking through the mist, I couldn't help but think of another voice beyond the grave, A. E. Housman's 'Is My Team Ploughing', so eloquently set to music by Ralph Vaughan Williams in 1909, the year the composer visited Pembridge. The centrality of the image of a struggling ploughman across the centuries, and his almost Sisyphean task of turning the land over and over again, showed that the yearly cycle and its characters were absolutely fixed. Unlike the Victorians' harvest hymns, however, I had to avoid idealizing our home and the land around it.

THAT FIRST summer may have been thrilling for witnessing everything 'safely gathered in', but not every year was so generous, so easy. The small margins of those who picked the apples in the Elizabethan era or sowed, reaped and ploughed the village's fields were severely tested, both by the bountiful harvests that brought down prices and by the famines that similarly dogged their lives. After 'hats full, caps full, three bushel bags full', as an old wassailing song would have it, the following year produced just one apple on the trees in our garden, thanks to bud and bloom damage caused by a spring hailstorm, and a comparably pitiable crop in the village orchards.

In the 16th century, when the annual harvest failed, villages such as Pembridge failed. An equilibrium had to be struck, else food prices went up rapidly and, without a surplus, even among yeomen, scarcity and death followed. The husbandman's ten acres might have simply provided enough for bread, with little opportunity to buy other produce at market, to say nothing of planning for the following year. Or he was forced to prepare for a better then and cut back on the now. Either way, it was a challenge to balance the books, though the women in the family normally undertook that task, as well as doing the same for the accounts of the village church. They were also responsible for attending and bartering at market, as witnessed in one of the chapbook woodcuts of the age. Especially tough were the years when harvest failures were replicated further afield. Starvation could blight society in the late 16th century, with its expanding population, and small farmers found themselves in deep debt, particularly in the undulating west, where agriculture, despite years of abundance, proved arduous due to prevailing wet weather fronts from the Atlantic – that too has not changed. There were few reserves and grain had to be imported, which only exacerbated the problem.

In this enclosed, divided and, often, penurious world, the security of our home must have been crucial. Rationing of grain and apples would have been part of daily life and, when the market wasn't open, the careful storage of its produce was paramount. And it wasn't only about life in the village, at least when good harvests came in. Storage was key to the larger mechanisms of the mercantile sphere, through which villages were able to levy the value of their produce against that of other centres. Our home and the Hall outside the window were just two cogs in such a scheme, connected from town to town, and born specifically from need rather than curiosity, to diversify for the sake of survival.

As our building was coming into being, market forces in Elizabethan society were reaching their peak. The shift from a predominantly self-sufficient system to a more doggedly commercial one was the result of both local and national concerns, but it was also responding – or at least trying to respond – to a wider, global crisis. During the second half of the 16th century, a phenomenon that had long (but quietly) been present became forefront and centre. It was later to be known as the Little Ice Age and was one of the defining occurrences of the period. It brought with it bitterly cold winters, when the populace's hand-to-mouth existence was tested to the max. Rainy summers followed, when, quite unlike Bruegel's idyllic August of earlier in the century, unharvested wheat rotted in the fields or, in some cases, was destroyed by hailstorms. A two-degree drop in mean temperatures meant that all growing processes slowed, including the oaks from which our home was built, and the arable harvest, one of the most crucial aspects of Pembridge's economy and power, didn't return to pre-1570 levels until well into the 18th century.

What was immediately apparent about these dates was that they tallied almost exactly with the two most significant moments in the life of our building: 1570, when the harvests began to dwindle, was when storage and forward planning became paramount and our home was constructed; and the mid 18th century, when the harvests finally began to recover, was when the importance of the market in Pembridge came to an end and our building had its chimneys added and the roof raised so that it could begin its new domestic chapter. As such, the house may well have been part of a large number of (again nameless) properties surrounding the Broadstone and Buthall Hill that were sold between 1749 and 1867.

Broadstone still provides the name of an early-18th-century house behind The New Inn, taking its moniker from the large flat stone – the mark, march or merch stone – that would have stood both on West Street, once part of the marketplace, and on the south-west edge of the extant Market Hall, to indicate the village's original points of exchange. The second of these stones sits diagonally opposite the north-east angle post that is presumed to rest on the base of a medieval market or preaching cross. Buthall Hill, a name no longer actively used in Pembridge, though already noted in various rent rolls, referred to the hill on which the booth or market was situated, rising up towards the old castle mound above the church, or to the court, which was held at both The New Inn – the lock-up is now used as a beer cellar – and the appropriately named Court House Farm, where an even more extensive series of cells occupies the basement. As part of this system of local law and order, there would also have been a village pound for unruly animals and livestock, as survives just a few miles away at Staunton on Arrow – now, thankfully, out of use.

Vestiges of the village's mercantile life nonetheless survived beyond the Little Ice Age and our home's original role, with market house tolls collected well into the 19th century. But with better roads and the increasing dominance of nearby Leominster and Hereford, as well as a shift from a local economy to a national one, the original purpose of both our building and the Market Hall ended. There was a casual market every Monday until the 1920s, replicated in the charming though sadly abortive farmers' market of recent years, and the annual hiring fairs for harvest labourers continued too, particularly at the Cowslip Fair in May, but Pembridge's prime had long since ceased. Now, only when members of the Royal British Legion distribute poppies in November, or when people come and sell wreaths, Christmas cards and handmade ornaments on an early December evening, do you get a sense of the Market Hall's original purpose. It had simply survived through neglect – there was no demand for its replacement – while our home was quickly repurposed. Like so many villages across Europe, Pembridge faded.

VI.

Across Miles

As the weekend came to an end and I felt the return of that strange tug, of homesickness, of being away from our new anchor, I was nonetheless able to turn to the comfort of my trip to Vienna. I would be leading a group of travellers who were as keen as I was on museums, art galleries and grand continental cafés. I had always felt at ease in the Austrian capital, ever since my first visit, aged twelve. Then and since, I'd been amazed by a city where so many histories and dynasties overlapped, like its ubiquitous tramlines, and the buildings seemed to assert (and appropriate) an extraordinarily tissued past. Vienna is another historical storeroom, with the Kunsthistoriches Museum, the city's principal art gallery, a crowning emblem for this gathered epic. And on this particular expedition, I would feel the tethers of our home in its midst.

I'd been to the Habsburg (turned state) collection of art and antiquities many times before. It's an astonishing place of wonders, displayed in a bejewelled case of a building. It is not, however, a museum testifying to great taste in art, though that is plain to see. The Kunsthistoriches Museum is a building of power – now disappeared – filled with objects that demonstrate the Habsburgs' predominance in parts of Europe. While you will look in vain for French or English paintings, given that they never controlled either country, there is, arguably, no better place for sweeps of Spanish, Italian and Netherlandish art combined, due to the Habsburgs' robust presence in all three areas. As such, many of the Bruegel paintings that were fascinating me had passed into the hands of the Central European dynasty.

Bruegel's original patron, Nicolaes Jonghelinck, hadn't been able to enjoy the fruits of his commission for long. Created in 1565, the paintings had hung on the walls of Jonghelinck's dining room for just over four years before he died in 1570. By 1594, the paintings, though perhaps not all six of them, had become the property of the City of Antwerp, before the originals were bequeathed to Archduke Ernest, who, as a Habsburg, was serving as governor of the Netherlands. When Ernest died in Brussels (also Bruegel's place of death) in 1595, the paintings were passed to his brother, Rudolf II, the Holy Roman Emperor, who masterminded the beautification of Prague – his chosen seat, instead of Vienna. A Renaissance man, Rudolf was as keen a patron of science and the occult as he was of art and architecture, more so, really, than ever displaying a talent for governing. Six years after his death, Rudolf's vacillations and indecisions had helped trigger the Thirty Years War, resulting in the slaughter of some eight million Europeans.

By 1659, eleven years after the Peace of Westphalia had effectively ended three decades of death in Central Europe, Rudolf's cherished paintings were in the possession of Leopold Wilhelm, another Habsburg governor of the Netherlands. Two of the sequence were kept in the castle at what was then Ofen (Buda), now one of the constituent parts of Budapest. And while one returned to the imperial collection in Vienna, it was held in storage with two others, having no immediate value. Eventually, *The Harvesters* was sold in Paris in 1816 and, through another sale, made its way to Brussels, until 1919, when it was purchased for the Met in New York.

Another painting, featuring early summer, had passed, perhaps as a gift, through the Lobkowicz princes of Bohemia, which they moved from their palace in Vienna to residences in the Czech lands. It was then exhibited publicly during the Soviet period (and remains for all paying guests to see in the Lobkowicz Palace within Prague Castle). The three 'Viennese' paintings were more or less forgotten, however, until the magniloquent Kunsthistoriches Museum opened at the end of the 19th century, all part of the Habsburgs' aggrandisement of Vienna, which focused on the construction of the Ringstrasse, the most pompous ring road in history.

Outside anniversary exhibitions and their suffocating crowds, the scale and grandeur of the Kunsthistoriches Museum allows its visitors a veil of anonymity and hush that is rare in equivalent galleries. Walking up the imposing main staircase, which the architects based on a Neapolitan model (another area linked to the Habsburgs), and later decorated by the young Gustav Klimt, you make your way along a galleried landing to one of the museum's enfilades. Each wing unfolds like the rooms of a Renaissance palace, providing a glimpse into the lives of the commissioners of the building, as well as their immense wealth and power.

The section dedicated to Northern European painting is, counter-intuitively, in the south-east corner of the gallery – the majority of Southern European painting is, conversely, on the other side of the museum. I knew the drill, swinging through the towering doors of the first room. It was filled with the finest examples of portraiture from the 16th century, including one of Holbein's no doubt flattering images of Jane Seymour from around 1536 and the 73-year-old Dr John Chambers, one of the physicians to Jane's husband Henry VIII, from 1543. Moving past these paintings, both of which were acquired after the death of a British courtier and grand tourist, Thomas Howard, the 14th Earl of Arundel, by the even more acquisitive Archduke Leopold Wilhelm, you enter the Bruegel room, featuring more of the governor's spoils.

It is a lofty, grand space, quite contrary to the *sancta rusticitas* of the images contained within. Pale grey-blue banquettes enclose large grilles. The walls are also grey, albeit with a purple tinge. Above, a gilded ceiling speaks of the Ringstrasse's strident historicism. Such a haughty space engenders silence – though, admittedly, not during a blockbuster exhibition. Ordinarily, and when returning since, there is a distinctive soundtrack to the Kunsthistoriches Museum, and this corner in particular: the slow but continual creak of the parquet beneath the visitors' feet. Equally unique is the smell of the place. From the grilles in the ensquared banquettes comes an aromatic scent. It's slightly acidic, catching at the back of the throat. But it's full of spice too, a reminder of Antwerp, Bruegel and Nicolaes Jonghelinck's home, and its trade roots, bringing back the nutmeg, cinnamon and bitter lemons that fragrance the gallery's air, and the bolts of wool from centres such as Pembridge, as well as spreading printed images from the city's studios, even as far as Herefordshire.

Here, sitting alongside two other images originally in Jong-helinck's collection, the larger *Tower of Babel* and *The Procession to Calvary*, are three of Bruegel's season paintings, by far the gloomiest from the surviving quintet. Not for Vienna the sun-filled glories of the Lobkowicz family's *Haymaking* or the Met's *Harvesters*. No, for the Habsburgs and their grandly serious gallery, it had to be *The Hunters in the Snow* of deep winter, the aptly named *The Gloomy Day*, depicting spring's slovenly arrival, and *The Return of the Herd*.

It was to the last of these paintings that I was drawn. As an October day sank outside the Kunsthistoriches Museum — though, largely lacking windows, except onto internal courtyards, the building conveys artificial rather than natural vistas – it was apt to feel an affinity for this image of autumn. Reliably, Bruegel captures the shift in seasonal activity, weather and mood. Dark, scudding clouds on the right-hand side of the painting deny the last vestige of summer on the left. But it is not only the clouds that are moving. In the foreground, passing among trees that could be from the very same copse viewed in *The Harvesters* – like a symphonist, Bruegel relishes interconnected motifs – is a herd of cattle being driven into a village of timber-framed houses.

This is the act of transhumance, the transfer of cows (or sheep) from pasture to pasture. In Alpine areas, including Austria, the tradition takes two constituent parts: in spring, there is the festival of *Almauftrieb*, where cows are taken from the village up into the higher pastures to spend the summer gorging on the meadows' rich herbs, grasses and flowers; in autumn, the reverse happens, with the *Almabtrieb*, as the cows are brought down from the mountains, to be protected from the worst of winter and milked in the sheds at the farm. Bruegel must have witnessed these processions, which continue today, when he travelled through the Alps with Jonghelinck's brother Jacques on their way to Italy, for it wasn't a tradition followed in the flatlands of his home.

Around the returning herd – the German name for the painting, *Heimkehr der Herde*, underlines the sense of home or *Heim* – are all the markers of autumn. The leaves have largely fallen. In the vineyards down by the river, workers strip the last vines of the *Auslese* harvest. On the opposite bank, the first frost is already in evidence. Bird traps are being laid, while nets are left to catch the larger game. But as much as there is promise of plenty, a gallows and other implements of torture positioned by the river portend trouble, as do the clouds above. And yet there is a transfiguring rainbow. Also of comfort is the herd itself, into which we, the viewer, are invited, thanks to the unblinking stare of a dappled white cow. A collective view, of working together, of facing the encroaching cold as a united village, is implied.

MINUTES PASSED in the gallery's solid air and I continued to look at Bruegel's autumn. While most of my group had huddled around the two versions of the *Tower of Babel* that had been placed next to each other, a couple of fellow travellers came to join me. Their appreciation was shared but silent. Annabelle, a charming if somewhat frank Australian, had come to Vienna with her daughter to pay homage to her late husband's roots. Eventually, it was she who broke the quiet.

'It's like the old bush stockmen.'

'Really?' I said, preferring the hush.

'Their routes are still there, right past our land,' she mused, with a hint of homesickness.

'Your land?' I asked, thinking of Alastair and Toby at home in Pembridge, enjoying the last days of half-term.

'My father's,' Annabelle continued. 'He was Scots.'

'But it's Alpine, surely?' queried Richard, another member of the group, who had otherwise spoken little on the trip.

'I wasn't saying it was Aussie,' Annabelle laughed.

'No. Quite so.'

'It's funny,' I responded. 'Bruegel did probably base this on the Alps – it's certainly not the Netherlands with those mountains – but he was doubtless aware of other systems.'

Transhumance, or a form of it, is also there in Spenser's *The Shepheardes Calender*. In June and July, the hapless Colin admires his friend Hobbinoll's ability to graze his sheep in the open countryside, but the shepherds are much closer to the farmhouse by September and October. Come December, Colin, 'weary of his former wayes' and comparing 'his life to the foure seasons of the yeare', sits alone with his sheep, who are pastured immediately outside the gate. But Annabelle's response, as well as the painting itself, had reminded me of another shifting herd, another *Heim*.

The practice of transhumance has continued in the valleys around my mum's birthplace at Bwlch-y-rhiw, where flocks of sheep are transferred between pastures: the *hafod* of the summer months, high up in the hills; and the *hendre*, down by the main farm, to which, in late-autumn, the shepherd would return his flock. Even I can remember the sheep being much closer to the house during the winter months, when the top of my grandfather's mountain, Mynydd Mallaen, was left exposed, regardless of a good fleece. Around Pembridge, village livestock is likewise moved from field to field, though there isn't quite the same differentiation of lowland for winter and highland for summer as practised in the hillier edges of the county and further into Wales.

Much more familiar to Pembridge was another farming practice that Bruegel evoked: the drovers. It's a tradition that counters any claim of the emergence of a modern market society as late as the 16th century. Beginning at least three hundred years before, farmers from the uplands of Scotland and my grandfather's corner of Wales, as well as Cumbria, had driven their cattle and sheep to where they could command much higher values. Arduous and often dangerous, the droving life nonetheless had its rewards. It is a truism that an Englishman's love of roast beef furnished the coffers of many Celtic farmers. It also created an extraordinary network through the British Isles, the routes of which remain etched in the landscape, as are its clusters of Scots pine.

These evergreen trees were chosen to mark the way, like the single surviving example at the top of May Hill, one of Robert Frost and Edward Thomas's sacred sites, west of Gloucester, on the border with Herefordshire. The trees were unique features on the horizon, given their distinctive crown, and could grow quickly, thriving on relatively poor soil in exposed areas. While the drovers' originals, like that on May Hill, have largely gone, their descendants remain, marking various junctions and streams along the routes, as well as fields near pubs and farms that were welcoming to the drovers (which was not always guaranteed).

Shortly before I'd left for Vienna, an old farmer called James, born in Hardwick, a hamlet beyond the orchards in Pembridge, told me about the last of the drovers that his father remembered. Standing in the back bar of The New Inn, he explained that they were all relatively poor men, some only speaking Welsh and unable to pay for rail transport for their livestock. Like his ancestors before him, James's father had offered them shelter, as the driving team journeyed from mid-Wales to Hereford and beyond.

Finishing his pint, James told me where to find the pines that the drovers had planted – 'left at the top of the orchard, along the back lane; you'll see them' – and the following morning, I went to locate the spot.

It wasn't far from where Vaughan Williams had been recording traditional Herefordshire airs in 1909. One of them, fittingly heard in versions right across the British Isles, but which he collected from one Mr Hirons nearby, even seemed to refer to the non-deciduous pines:

> The trees they do grow high,
> The leaves they do grow green.
> Many is the time my true love I've seen,
> Many an hour I have watched him all alone.
> He's young,
> But he's daily growing.

The thicket in question was so compacted that it was hard to get inside, even for Toby, with rotting bracken and long brambles. But I could see the clear outline of the Scots pines above, some with a breadth like the acacias of the Serengeti. There were taller, narrower trees too, shooting up through the canopy, but they must have multiplied over the last century or so. There wasn't any space for cattle or sheep now, though it provided perfect cover for a mob of sheltering deer, deep within the copse.

The drovers' herds and flocks could be surprisingly vast in number and require several men on horseback to ensure a safe and profitable journey, with packs of stumpy but loyal dogs, not spaniels like Toby, but heelers such as the Welsh corgi, coming along to bite or 'heel' the cattle and so drive them onwards. The dogs had such a sharp sense of direction that they would come to know the routes much better than their owners and, having reached market, they would run home, traversing hundreds of miles. Bounding through southern and central England, all the time feasting on vermin, they would eventually cross back into Wales, leaping over streams, rivers and hills, and appear at home to warn their mistress that the master was on his way. As such, the farmers' wives near Harlech on the Cambrian coast said they could accurately predict their husbands' time of arrival after the dogs had slumped by the hearth.

Due to the demands of the journey, cows would have to be shod, requiring a whole network of smithies across the countryside. An entire industry, in fact, arose from the tradition, including bridges and tollhouses. One, now at the National Museum of Wales in St Fagans, but originally built on the southern outskirts of Aberystwyth, indicated that 'For every drove of Oxon, Cows, or Neat Cattle, the sum of Ten Pence per Score, and so in proportion for any greater or less number' was charged, while a drove of 'Calves, Hogs, Sheeps, or Lambs' cost half the amount. Journeying from Wales to the markets in London, as well as elsewhere in the south-east, could quickly become expensive, so many droves took to the hill paths, even if such detours risked encountering thieves.

One of several routes over the Welsh uplands went directly through my grandfather's farm. Travelling across the area, most of the herds had arrived from Tregaron and the coast, a place used for fattening mid-Wales livestock. They came south through Lampeter, after which the animals would be shod at Pumsaint, where the old forge later became a garage – a modern-day equivalent of sorts (though my grandfather still took the farm nag there, well into my childhood). The drove would then pass over the mountains, through the land of the Welsh Robin Hood, Twm Siôn Cati, himself a drover from the late 16th century. Climbing to the north of my family's farm, the team descended into the valley through the top of the yard and on, down past the chapel, where my grandparents are buried and where, one day, my parents will be too. Every time we went to place flowers on Dadcu and Mamgu's grave, we crossed the path of the drovers.

Sometimes, the team would bypass the farm altogether, travelling over the mountains in front or behind. But whichever way they went, it was only the beginning of a much longer journey, across Abergwesyn Common, where the drovers could rest by the River Irfon, and then to Builth Wells and into England. As they came over the border, the route traversed an even more ancient track, Offa's Dyke – named after the 8th-century Anglo-Saxon king of Mercia – at one of its most spectacular points, Hergest Ridge. Below is Herefordshire and, within it, one of the first ports of call in England: Pembridge.

From our village, the drovers would have moved on to Hereford, where some of the cattle were marketed and slaughtered. They also went across to Worcester and to Shakespeare's birthplace at Stratford and down, past my parents' home in the Vale of Aylesbury, another area used for fattening cattle, into London, right by the front door of my old flat at the bottom of Hampstead Hill.

To me, the drovers' routes weren't so much marks of transhumance on a massive scale as they were the arteries of a collective body or family tree over time. The pathways provided points of connection between histories, periods and customs, and, through the imaginary highways and byways of Bruegel's paintings, a network between places that I had known and loved – and would come to know and love. Our home was just one of its hubs.

THE ANCIENT pathways of the drovers, of transhumance, link together thousands of places of residence, gathering, worship and battle. And they join other paths and strands. The author and archaeologist Alfred Watkins, whose birthplace was Hereford's Imperial Hotel – later the Berni Inn where my family and I ate during the 1980s – thought that a whole sequence of straight lines could be drawn between these historic structures. They represented routes created by ancient British tribes and civilizations, precursors even to the Roman roads that are still in evidence across the landscape, including from Caerleon to Wroxeter through Canon Pyon near Pembridge (where, thanks to the straightness of the road and a lapse in concentration, I was caught speeding by West Mercia Police). Watkins was convinced of the power of these paths, this 'alignment across miles of country of a great number of objects, or sites of objects, of prehistoric antiquity'.

Traversing Offa's Dyke and the very tracks along which the drovers had come, spotting the grids between mounds, water sites, trees, camps, churches and mark stones, including the corner of the Market Hall in Pembridge outside our home, Watkins eventually published his ideas, specifically in *The Old Straight Track*. Although he had great passion and conviction, 'beyond the possibility of accidental coincidence', his ideas were repeatedly

debunked by established archaeologists. The theories nonetheless found an avid following among neo-pagans believing in earth
mysteries and in the spiritual significance of fault lines, hills
and rivers. I was on the side of the spiritualists rather than the
sceptics, finding it impossible to ignore the paths that had led
directly into my own geography, not only suggesting the people
who had occupied my home at the end of the 16th century, but
also the people further west who travelled through, bringing with
them their own topographies and histories, including memories
of my ancestors whom they would have met.

Such an intense connection to the land was something my
grandfather sensed in his bones. The energy Dadcu, like my
uncle today, had to muster to continue the Welsh hill-farming
traditions – now under threat, despite all government promises – or that the drovers felt, treading in the same paths as their
forebears, had to have been ancestral, primeval even. It was like
the path, according to Milton, that our first parents 'hand in
hand with wandring steps and slow, through Eden took thir soli-
tarie way'. And it was there in the tracks that had crossed the
Australian bush from time immemorial, long before stock was
driven past Annabelle's father's land, those songlines, with their
antediluvian words and tunes that are still perceptible to the
Aboriginals. Bruce Chatwin, another surprising aficionado of the
Marches and the area around Pembridge, called them 'a spaghetti
of Iliads and Odysseys, writhing this way and that'.

But in the midst of their slog from west to east, would the
drovers have felt that connection? Would they have heard the
songlines of the Marches, as Vaughan Williams later did, when

intervening centuries had erased or added to the marks of the men and beasts that had travelled the roads before them? What would they have thought along the way? Was there a simple familiarity to the journey? Or was romance trounced by drudgery? Surely, certain points of call, features in the landscape, even those they had personally etched into soil and stone, as well as the faces they passed, would have prompted memories, happy and sad. One thing I did know was that the drovers were indeed heard to sing – loudly – in turn giving rise to an entire repertoire of folk songs and poems by and about them, another songline in the lay of the land.

Infinitely less tuneful were the packs' calls, heard for miles around, to warn the locals of their arrival. Farmers, after all, didn't want to see their own livestock swallowed into a drove. Combined with the cattle's mooing, bellowing and grunting or the incessant bleating of the sheep, which still rings around Pembridge as lorries drive lambs to slaughter along the A44 at the bottom of our garden, the drovers' call 'was something out of the common', as one early-20th-century observer remembered; 'neither shouting, calling, crying, singing, halloing or anything else, but a noise of itself, apparently made to carry and capable of arresting the countryside'. Those hollers of 'heiptro ho!' would have sounded in Pembridge too, right outside our front door, as the drove passed through the Market Square, perhaps to have cattle re-shod, or the farmer's horse re-saddled by George Rowlands, one of the previous owners of our home.

Rather than Stepps House, however, it is on Hergest Ridge, five miles west, that the drovers' presence is strongest. There, they carved a sort of etching plate for a map so densely woven it could no longer be read. Standing on the heathland, looking back to Wales and forward to England – or is it the other way around? – you can see the map in full-scale counterpart, where the ground near the trig point is packed with foils, missives and monograms. There are the marks of sheep, now left to graze on Offa's Dyke rather than being driven onwards. The paths of their woolly ancestors are visible too, with many abandoned pens and shelters. And in the near distance, I can see the road that leads from Kington to Pembridge, scarred with tarmac and much faster vehicles. Other wanderers would have carved an alternative line over Wapley Hill, following Glyndŵr's prowling troops. Yet despite all the lines and layers, the heaviest (perceived) mark in the landscape, the border between Wales and England, is invisible to the human eye, a mere construct of politics rather than the foil of ancient nomads.

Whenever I go up to Hergest Ridge or to Hay Bluff, taking Toby for a walk, I spring between Wales and England without a thought as to which side of the national divide I stand. Meanwhile, as Toby darts through the gorse and the wild horses, I feel a sense of elation – what John, my old chaplain's widower, described as being on top of the world. Sometimes, in the evening, Alastair and I take a bottle of wine up to Hergest with a couple of plastic cups, shelter behind the monkey puzzle trees or by the trig point, if the wind is down, and watch the sun set over Wales, casting the Bluff, Pen y Fan and Picws Du in bronze, before falling behind the Cambrians and into the Irish Sea. One of the other villagers, called Osian, often found drinking in the pub or under the Market Hall, even sleeps on the ridge when the weather is fine. Every spring, with nothing but an old feed-sack for shelter, he, his wife and their two daughters have a night under the stars, with unclouded views into several counties.

THAT APPARENT freedom, of the limitless right to roam — the modern-day, recreational equivalent of droving — is, sadly, an illusion. For all the spirit of a shared land, 'of my fathers' or of 'feet in ancient time', people have more often than not been denied such independence. There are primal pathways intersecting the land around Pembridge, right across the British Isles, but there are also fences and boundaries. It was this lack of freedom against which Thomas More railed, denouncing private property, advocating a share of wealth and labelling the Tudor hierarchy, of which he was doubtless a part, the 'conspiracy of the rich'.

The intensification of seizing land from common purpose during the 1500s didn't only affect those who had previously enjoyed direct grazing access within the confines of a village, it also changed the lives of everyone in Britain. Where, previously, there had been an implied right to pasture and to roam, there were suddenly barriers, even blockades. The drovers were often forced to detour as a result of enclosure and their very way of life was called into question. One of the paths they might have followed after leaving Pembridge, having sheltered in the pines at Hardwick, would have risen over Winsley Hill, south of Leominster. Travelling under the ridge that continues to Dinmore, the drovers would have skirted acres of ancient woodland and orchards.

That was until 1604, when the land was summarily enclosed. It had supposedly been part of the villages of Winsley and Hope, but the ownership was fiercely disputed by a landowner from nearby Ivington (nowadays the site of Monty Don's garden of Longmeadow, as featured on *Gardeners' World*). While the dispute concerning the ownership of Winsley Hill was largely irrelevant to the drovers, the enclosure itself proved hugely problematic.

Even today, it can be tedious to cross this beautiful part of the county, with its views north to Shropshire, given the sheer number of stiles, gates and ditches that mark this 400-year-old robbing of common land. With a dog, it's an even trickier business, and Alastair and I have had to become dab hands at passing Toby through and over fences, his fur wet with mud or matted with teasels. Sometimes, he defies the assault course entirely and darts through the hawthorn and blackthorn and hazel without a care for the grazes or the broken twigs. But it wasn't quite so easy with a flock of sheep or a herd of cattle.

Added to an already strenuous journey, the drovers were even more tightly monitored during the reigns of Edward VI and Elizabeth I. All itinerant farmers had to be householders and, furthermore, married and at least thirty years of age. In order to carry out their arduous work, walking from West Wales to the meat markets of London – Smithfield Street is still the name of the main road through the Welsh town of Llanidloes – they were required to hold an annual licence. When a drover carried this document, issued by the local jurisdiction, he was unlikely to be confused with a vagabond, though the term was also indiscriminately applied to anyone Welsh. There were other tags too, with travellers termed 'Egyptians' in Acts of 1530 and 1562, who ran the risk of being killed on the roads until as late as the end of the 18th century due to no other offence bar their nomadic life. In Herefordshire, however, the travelling community proved very useful for seasonal work in the orchards and hop gardens, right into the 20th century.

Although the lives of drovers and travellers were frequently compromised by changes to the law, including enclosure, this centuries-wide policy doubtless had an even more marked effect on the sedentary peasant. In the Welsh borders, the practice became the norm and resulted in the destruction of local economies, even entire villages. Luckily, Pembridge was big enough and just about affluent enough to ride out the change – at least for a time – though the Marches are filled with examples of completely abandoned villages. The former Shropshire settlement of Upton Cressett, thirty miles from Pembridge, was deserted in 1517 when Thomas Cressett emparked forty acres of its arable land. The seizure was listed in Cardinal Wolsey's Inquisition of Enclosures, but by 1647 nothing had been done to reverse the process and maps now show the former site of Upton Cressett within the deer park of the landowner's descendants. That was a relatively rare case of seizing land for personal use. More often than not, the powers that be enclosed land but continued to allow access through payment. A profligate court needed the income, especially when the debasing of currency had failed to shore up its ruin. But such an obvious disparity between the rich and the poor provoked rioting, and enclosure became as much a moral conundrum as it was an economic one.

Like Cardinal Wolsey, his predecessor as Lord High Chancellor, Thomas More's attempts to protect the underprivileged led to tension at court and inevitably – and for other significant reasons – both figures fell from Henry VIII's favour. Wolsey died in 1530, the year after he had been removed from office, while More was executed in 1535, due in part to his intransigence, as well as the machinations of Anne Boleyn and the members of her family who formed a significant portion of the twelve councillors, alongside seven justices, presiding at Sir Thomas's trial. Many aristocrats and landowners rejoiced at the downfall of both Wolsey and More, even though most couldn't have cared less about matters concerning the King's supremacy and the freedom of his marital bed that pushed him and, moreover, Boleyn to such ends.

Given the controversy and subsequent bloodletting, it was something of a surprise that the tenacious and ambitious Thomas Cromwell, also a councillor at More's trial, endorsed his predecessors' mistrust of enclosure. Eventually, however, he too had no choice but to turn his attentions elsewhere and abandon his profession to Henry to 'do the most profitable and beneficial thing that ever was done to the Common wealth of this your realm'. By the Dissolution of the Monasteries, such sentiments had been forgotten almost entirely, when land was moved from sacred into secular hands in an act that infinitely favoured the rich over the poor and consequently increased the wealth disparity of the age.

As a result of all these policies combined, the make-up of the British landscape changed precipitously during the 16th century, with intensive felling of timber making further dents in the countryside. Trees, woods, entire forests were cleared to create arable land and to furnish the material for buildings like our home, as well as for maritime use, with some six hundred oaks being required for every warship. Today's arguments about the felling of uplands and consequent flooding of lowlands were very much born during the 1500s, with the inundation of low-lying land aggravating the poverty of its peasantry. And the disputes between the people and the powerful only became more heated as the population expanded, from 2.4 million in the 1520s to 4.11 million at the beginning of the 17th century, the result of a combination of factors, including a comparable absence of major wars and epidemics, the relaxation of sexual morality during the Reformation and, for some (but not all), the ready availability of food.

Once land had been seized from common ownership, its possession was closely (and sometimes violently) guarded. Nowadays, the narrative is characterized by unmaintained footpaths, padlocked gates and barbed wire. But it is more pervasive than these simple but irritating obstructions to a friendly hike. Since the 1980s, there has been an equally determined privatization of large swathes of publicly owned land. In total, only 10 per cent has open access. Thousands and thousands of miles of public pathways have been lost due to years of land grabs, neglect and intensified agriculture. And although Devon and North Yorkshire have seen the most marked reduction in their footpaths, Herefordshire was third in a recent survey by the Ramblers, having lost 2,253 miles of public track.

Armed with these figures, Alastair and I began looking back at maps of the village, some over a century old, which we'd found among the piles of conveyancing papers. Over time, the path that had become our usual route in the morning with Toby through the first of the arable fields beyond the churchyard had actually diverged from its earlier course. Previously, it had split in two directions, one to the orchards and another, perhaps trodden by Vaughan Williams, to the farms and barns at Hardwick, thereby avoiding a (now) dangerous stretch of road. A path accessing a coppice that is often filled with rabbits, hares and deer, as well as an echoing owl, if I've left Toby's second walk too late, had also gone. Perhaps the advent of the car diminished such a need for paths between outlying hamlets, though I couldn't help but miss these variations on a walking theme that time, unconsciously, and the local landowners, more knowingly, had erased.

'Come back, Tobes,' Alastair shouted, while skirting one of the fields near Bearwood. But Toby had already vaulted towards the thicket in question.

'What's this,' I hissed, a normally foolproof way of bringing him back, with the promise of a gravy bone from a linty pocket.

Despite our efforts, Toby and his brown markings and docked tail had stolen into the trees after a rabbit colony. Alastair's endearingly gappy teeth meant that it was always left to me to whistle and wait for the dog's return. Luckily, Toby had a sharp sense of recall, but I was quietly thrilled at his wanton disregard for change, finding his own paths along tracks that had been laid down for centuries and since disappeared.

For those today who, against all odds, preserve a life on the road, their freedoms have been curbed even further, as Parliament has sought to make acts of trespass a criminal offence rather than a civil matter. As in the Tudor court, a legislature filled with landowners has played to the majority's fear of a small minority in order to outlaw wider access to the nation's land – its removal from public hands already overseen. While Scotland introduced and successfully maintained the right to roam, offering ready contact with uncultivated land, excepting domestic gardens, sports fields and school property, the English government has gleefully prevented the populace from accessing its own mountains green, to say nothing of a wider freedom of movement.

For the villagers of Pembridge in the late 16th century, openness was crucial: to cross the border into Wales; to follow a drove to market; to journey to the Continent; to benefit from knowledge of tomes by Hieronymus Cock and pictures by Bruegel; to embark on adventure and trade; even just to walk across the fields to neighbouring Eardisland or Weobley. Nonetheless, for the majority of the population, their world, like ours, was contracting just at the moment it was meant to be expanding. The figures peering out of Bruegel's paintings, like the faces of my own imagined workers in Pembridge, stacking the bags of grain downstairs and the apples and pears in the loft, felt very close to home. You can hear their calls, that 'noise of itself', echoing down the years, but the songs they're singing, the songs they have left in the hedgerows, aren't necessarily happy ones. Winter, after all, is only around the corner.

VII.

The Dead of Winter

I N VIENNA'S KUNSTHISTORISCHES MUSEUM, winter is,
indeed, just around the corner. The autumnal and the hibernal sit side by side or, to use the now established titles for the
paintings, *The Return of the Herd* hangs to the left of *The Hunters
in the Snow*. Winter strikes a chill. Gone is the ruddy warmth of
the wine harvest and the cows coming home to the consolation of
the barn. Instead, what Edward Thomas described as 'the gloom
of whiteness' slaps you in the face, reminding me of the first time
we saw Stepps House, on an icy afternoon. And while I hated the
thought of the year turning to winter, I was nonetheless excited
at the prospect of getting to know the village, our home and its
history through another season. Bruegel's vision aided that process.

As in *The Return of the Herd*, as with all the paintings in the
series, we stand on top of a hill in *The Hunters in the Snow*, looking down on a village. But where, in autumn, there was industry,
here, in winter, there is interruption. Everything is frozen. In
the bottom right-hand corner of Bruegel's intensely detailed
painting, a millwheel is rendered stationary. Work struggles to
continue, with various figures gathering firewood. They may
simply be trying to survive or perhaps their finds will help scorch
the hide of a pig that is about to emerge, petrified, from the inn in
the left-hand corner. You can smell the wood burning and hear its

crackle, before you turn away from the inevitable stink of singeing flesh. Unsurprisingly, other villagers have chosen to ignore the desolation and play on the frozen ponds, the same water they bathed in during harvest. But the withered tendrils of the brambles, the bare branches and the bare poles the hunters carry, with one derisory fox to show for their efforts, reveal paucity rather than plenty. Cracks are beginning to appear in the ice.

Standing in the grand, evocatively scented room of the former Habsburg gallery in Vienna, my eyes flicking from season to season, I got a sense of how this and the other paintings in the series were first seen, in Nicolaes Jonghelinck's dining room at Ter Beke: each showing a window onto the world outside, albeit a much broader, more varied vista than was visible in 16th-century Antwerp (or now). Bruegel shows Jonghelinck something the merchant banker (and his guests) would not have experienced: abject poverty. There are no aristocrats in the paintings. In winter, we imagine they're carefully concealed in the castle under the mountainous outcrop, to which the hunters are, ultimately, tending. But as clearly as we see that now, we cannot perceive what Jonghelinck and the other diners would have known culturally and instinctively about these paintings: that they encapsulated a calendar of specific labours associated with the passing of the year. It is a tradition lost to us, though it was a tradition that was absolutely intrinsic to the visual language of the 16th century, as well as to literary responses such as Edmund Spenser's *The Shepheardes Calender*.

Bruegel's sequence had, in many ways, no direct precursor – the series is so original in its breadth, its focus on society within the landscape daringly modern – yet its themes and motifs were rooted in illustrations familiar from medieval Books of Hours (*horae* was the Latin name), the often lavishly illustrated lay person's equivalent of a monastic breviary. These publications would have drawn on the prayers, psalms, hymns, antiphons and all the other textual paraphernalia of the liturgy, as well as providing voluntary devotions; in turn, they offered a relatively uncomplicated spiritual timetable, including a calendar that was customarily placed at the beginning of the book, much as in contemporary almanacs.

William Langland, the 14th-century poet of *Piers Plowman*, who was a lay chantry clerk and based around the Malvern Hills at the eastern edge of Herefordshire, professed the power of his copy of such a publication:

The lomes that y labore with and lyflode deserve

Is *pater-noster* and my prymer, *placebo* and *dirige*,

And my sauter som tyme and my sevene psalmes.

This y segge for here soules of suche as me helpeth.

Even those who couldn't read the Lord's Prayer in Latin – the language, of course, of all such pre-Reformation texts – were, in their almshouses and at Mass, able to glean something of its meaning through repetition. Previously only the domain of the gentry, and consequently of great value, Books of Hours became one of the most widely published and lucrative products of the printing revolution at the beginning of the 16th century and were owned by learned reader and illiterate layman alike. Even if an individual were not able to follow the text, they would have been able to understand its content through the illustrations: originally, full-page miniatures, some of the finest art of the Middle Ages; later, mass-produced woodcuts or etchings (not unlike the ones featured in Spenser's *The Shepheardes Calender*). The pictures not only represented stories from the gospels, the Virgin Mary and the saints with their identifying symbols, they also showed idealized images of a predominantly rural life. As the months progressed and the Church's feasts came and went, so too did a vision of a non-spiritual life, viewed through the lens of the same ordered humanism promoted by Bruegel and his contemporaries, with each figure assuming a place within society and, in turn, reflecting the order of the heavenly realm.

In one such image from around 1400, painted not for a publication but for the interior of a castle in northern Italy, the artist, known as Master Wenceslas of Bohemia, shows January clad in snow, though the gardens of a nearby castle remain verdant, benefiting from their own microclimate. The aristocrats are having a snowball fight, while their servants go hunting with the hounds, carrying the same poles viewed in Bruegel's later painting. For it is the peasant who is sent out into the cold and forced to fight against the season in order to furnish the table for winter banquets. And January was traditionally the month of feasting, while December was for killing pigs and baking – hence the hapless swine and, perhaps, the chimney fire in the house to the left of the village church in Bruegel's painting, which conflates the two months.

The patterns remain the same, even today. In Pembridge, Alastair was dealing with a wood delivery and the sweeping of the chimneys on the last day of his holiday, before driving back to school. Normally, he missed the arrival of the firewood in our house in Bedford, where I had to carry it from the roadside to the shed at the bottom of the garden, so I was delighted that he now had to contend with piling up a crateful by the back door like a game of giant Jenga. Chatting to Alastair on FaceTime as I walked around the Ringstrasse, the snowy winds already hurtling into Vienna from the Alps, I could see Toby wasn't being at all helpful, picking up the smaller pieces of kindling and running around the garden with them.

'Just think, you're continuing a long and august tradition,' I said.

'I'd have preferred a couple of strapping youths to help,' he responded. 'How were the Bruegels?' he asked, enviously.

'Fabulous. It was overcrowded. But they were fabulous.'

I had stood in front of *The Hunters in the Snow* for so long, resisting any attempt to be moved on by the other visitors, that my retina had stored a negative after-image of Bruegel's winter. It merged with Alastair's preparations for the same, much like the tropes, harking back two hundred years (and more), that Bruegel had similarly relied upon. I missed being with Alastair and Toby at these crucial moments, however much I knew they would come around again.

It wasn't so pleasant for our Pembridge predecessors or Bruegel's peasants, with the artist notably sympathetic to their lot. After all, the distant, fun-seeking skaters do not command

his – or our – attention; that is given to the hunters in the foreground and, in a more heart-wrenching gesture, one of their
dogs, who turns to face us, asking, why me? The animals, as
ever, speak for everyone, just like the dappled cow in *The Return
of the Herd*. For even in a temperate winter, the life of Bruegel's
villagers, like those in Pembridge – anywhere, everywhere in
Europe – was severely tested during the 16th century.

Margins were tiny and while such a situation could spur
enterprise among the population, including the expansion of
local markets and trade, perhaps even prompting the construction of our home, they were also hampered by the paucity of the
roads and, particularly, their impassability in deep snow. Horses
were expensive and scarce, though The New Inn in Pembridge
may well have stabled and hired them to trustworthy clients.
Yet even on horseback, with sunlight (or a pale suggestion of it)
only available from eight in the morning to four in the afternoon,
a traveller could make just twenty miles a day in winter, having spent most of the time skirting around muddy furrows, as
opposed to a hundred miles during the summer. From Pembridge,
twenty miles of concerted travel as the crow flies – but not as
the horse canters – wouldn't even reach Ledbury or Ross-on-
Wye at the furthest edge of the county, while a hundred miles
would take you as far as Oxford, even beyond. Markets on the
other side of Herefordshire, to say nothing of further afield, were
therefore difficult to reach in winter, which forced everyone to
rely on the locality. In Pembridge, as in so many rural villages,
that meant good neighbourliness and a shared sense of obligation.
This may have sat at odds with the commercialism engendered

by even the most basic market economy, but it was, at least during the first years of our home, an essential part of the nation's connectivity.

Cooperation was the core of social contact, both professionally and philosophically: from the yeoman paying his tenancy to the manor, to the husbandman who was both employed by the yeoman and bought some of his crop – or worked for it – out of the couple of pounds he had each year. While this was largely beneficial and created strong local identities, it also meant that villages, hundreds (the subdivision of a county) and entire counties could likewise suffer when the harvest had not been profuse and the huntsman came home empty-handed. Isolation and insularity could inevitably lead to selfishness, theft and other crime.

Judging by reports kept in the National Archives in Kew relating to the Star Chamber, an English court that sat at the Palace of Westminster from the late 15th century to the mid 17th century, most criminal cases during the period related to the eighth and tenth of God's commandments: stealing and coveting. In 1608, two Shropshire yeoman brothers called William and George Passand broke into William Murcott's house outside Pembridge, where they assaulted both husband and wife and then, for whatever reason, decided to kidnap their son. The Passand pair were promptly charged with assault, destruction of property and unlawful assembly. But theirs was hardly the only such crime. Four years earlier, a Pembridge gentleman called William Lockard living at a large house called The Byletts and who was also named as a recusant Catholic, was part of a ragtag bunch who made their way over the border into Wales, specifically to the village of Disserth, south of Llandrindod Wells, to assault and destroy the property of David Lloyd ap Lewis.

Fraud, rent dodging and racketeering were also widely reported. And if Stepps House was originally a market storehouse, it would have been another prime target for robbery. Indeed, the creation of our home may well have been a way of centralizing security in the village, to ration and stretch out provisions for as long as possible. But for the first owners, it wasn't only about dealing with security or with winter as a boring annual occurrence, with its customs and demands. Winter was becoming much harsher during the period in which our storehouse was built, which brought further confusion and disruption to the lives of everyday citizens.

THERE WAS a fashionable preponderance of winter images in the late 1500s, chiefly because there was a preponderance of winter. In 1565, the year that Bruegel painted *The Hunters in the Snow*, Europe saw the coldest winter on record to date, with everything bleached of colour and life. Shocking though it was, it was nothing compared to what was to follow. Although the history of the Little Ice Age has a much broader scope, its most focused studies deal with events during the 16th and 17th centuries. The concept of the period's intemperate climate was born, however, much later, during the 20th century, as temperatures began to return to levels experienced during what was known as the medieval warm period. Noting these changes, especially in the shape and size of glaciers in Yosemite in Northern California, the Dutch-born geologist François Matthes was the first to coin the term the Little Ice Age and ratified the idea with his colleagues through years of painstaking research, including the problematic act of re-creating weather trends. While lacking contemporary scientific data comparable with that of today, these historians and scientists were nonetheless able to call on various other forms of evidence to show that, from 1500 onwards – and particularly at the end of the 16th century – median temperatures nose-dived and, crucially, why such a change had occurred.

Some of their findings pointed to reduced solar radiation. Others observed that volcanic activity during the era increased, with a series of major eruptions between 1580 and 1600 that threw ash into the atmosphere, blocking the light and heat of the sun. Consequently, glaciers encroached on and destroyed villages in the Alps, the Rivers Rhine and Thames froze and harvesting processes had to adapt. Almost overnight, the majority of northern areas of Europe, including England, which had previously been able to prosper from winemaking throughout the Middle Ages, were unable to grow a single grape. The Little Ice Age thereby intensified the wealth divide and the already marked differences between urban and rural life, as Virginia Woolf's account in *Orlando* (based on a pamphlet called *The Great Frost* of 1608) makes clear:

> Birds froze in mid-air and fell like stones to the ground. At Norwich a young country woman started to cross the road in her usual robust health and was seen by the onlookers to turn visibly

to powder and be blown in a puff of dust over the roofs as the icy blast struck her at the street corner. The mortality among sheep and cattle was enormous. Corpses froze and could not be drawn from the sheets. It was no uncommon sight to come upon a whole herd of swine frozen immovable upon the road. The fields were full of shepherds, ploughmen, teams of horses, and little bird-scaring boys all struck stark in the act of the moment, one with his hand to his nose, another with the bottle to his lips, a third with a stone raised to throw at the raven who sat, as if stuffed, upon the hedge within a yard of him. The severity of the frost was so extraordinary that a kind of petrifaction sometimes ensued; and it was commonly supposed that the great increase of rocks in some parts of Derbyshire was due to no eruption, for there was none, but to the solidification of unfortunate way-farers who had been turned literally to stone where they stood. The Church could give little help in the matter, and though some landowners had these relics blessed, the most part preferred to use them either as landmarks, scratching-posts for sheep, or, when the form of the stone allowed, drinking troughs for cattle, which purposes they serve, admirably for the most part, to this day. But while the country people suffered the extremity of want, and the trade of the country was at a standstill, London enjoyed a carni-val of the utmost brilliancy.

Far from the gaiety of the capital's frost fairs, isolated market towns such as Pembridge were at risk of being cut off entirely. As Woolf stresses, the long, hard winters of the late 1500s and early 1600s brought absolute devastation to livestock. In a similarly remote Devonshire village called Morebath, the focus of a pioneering study by Eamon Duffy, an annual sheep count of the period records animals 'lost and gone', 'drowned' in nearby swollen streams and rivers or 'lost at crystmas'. But human selection also came into it, as many villagers, particularly husbandmen, realized they couldn't afford to feed their flocks during the winter months. It made for tough choices, given the (admittedly fetid) warmth that sheep and cattle offered a farming household – the animals of *The Return of the Herd* are notably absent in *The Hunters in the Snow*, perhaps having been brought indoors. And the flooding that claimed the lives of the sheep of Morebath – and no doubt Pembridge, with the swollen River Arrow during the darker half of the year – also created environments in which epidemics thrived among humans and animals, exacerbating comparatively poor levels of sanitation, even if the countryside was, on the whole, healthier than the city.

The death of livestock, the flooding of land and the plummeting temperatures all triggered falling levels of natural fertilizer too, which made for even poorer harvests come the following summer. By reversing the trend of enclosure in some areas, there was increased land given to common arable farming to compensate for the loss, though this proved more labour-intensive and provided even less space for the pasturing of sheep and cattle, which prompted yet more slaughter. And it wasn't only during winter that these problems became apparent. The wet summers of the Little Ice Age did nothing to help the process.

· · ·

WHILE TODAY'S citizens in Pembridge are spared most of these indignities, even if flooding remains a significant problem for farmers in the Arrow Vale and many a winter shoot going into The New Inn looks rather thin on birds shot and retrieved, there is one phenomenon that the village's current inhabitants share with their predecessors: SAD, seasonal affective disorder. The affliction may reflect generally poor mental health, but it is (and was) worsened by the onset of winter. Depression, indolence, inactivity and, for me certainly, the craving of carbohydrates and melted cheese – and subsequent weight gain – have been the hallmarks of many black ends of the year. I have a particular loathing for November.

A complex condition, SAD is directly linked to the absence of light during the winter months. The hormone melatonin, created by the pineal gland, is released at night and provides an internal signal of darkness. Exposure to light resets melatonin's circadian rhythm and inhibits its synthesis. During winter, the body's rising and more prolonged levels of melatonin prompt sleepiness, while, at the same time, falling levels of serotonin, linked to mood and appetite, as well as sleep patterns, combine with the body's internal clock, lacking the trigger of sunlight, to create a debilitating cocktail. So while the outward signs of SAD are often perceived as characteristics of modern living, the disorder is nothing new.

During the worst years of the Little Ice Age, depressive symptoms now associated with SAD led to observations of a malady known as melancholy, not least in Robert Burton's 1621 tome on the subject, *The Anatomy of Melancholy*. A lengthy self-help book, it supposed that idleness was the sickness's primary cause, and, consequently, that busyness was its cure. By composing the text, Burton was trying to treat his own condition through immersive therapy. While he did not necessarily align the absence of light with melancholy – seasonal affect, as such – he certainly understood the general effect of weather:

> We may gather, that to this cure of melancholy, amongst other things, the rectification of air is necessarily required. [. . .] The medium must needs be good, where the air is temperate, serene, quiet, free from bogs, fens, mists, all manner of putrefaction, contagious and filthy noisome smells.

Without modern knowledge of hormonal disparities, Burton's argument focused instead on an imbalance of bodily humours. It revolved around the idea that while melancholy was an essential facet of anyone's make-up – and integral to the body's equilibrium – too much melancholy was sapping. According to Burton, this wistful sadness derived its power from black bile produced by the spleen – the Greek root of melancholy, or *melaina kholé*, actually means black bile. So it is little wonder that I am an inveterate melancholic, given that I have a splenunculus – not just an enlarged spleen but a secondary one, likely caused by an extended period of glandular fever, too much alcohol, or a combination of the two. Like nostalgia, black bile pumps through my veins, instead of being balanced with the three other bodily humours: blood, phlegm and yellow bile. Burton took a particularly puritanical approach to curing the malady through hard graft, but he was also steeped in classical studies, specifically the medical theories of Hippocrates, and advocated more pleasing treatments, including exposure to music.

One of the leading exponents of such a cure was the lutenist and composer John Dowland. Assumed to have been born near Dublin around the time that Bruegel was creating his season paintings, Dowland's early career is (familiarly) poorly documented. By the 1580s, however, he was making his name on the English music scene and had been noted by Oxford academics and poets alike. Even Queen Elizabeth had heard one of his songs by 1590, though Dowland was as drawn to the European courts – and to Catholicism – as he was to his adopted homeland. It wasn't always a charmed life, nor was music entirely curative. Dowland was notorious for moping, like the 'inamorato with folded hand' in Burton's text:

> Down hangs his head, terse and polite,
> Some ditty sure he doth indite.
> His lute and books about him lie,
> As symptoms of his vanity.

Following suit, the lyrics to Dowland's songs, with such titles as 'In darknesse let me dwell', 'Vnquiet thoughts' and 'Sorow sorow stay, lend true repentant teares', profess a miserable figure. But just as depressed musicians beguile us now, so it was in late-16th-century England – and Europe – that 'such a woe [. . .] wins more hearts than mirth can do'.

The fashion for lovelorn lutenists was far from limited to the court and the city. In Herefordshire, John Attey followed in those footsteps and won local hearts, even if his renown was outrun by the music of Dowland and other contemporaries. Notably, one of the most melancholy songs in Attey's *First Booke of Ayres*, published in 1622, though doubtless composed over a number of years, is a winter lyric:

> For my sense sees no other sun
> But that which in thine eyes,
> That in another sphere doth run,
> And clouds thy native skies.
> Then come again, then come again,
> Display thy pleasing beams.
> Else all my pleasures are but pain,
> My comforts are but dreams.

Unrequited love was the modus operandi of the melancholic, which found no more persuasive a subject than same-sex desire. Although men could be hanged for penetrative sex with another man (following the Buggery Act of 1563, an Elizabethan return to Henrican law), what we would now term homoerotic sentiment, as well as more flagrant expressions of homosexual behaviour, did find their way into the literature of the age. Shakespeare's Sonnet 97, 'How like a winter hath my absence been', is one of many the bard addressed to 'my lovely boy'. Such texts encouraged a reading of queerness as a mark of intellect, which could also manifest in gender fluidity and cross-dressing, evinced by further chapbook illustrations.

So as much as winter was pervasive, and melancholy could be seen as a psychological Achilles heel, the latter was also immensely fashionable. Both Orsino in Shakespeare's *Twelfth Night*, first performed during the winter of 1601–2, and, less amusingly, Hamlet show a melancholy that was persistent and chic. While Orsino is able to shrug his off, thanks to music, 'the food of love', and the requital of his passion for Olivia, Hamlet tells his mother that his 'customary suits of solemn black', seen in Elizabethan miniatures of sulky youths by artists such as Nicholas Hilliard and Isaac Oliver, are nothing compared to his feelings:

> I have that within which passeth show,
> These but the trappings and the suits of woe.

For those of a lower rank, melancholy or SAD, as we would call it, was not so easily flaunted. It was deeply felt and, worse, indicative of the ruination that came with winter. Little wonder the crowds in Bruegel's painting try to make the best of the season.

NOT ALL of the modish winter paintings of the era were able to offer a smile. Particularly bleak is a Bruegel image known as *The Massacre of the Innocents*, which was subsequently copied by others, including the artist's son. Depicting events from Matthew's Gospel, when Herod, learning of the birth of Jesus from the Wise Men, decides to kill the entire firstborn of Judea, the painting likewise provided a bitter commentary on the Spanish Duke of Alba's suppression of the Dutch Revolt during the 1560s. It marked the start of the Eighty Years War, stoked by resentment of the Iberian branch of the Habsburgs – the very dynasty who came to own the majority of Bruegel's work – and the Catholic Church and Holy Roman Empire for which it stood. That Bruegel set his image of the slaughter of innocent children in deepest winter reflected not only the timing of both the Feast of the Holy Innocents, on 28 December, but also the debilitating ferocity of winter during the 16th century.

Light may bounce off the snow in these paintings, but they were created in a world starved of literal and, at times, spiritual light. When night descended, the suffocating shadows encroached. Our home would have gone dark long before the end of the day, the business of the market over, but there would have been glimmers around the square, not least from The New Inn (analogous to the hostels in Bruegel's icy images). So it remains. As in many villages of the age, the pub was the principal hub of entertainment, complete with a fire and meat spit. It could also be a place of commerce. And it provided respite from the crowded atmosphere of home, where separate bedrooms were yet to be the norm, certainly within the houses of husbandmen. With candles at a premium, it was often cheaper to go to the pub for the evening, to buy ale and benefit from shared light and the warmth of shared company.

In the depths of winter, light was particularly cherished. Published in 1582, Thomas Bentley's *The Monument of Matrones*, a collection of writings by Elizabethan women, praises the gift of candlelight in lilting Book of Common Prayer style:

> Thanks be given to thee O Lord, which after daie, when night commeth, hast given us for the remedie of darknesse this artificial light of the candle or lampe, whereby we see and discerne those things in this night of our bodies, which are expedient for us to use.

The expense of candles could be somewhat mollified by killing yet more livestock, even if that in itself could be a risky commercial proposition. As well as saving grain during the winter, slaughtering animals early in the season could provide tallow, which was cheaper than beeswax, to guard against the 'perils and dangers of this night'.

But it wasn't all bad. The recovery of backgammon boards from Henry VIII's flagship, the *Mary Rose*, which sank in 1545, and a die discovered in a 2009–15 excavation around Shakespeare's birthplace in Stratford speak of the popularity of gambling during the leisure time of the average Elizabethan. Often, winning games of bowls, as well as now obsolete rounds of tables and maw, was a way of affording snacks in the pub, many of which were preserved and kept in the servery or buttery during the darker months – hence the pickled eggs and onions still in evidence today. And there were more violent games on which to gamble too. The rounded settle in the back bar of The New Inn is thought to have formed part of the seating for a cockpit – providing the old name for our neighbour's house – though its high back also acts as a perfect shield against the winds that dress Hergest Ridge and Hay Bluff in snow before whistling down Buthall Hill or along West Street to whip around the Market Square. The unadorned oaks of the timber-framed houses look like the surrounding woods as Pembridge loses its bloom. The furrows are naked and the swallows that gladdened the sky in summer are gone.

VIII.

Bare Ruin'd Choirs

DESPITE MY INCIPIENT DEPRESSION and loathing of winter, I felt just as glad to return to the house after my trip to Vienna as I had been in September's gasping summer. Alastair had done a fine job of stacking the wood for the fire while I was away and I repaid the debt by busying myself in the kitchen. I made endless soups, from turnips with garlic and a glug of white Burgundy and from beetroot with shavings of nostril-stripping horseradish. And then I boiled a gammon in local cider, with a clove-studded onion and bay leaves from our own tree, still perfect in its knot-garden plumpness, before roasting the joint in sugar and mustard. Like Bruegel's hunting painting, my mum reminded me that it was the season for killing pigs, as she'd witnessed on the farm as a child, with the hog's roaring scream ringing down the valley like a voice in the wilderness.

In Pembridge, the cawing crows provided yet more barbed language. As we walked the orchards for the first time in weeks, we also saw fieldfares picking at the windfalls, the same fruit Toby substituted for his beloved tennis balls. And further beyond the village, there was the *pup-pup* of several shoots, with abandoned cartridges littering the Somme-like churnings of the fields. Everywhere, there was a dance of decay, the landscape almost stripped to the bone. The growth of the emergent rapeseed and wheat, planted just weeks before, was temporarily halted as the late sun found itself netted in the poplars, defying even Max Ernst or René Magritte with its burning surreality.

There was such malice in the display. Arriving here in summer, we had been embraced by the landscape, with its echoes of individual and wider roles within an agrarian pattern. Yet the year's midnight, for all its ruddy, late-afternoon flush, negated the reflection, offering only vague memories and rotten fodder. The link between humanity and nature was broken; the mirror's film had foxed and become as thin as the ice that stretched across the puddles – until Toby's paws cracked it and he slipped through, like one of Bruegel's skaters. December was a time for indoors, a time to leave hemiparasitic plants to gorge rampant on the year's remains.

Mistletoe, or *Viscum album*, is now much more widespread than it was in the Middle Ages. The increase is largely the result of deforestation, with oaks having been felled for construction and other woodland cleared for more utilitarian pasture and fields. Immediately around Pembridge, the reason for the predominance of mistletoe is that it craves light, with sparsely planted orchards providing the perfect home. Here, the aptly named mistle thrush, as well as other birdlife, can find food and, in turn, help spread the plant by regurgitating and excreting the seeds, or wiping their sticky beaks on the branches of the trees. With so many orchards in this corner of England, mistletoe has consequently become ubiquitous, so much so that it's the county flower.

There are also climatic reasons for these explosions of mistletoe, with Herefordshire the epicentre. It is a relatively low-lying county, caught between hills and enjoying prevailing warmth and dampness from the west. Yet for such a mundane plant, it still holds the mystic appeal of scarcer days, which prompted Pliny the Elder to remark that 'mistletoe is rare and, when found, gathered with great ceremony'. The rituals endured, with the idea that the plant could provide a ward against evil spirits, a good-luck charm during the dark winter months, even a cure for melancholy. It was promptly hijacked for Christian purposes and the decoration of houses at Christmas, though it also retained its primeval associations with fertility, the viscosity of the berries being likened to semen.

Having lived for most of my life in the east of the British Isles, where mistletoe is much more unusual, I was enchanted by its preponderance in Herefordshire. Locals may be more blasé and dismissive of this notoriously invasive plant, though the divesting of mistletoe from local orchards has threatened to rob them of their unique combination of flora and fauna, stemming from both the apple trees and the animals and plants that feed off them. Nonetheless, I needed some to decorate Stepps House, while making sure to spread the seed from the berries on a suitable branch and thereby continue the cycle.

'Cover me,' I said, 'I'm going in.'

'What if someone comes?' Alastair jittered, as I began reaching into the branches.

'This one's a beauty,' I said, lopping off a vast bundle.

'Where the hell are we going to hang that?'

'Above the stairs,' I said, proudly, if a little concerned at how obvious my thieving would appear when we went back into the village. As it was, nobody batted an eyelid and the mistletoe swung from one of the beams during the festive season like a Louis XVI chandelier.

The Norwegian spruce is a new decorative element, of course, but bringing in boughs of other trees at Christmas was well established in Herefordshire – and beyond. Towards the end of the 16th century, the 'kissing bough' regained previous currency, as pagan and Druidic symbols were again countenanced over and above Christian (and specifically Catholic) iconography, which had become anathema to modern life. All of it, however, pointed not to orthodox spiritual sustenance but to a yearning for continuing sources of transcendence in lives dominated by darkness.

LIKE OUR own celebrations of the great winter feast, 16th-century Christmases, particularly those of earlier in the century, would have been lavish, community-based affairs. Ecclesiastical accounts from the time detail the purchase of larger numbers of tallow candles than at any other season – Easter and its sequence of feasts perhaps notwithstanding – for the lighting of statues, the rood screen, shrines and side altars within parish churches. While places of worship in cities detailed additional costs at Christmastide, such as holly, ivy, bay, box and mistletoe, brought in from the countryside and sold at market, there was no need to use Pembridge money on things that were so easily collected from nearby woods and fields.

Instead, rural centres could focus on the enhancement of what was already in the church, raising additional funds for the

lights in front of each of the images that adorned the walls. Faint, chalky evidence of these is still present in the church of St Mary's in Pembridge. While many were subsequently white-washed or replaced with doggedly Protestant panels spelling out the Creed or the Lord's Prayer, these were never able to elicit the same fervour with which the church's pre-Reformation adornments had been admired by the laity.

Often, the followings and decoration thrived on the simplest of means. While there may have been an element of competition among village guilds, as well as individuals, to support the liturgy through rent from parcels of land, the sale of a bushel of barley or a cloth of wool – even certain income from the pub – a parishioner or guild was rarely denigrated for being poor. Nationwide parish records demonstrate that priests were as happy to receive the smallest amount deemed appropriate for a 'good doer' as they were larger bequests. Active parishioners were decent parishioners, whether operating alone or in groups, though 'membership' was as much about socializing and showing devotion to the community as it was about worshipping God.

There were two main chantry funds in Pembridge, at least according to official endowment valuations from 1547, which were taken by a commission from Edward VI. The first was 'Our Lady Service', no doubt relating to the (now reclaimed) Lady Chapel in the church's south transept, with its traces of white Marian roses. To this, twelve parishioners contributed funds. And there was also the 'Trinity Service' for the chapel in the north transept (now a vestry and a place for stacking chairs), though this was a much more modest affair, judging by the income from just two benefactors. There may also have been a separate chantry chapel outside the village, at least according to a 'Chantry Route' listed in a rent roll for burgages and tenements in the adjoining hamlets of Bearwood and Broxwood. In Broxwood, too, evidence exists of a sanctuary dedicated to St Peter, and there were supposedly chapels in both Marston (dedicated to the Feast of the Translation of St Thomas of Canterbury) and Weston, though these had vanished by the mid 16th century.

In St Mary's itself, all the endowments for the two transept chapels came from 'certayn lands with thappurtenaunces in Pembryge' and 'medowes leasows & pastures', as well as 'tenementes'. The money was paid for the saying of prayers and the lighting of lamps and candles, with the intention of limiting the time that deceased loved ones had to spend in purgatory. 'Obits' were the costliest, compensating a priest for the perpetual recitation of prayers for the departed. The next category, 'anniversaries', likely focused on the date of the departure in question – the word is still mentioned in intercessions at Mass today. And, finally, 'lights' were the cheapest and most literal of the endowments, concerning either the constant or intermittent burning of a candle, which would have certainly increased at Christmas and other feast-filled points of the year.

It was all part and parcel of what the new Chantries Act of 1547 called 'phantasising vain opinions of purgatory and masses satisfactory, to be done for them which departed'. Even though the parish priests benefited from the system, as did the village church entire, it was an abomination in the light of unfolding changes during the 16th century and all the income from the chantries was promptly transferred 'to the kynges maieste', with many of the spaces destroyed or repurposed. Indeed, following the shifting religious principles of the Tudor monarchs, a whole system of parish arrangements was swept away, though such a move destroyed the majority of lay religious activity. It also robbed the accountants for these funds, often women familiar with bookkeeping on a domestic front, of an important role in the life of the church. Overall, the effect that these and other reformatory decisions had on the daily and spiritual life of middling and poor members of society is therefore difficult to overemphasize.

For villagers in places such as Pembridge, the entire Reformation not only marked major religious and political change – in the main, the political elements of the divorce from Rome were easier to swallow – it also prompted painful visual and cultural transformations. Liturgy was one of the most cherished forms of entertainment, not least at Christmas, with the imagery in church providing a rare glimmer of transcendence in otherwise plain lives. The sheer fervour with which pre-Reformation rituals and iconography were held can be gleaned from the words of the anti-papal priest Simon Heynes when he noted that 'it may appear that the common people have a greater affiance or trust in outward rites or ceremonies than they ought to have, and that they esteem more virtue in images and adorning of them, kissing their feet or offering candles unto them'. Suddenly, according to the *Bishops' Book* of 1537, officially entitled *The Institution of the Christian Man* and published by the synod under Thomas Cranmer as Archbishop of Canterbury, the people were 'utterly forbidden to make or have any similitude or images, to the intent to bow down to it, or worship it. And therefore we think it convenient that all bishops and preachers shall instruct and teach the people [. . .] that God in his substance cannot by any similitude or image be represented or expressed.' While Cranmer's first monarch Henry VIII could, at times, appear to have a foot in both camps, eschewing the control of Rome but not all the trappings of its worship, his son, Edward VI, made it absolutely clear that the Church of England was going to be very different in hue and went much further along the path of reform.

During the summer of 1547, the year Edward came to the throne, a royal visitation of the entire country was proposed, with a new set of injunctions that may, on the surface, have tracked those of Henry VIII, though some, in fact, had no precedent whatsoever. One of the most damaging changes to parish life was the abolition of all processions, as would have taken place before the principal Mass every Sunday and on feast days such as

Candlemas (seen in a Flemish Book of Hours from around 1550). Even the traditional and important act of crossing the fields, praying for plenty at harvest and beating the parish bounds at Rogationtide, which fell on the Sunday after Easter and in the days immediately preceding the Feast of the Ascension, was banned (though the act was later restored). This was a seismic change in a rural parish such as Pembridge. Bells were not to be rung during the services either – again, with its detached belfry, St Mary's Church would have felt the loss keenly – and those ignoring what 'the King commanded to be observed' would be condemned, particularly those who went about:

> Casting holy water upon his bed, upon images, and other dead things; or bearing about him holy bread, or St John's Gospel, or making crosses of wood upon Palm Sunday in time of reading of the Passion, or keeping of private holy days, as bakers, brewers,

smiths and shoemakers, and such others do; or ringing of holy
bells, or blessing with the holy candle, to the intent thereby to be
discharged of the burden of sin, or to bribe away devils, or to put
away dreams and fantasies.

As the visitation made its way around England, the thirty commissioners enforced the King's will with significant aggression,
crudely destroying the cherished images they found, as well as
extinguishing the lamps the villagers had funded for generations,
sometimes by killing their own livestock, and abolishing all the
traditions that guaranteed the individuality and spiritual identity of rural centres.

From 1549 to 1553, Edward continued his project with an
inventory of the entire wealth of the infant Church of England,
not just that of the chantries, but also all manner of 'goodes,
plate, juells, vestyments, bells and other ornyments within every
paryshe belonging or in any wyse apperteying to any churche,
chapell, brotherhed, gylde or fraternytye within this our realme
of Englond'. With the reported intention of stopping private
embezzlement of church goods – normally by families reclaim-
ing what they had donated in the first place – the commission
professed to ensure the preservation of these treasures for use
within the parish (and the Church of England at large). But
Edward was very much his father's son when he was informed of
ecclesiastical prosperity and the commission promptly ordered
the valuables to be seized, 'for as muche as the King's Majestie
had neede presently of a masse of mooney'. Only the barest
essentials were left for church use. All remaining plate was sent

to the Jewel House in the Tower of London, where it was melted down, while the money from goods sold locally was sent to the treasurer of the Royal Mint. It was an enormous endeavour, which included the complex weighing of church bells, and while Queen Mary reversed the commission, much as she did the majority of Edward VI's religious proclamations, the damage was done.

The commissioners appointed by the King to record the contents of the city and county of Hereford were Sir John Price, a Welsh notary public who had worked for Thomas Cromwell and variously served as MP for Breconshire, Hereford, Ludlow and Ludgershall, and Sir George Cornewall, another of Cromwell's hoodlums, who had been a member of the household of Charles Brandon, the 1st Duke of Suffolk (played by the dreamy Henry Cavill in the recent TV romp *The Tudors*). Assisted in their work by Thomas Dansye, they went through the county noting that much 'church stuff' had already been squirrelled away, with some villagers calling on their neighbours to testify to their true ownership of the valuable metal and jewels in question.

That may well have been the case in Pembridge too, though such a large church still boasted a number of treasures by the time the commissioners arrived. Visiting the parish on 26 September 1552, Sir John Price noted: a gilt chalice; a silver pix used to carry the consecrated host at Mass (rendered obsolete by Edward's changes to the liturgy and its import); four bells, which would have had to have been weighed; a copper cross; two brass thuribles for the burning of incense; a metal ewer (a jug used to pour water into the font for the sacrament of baptism);

a tynacle of brass, though the word, variously spelled in other inventories of the time, was more usually associated with a tunic or tunical for the sub-deacon at Mass and made of silk or satin; two brass candlesticks; a Sanctus bell, which would have been rung at the consecration; a set of white damask vestments; a set of black funeral vestments, albeit without the cope; a white satin vestment; a red silk vestment; a yellow silk vestment; a white vestment made for a particular use that is sadly illegible; a blue velvet cope; a cope described as being of 'changeable color'; two altar cloths and two towels.

From this extensive though by no means complete list of pre-Reformation treasures, the parish of Pembridge was allowed to keep only the chalice, two copes and two altar cloths. Everything else was seized for melting down or destruction and by 1903, when another comprehensive survey of the ecclesiastical riches of Herefordshire was created, Pembridge had no remaining treasures, except a chalice made in 1751. All bar one of the original bells had been taken from the village belfry in the 16th century, only to be replaced slowly over time: the first substitutes were made in 1658, after yet more atrocities and damage during the Civil War; and the last installed in 1898, at which point the 17th-century replacements were recast.

While there were many parishioners snaffling precious chalices and pixes, all the time weeping over the loss of a dramatic liturgy of vestments, candles and processions, there were others who relished the freedom of the Edwardian Reformation. It was a moment of liberty and vigorous discussion, of ready printing and of the (temporary) abolition of heresy laws and censorship, barring the sheer number of Catholic publications destroyed. Priestly celibacy was over and there was a similar freedom within the laws of marriage for the laity, following the example of Henry VIII. It spoke of the youth of the monarch and the zealousness of his advisors, even if Edward VI would not remain as vigorous as he first appeared. Nonetheless, it was a time of sweeping change. Pembridge, as a relatively important mercantile hub, may well have adopted the reforms quite readily, following the lead of London and the south-east, as well as Bristol and other centres of power, though there is, to this day, equal evidence of a cherished regard for the trappings of traditional religion, not least at Christmas.

WE HAD left our old decorations in the accommodation that came with Alastair's job, so I put my mind to creating new ones for Stepps House. I threaded a needle and sewed red ribbons to two dozen dried oranges – my own attempts to dry them in the oven had failed, creating only a sticky mess, so I'd been forced to order the fruit online. And I added to this a clutch of stars made from straw, which I thought provided a fitting reflection of the village's agricultural life.

'Looks stunning,' Alastair said, as he passed me a glass of the damson gin we'd set for steeping in the autumn.

'I thought we should lead by tasteful example,' I responded.

'Indeed.'

'Though we might want to tell the rest of the village,' I said, nodding to the window.

'Oh, come on, it's lovely,' he reacted, gazing out at the extraordinary display under the Market Hall.

'You only like white lights!'

Some of the coloured variety looked like they had more or less been thrown at a huge tree that was squeezed under the roof of the early-16th-century structure, though they may well have worked their way free, the result of strong seasonal winds, which had caused many of the white lights, resembling icicles, to swing wildly.

'Maybe we should intervene next year,' I offered.

'We? No! PIPS has done us proud!' Alastair said with a flourish, citing the group who dutifully planted the village's bulbs, swept the Market Square and decorated the place for Christmas.

PIPS was the jolly acronym for Pride in Pembridge. We had initially mistaken it for a local LGBTQ+ organization, though the girls at the pub disabused us of the presumption. The members of PIPS clearly took great pleasure in looking after Pembridge, much as the village's medieval parishioners had done, with trees displayed the length of London (now East) Street and West Street, lit here in shocking blue, there in dazzling red. Outside the porch to St Mary's, thanks to Gill the churchwarden's handiwork, there were two elegant trees with white lights, the extension cable popping through one of the Civil War musket holes in the church's west door. And we did our bit too, handing out coffee and fruit cake when the teams took a break from their decorating work.

It all contributed to the beautification of the village, much as wax and tallow had done in the church five hundred years ago. It wasn't just about the trappings, the outward show of the feast and the liturgy in all its finery. Then, it had also satisfied an intense familiarity with rites and rituals that were intrinsic to society. At Christmas, despite all our manifest differences, the veil between the periods becomes thinnest and an understanding re-emerges in carols such as 'There is no rose' and 'Adam lay ybounden' with their evocative, pre-Reformation juxtaposition of Latin and English. Such texts, handed from generation to generation, showed that the connection to worship, as well as its prayers and antiphons, was so intense that it could be internalized. While, as Eamon Duffy explains, 'the centrality of the liturgy in lay religious consciousness was not confined to Christmas', it nonetheless remains clearest during winter.

Herefordshire has its own rich tradition of Christmas music, including one carol that, like 'Adam lay ybounden', concerns Adam and Eve's actions in the Garden of Eden and our consequent need for redemption: 'The Truth Sent from Above'. It was one of many such songs collected in and around Pembridge as late as the beginning of the 20th century. Ralph Vaughan Williams and his colleague Cecil Sharp were part of a concerted project to collect the folk tunes of the British Isles before they vanished in the face of modernity. In Herefordshire, particularly around Weobley, various songs and carols had been recorded by folklorist Ella Leather since 1905. Four years later, Vaughan Williams decided to come and hear for himself. Some of the tunes were on phonograph records and notated after the event, including 'The Moon Shines Bright', which one Mr G. Vaughan had reportedly sung in March 1907. 'The Truth Sent from Above', however, was heard both on record and at various destinations in this corner of the county. Sometimes, as at King's Pyon, it was performed with the words that are often sung on Christmas Eve at King's College, Cambridge, along with many other ancient texts and tunes:

> This is the truth sent from above,
> The truth of God, the God of love;
> Therefore don't turn me from your door,
> But hearken all both rich and poor.

At other times, Vaughan Williams heard a variant of the same modal music, including at Hardwick outside Pembridge, sung to the words 'There is a fountain of Christ's blood'. Equally sombre was what Caroline Bridges performed for Vaughan Williams at The Swan Inn in Pembridge during July 1909. Sadly, The Swan no longer exists, one of many such pubs to have vanished from the village's streets, but a cygnine statue continues to sit in the window, marking where the composer heard a familiar tune with rather unfamiliar words:

Awake, awake, sweet England, sweet England now awake,
And do your prayers obediently, and to your soul partake;
Our Lord our God is calling, all in the sky so clear,
So repent, repent, sweet England, for dreadful days draw near.

Vaughan Williams might have been chilled by the message, though he quickly noted the melodic contours, which followed a somewhat ungainly path around the tune we would more readily associate with 'God Rest Ye, Merry Gentlemen' – though that carol was also collected separately. 'Awake, awake, sweet England' had begun life in the late 16th century as a penitential song by the ballad-writer Thomas Deloney, for whom London's 'Great Earthquake' of 1580, toppling part of the old St Paul's Cathedral, was a sign of God's displeasure. The stark contrition of Deloney's song has thankfully vanished, though the cheerier Christmas variant, likewise originating from the 16th century, has endured. With its rousing refrain of 'tidings of comfort and joy', it was the very song we heard booming out of the back bar of The New Inn a few days before our first Christmas in the village, sung with gusto by a group of teachers accompanied by ukuleles, sleigh bells and the pub's honky-tonk piano.

· · ·

EVEN TODAY, in a supposedly secular world, the notion of divesting rituals such as Christmas of their richness would be met with abject horror – as it was under Thomas Cromwell's descendant Oliver, who made even more marked bowdlerizations of the remaining Catholic elements of the liturgy of the Church of England. But to a 16th-century parishioner, the changes within a year-wide liturgy that had previously been central to lay consciousness, and not just at Christmastide, were very drastic indeed. Unsurprisingly, the Reformation was rejected with great passion in many areas of England, not least the remoter west.

In 1548, William Body was busy removing images from the churches of Cornwall's Lizard Peninsula when he was attacked and killed in Helston in one of a series of uprisings. For common people who had seen common land stripped from them and were now witnessing the degradation of their village churches – 'What next? The pub?' they might have thought – insurrection was the only option. The result, however, was merely an intensification of the original injunctions and in 1550 'images of stone, timber, alabaster or earth, graven carved or painted, which heretofore have been taken out of any church or chapel or yet stand in any church or chapel' were to be destroyed and all books 'heretofore used for the service of the Church' were to be surrendered, including the Books of Hours filled with the monthly and annual cycles of images that had inspired Bruegel's season paintings and many other series besides.

Little wonder these congregations returned to former papist worship as soon as they possibly could. In 1553, after the death of Edward VI, Queen Mary issued a decree of mutual tolerance and the Latin liturgy of 'the old religion' was permitted to coexist with the vernacular Book of Common Prayer. Consequently, many seized upon the restoration. In Much Wenlock in nearby Shropshire, the Old Rite was reintroduced just three months after Mary's accession. But when Elizabeth followed her half-sister to the throne, the very same parish decided not to adopt the new monarch's 'litanies in English after the fashion of King Edward' but instead celebrated the news with the singing of an anthem and a Catholic Mass.

Despite Protestant adherence within the bishopric of Hereford, the peripheral position of the county encouraged a particularly vociferous Counter-Reformation. According to local ecclesiastical records, a number of the gentry in Pembridge were presented at court for recusancy, of continuing to worship in the traditional manner, despite all change and prohibition. The residents of manor houses such as The Byletts, Mylton and The Leen, north of the village, as well as at The Court of Noke on the outskirts of Staunton on Arrow, and The Bury of Weston and Marston were all named as Catholics. As late as 1632, the owners of The Leen had been accused of hiding a priest in their home, doubtless the same one who was baptizing local Catholic children. But there were also non-gentry followers of the traditional religion, who perhaps took even greater risks maintaining their faith, given that they lived hugger-mugger with neighbours. And then there were those who took matters into their own hands when it came to expressing distaste and distrust of the reformed church.

One Pembridge resident called John Hall was presented as a

recusant at court on numerous occasions between 1605 and 1626, while Jacob Hall, who may well have been a relative, was accused of recusancy in 1613, along with his wife, who also appeared regularly at court until 1621. By 1636, they may have been attending services in Pembridge church, but both gentlemen were wholly ungentlemanly in their defilement of the churchyard. John, for instance, 'built up a goose-cubbe with a sinke whereby the filthiness' drained through the graves, while Jacob, according to Acts of Office discovered by Wendy Brogden, leased out 'certen tenements bordering on the churchyard' and filled them 'with beggarly people, [with] all filthynes and excrement' running onto 'the sacred ground'.

I read the reports to Alastair, who couldn't help but giggle at the recusants' methods but was fascinated by the thought that we, the current (unbeggarly) occupants of one of the properties neighbouring the churchyard, were likewise Roman Catholic, surrounded by more obedient – and more obediently middle-of-the-road – Anglicans. Certainly, our methods were rather different from our predecessors, wholly respecting the current use of the church. And we always made sure to clean up whenever Toby deposited his 'filthynes' on holy ground. The consequent ire of the wardens simply wouldn't make our lives worth living.

Petty though local fights might seem, they could also take on a violent edge. In 1605, there were Catholic riots around the Feast of Whitsun. The events began on Tuesday 21 May, when 'some fourty or fifty persons (many weaponed in offensive maner)' were seen 'accompanying a Coarse [corpse] round about the church' at Allensmore, south-west of Hereford. They had come to bury a fellow recusant called Ales Wellington, whom the parish priest had refused to inter, following her excommunication in 1595. The priest, Richard Heynes, was in part doing the bidding of the Bishop of Hereford, who had been fighting the influence of large numbers of recusant Catholics across the diocese. Watching the funeral unfold from his rectory window and noting the weapons brought by the mourners, the priest decided not to challenge them personally, but reported their actions to the Bishop, giving the names of those he could identify. Over the coming days, arrests were made, though there were also ambushes of the justices as they made their way to the properties in question. Further south, on the border with Wales, a group of eighty-two recusants prepared to defend a Catholic stronghold from the Bishop's forces, though by the time it had got to ten o'clock in the evening and the troops hadn't arrived, most of them repaired to the pub.

Largely, the ecclesiastical courts were concerned with smaller fry, though it is impossible not to admire those individuals who sought other forms of transcendence. They include one of my heroes from the archive, Lewis Thomas, who hosted a dance in the church porch in Pembridge in 1617. Wading through the court records and their typically rough mixture of English and Latin – the continued use of the language, despite all changes in worship, speaks of further knowledge gleaned through old liturgy – it's easy to work out that Lewis Thomas, along with a minstrel called Matthew Steade, was summoned to a hearing at the priory in Leominster, some six miles away, and then excommunicated for his terpsichorean actions.

> Ludovicus Thomas daunced in the church porch amongst a companie of girles of the parrishe not knowne questitus &c in hos diem et locus preconizatus &c non comparuit &c vijs et modis in proximo citatus &c per publicum edictum in 3 diem Septembris predicti preconizatus non comparuit &c excommunicatus.

And he wasn't the only resident guilty of the crime of dancing on the Sabbath. Everyone was at it. In 1588–9, according to court records at Hereford Cathedral, Anne Gwillim of Kingsland, just a stone's throw from Pembridge, was charged with the same offence. Her relative Margaret was similarly accused and, although denying all knowledge, she, at least, had the grace to appear at court; Anne was nowhere to be seen.

Dancing often triggered the ire of the religious, who condemned it as a pagan practice that overpowered the senses and encouraged other sinful behaviour. There were old wives' tales about how dancing in the churchyard could eventually lead to you dancing yourself to death, in an echo of a slightly earlier era's *Totentanz* illustrations. Instead, it was better to wait for heaven and dance with the angels on high. But it wasn't just a country jig that flustered the courts; theatrical entertainments were equally bad, as witnessed in another incident in Kingsland. Detected by the churchwardens of acting 'a play with others upon the sabbath day at time of evening prayer', the painter – of a two-coats-of-whitewash rather than an oil-on-canvas variety – Thomas Waucklen chose not to appear at his hearing, though that did not stop the court from excommunicating him too.

Reformation life was ruthless. Given the comparative paucity

of the liturgy and decoration within the churches and the potentially fatal consequences of fighting against the reforms, it
was little wonder that encoded observations emerged describ-
ing England, like Zion, as a spiritual wasteland. The lives of
those who had relished the richness, ritual and beauty of the
pre-Reformation church had changed irrevocably. Far away from
court, experiencing the increasingly bitter wrath of nature, with
its failed harvests, famine and frozen months, and without the
joy of a gilded Catholic Christmas, there was a real sense that
'the city that was once thronged with people, the one-time queen
of nations has become as a widow'.

AT HOME in Pembridge, tucked up against the season's bite,
Alastair and I tried our best to rekindle some of the trappings
of the past. During winter, Stepps House can even feel like a
recusant chapel. Wrought-iron sconces suffuse the place with
candlelight, though we tend to buy ours from Ikea rather than
killing one of the village sheep to draw it for tallow. Often, we
also light a small brass thurible, like one of the two stolen from
the church by King Edward's cronies, which we fill with incense
to cloud the place with spice. The only disadvantage is that we
frequently set off the smoke alarms and alert our neighbours to a
potential conflagration.

We do the same on Easter Eve, the 'darkest day' of Holy
Week, when, at night, having built a bonfire in the garden, we
follow the tradition of lighting a single candle from its flames, as
well as the coals for the thurible, and bring both light and some

form of sacrality back into the house. It's cheaper than most scented candles for sure and helps reawaken something of a former age, perhaps even a previous chapter in the life of the house, not least when a motet by William Byrd provides the soundtrack or the candlelight catches one of our driftwood sculptures of Christ on the Cross, Doubting Thomas, the Archangel Gabriel and a Pilgrim, created by the Newark-based artist Peter Eugene Ball. With their tortured bodies, strange Romanesque hands and gilded faces, they look like the battered remnants of the vandalism of the Reformation. They also remind us of the strange position of the house.

When Duncan James first looked at the place, he noted that it was 'sited on land that may once have been in church ownership', which reminded me not to start dancing in the garden, for fear of death. The encroachment at the western end of the churchyard by small tenement plots bordering the Market Square, including ours, is likely to have begun at the end of the 15th century. Even now, we can find gravestones embedded in the hedge that separates our garden from the churchyard – and we've dug up other older fragments in the borders when planting spring bulbs. A few houses up, another unsuspecting gardener even uncovered a human skull. The coroners quickly swung into action, first to ensure that the object didn't relate to a more recent death and then to smooth the process of its reburial elsewhere in the churchyard. Luckily, neither we nor (more likely) Toby have yet found such a gruesome sight, though I have no doubt, with the house on a direct axis with the belfry, that there was once some connection to the churchly business of life and death. The most curious mark of a potential ecclesiastical use for the plot is the presence of a large yew tree at the bottom of the garden. Actually, it's more like several trees, climbing to six or seven metres, with various younger trunks rising from the rootstock, the offshoots of a more ancient stump.

It is impossible to age a yew in the same way that you can age oak, though the former has long been associated with churchyards. Practically, their thick trunks were seen to offer some protection from local livestock, often penned by parishioners and guilds on church land. An occasional runaway tup or ewe from the adjoining fields can still cause awkwardness today, either depositing their own brand of tribute on the remaining mausoleums or by ambling out of the churchyard and down into the Market Square, seemingly looking for a pint. The associations with yew, however, go much further back than Edward I, who was the first to order the increased planting of the tree in graveyards. The World Ash Tree at the heart of Norse mythology, and Wagner's *Ring*, may well have been a yew. And the Druids, like other groups, tribes and faiths, observed its innate ability to reproduce, even from seemingly dead wood. But it was the characteristic Christian appropriation of those connotations, just as with the mistletoe, that gave rise to the idea of the 'tree of life' seen within the death of the graveyard.

Why this yew-dominated corner of Pembridge's churchyard might have been transferred out of church hands is unknown, but it made me wonder what had stood here even before our modest house was constructed. It certainly could have been a small barn for the parish, storing a percentage of the villagers' harvest as payment to the rector. It might also have been a shrine to a local saint. Was there even a separate chantry chapel, predating the structure of our home, as in other market towns and Pembridge's own outlying hamlets? More chilling was the thought that it was the site of an old lychgate, where the dead would have rested until the funeral, with relatives warding off potential bodysnatchers. Perhaps that was what the old name for the house, Church Stile Cottage, had meant. There may have even been a rest house too.

Inside the church itself, it is also possible to see elements of a former life as well as what remained after the parish riches were stripped from the place and St Mary's was converted to the new liturgy. Prior to the Reformation, it must have been particularly glorious, an ecclesiastical treasure trove. When you walk up from the Market Square, past our old front door, the building looms large, exposed in the wintry winds that race around the churchyard. The porch where Lewis Thomas danced is grand, but once through the entrance, marked by the calligraphy of John, my old chaplain, the nave is even grander.

Standing under the towering chancel arch, you can see the last vestiges of the rood loft, where, according to various church histories, choristers sang during certain feasts or the deacon intoned the Gospel under the statues of the crucified Christ, his mother Mary (the church's patronal saint) and John the Evangelist, all illuminated by candlelight. Later, such figures were replaced by royal coats of arms, including at Abbey Dore, seized from the Cistercians in 1536, showing that the stamp of the monarch was more important than any godly image. Originally, in Pembridge, the screen itself, often the focus of Edwardian destruction, must have been dauntingly huge — there are staggeringly beautiful survivals in nearby Aymestrey and St Margaret's, as well as at Partrishow and Llananno just over the border, even further from the vandals' grasp. But all that remains in Pembridge are the plinths for the three statues and a locked spiral staircase in the south transept, rising up to a barred opening. To peer through the windows of the turret is to peer into a liturgical void.

Next to the door to the loft are further remains, the past impasto of the village's vibrant worship, coloured blood red and covered with the traces of white Marian roses that originally surrounded a towering statue of the Virgin. Scratched away with great vigour and violence, the roses are no more. A Yorkist friend was surprised when I uploaded a photograph of the scene to Instagram, insisting it was unlikely the flowers would have been targeted during Edward VI's reign, given that his grandmother was of the white rose. Yet this was, after all, a young king so convinced of Protestantism that he prevented Masses being said for the repose of his father's soul a year after Henry VIII had been buried. What would have stopped him ordering the expurgation of something only tangentially associated with the memory of his grandmother, however dear? Whatever the reason, Mary's holy blooms are gone, but the bracket for the original statue remains, now supporting a rather diminutive modern replacement. By the end of the 16th century, all such decoration would have been minimal at best, the altar no longer at the east end, but a table wedged at right angles near the congregation, strictures that Elizabeth notably avoided in the Chapel Royal. But it is still possible during the winter months to rediscover a glint of the complex liturgy and traditions of the pre-Reformation church. In Pembridge that Christmas, it was present in the light at the window, the smoke of a thurible and the sound of prayers, hymns and carols that had been spoken and sung for centuries.

THE 'CORPUS Christi Carol' is one of the strangest and most poignant texts from the 16th century. It was first written down by a grocer's apprentice and embraced the language and imagery of a number of feasts, including the days of Holy Week and the eponymous Solemnity of the Most Holy Body and Blood of Christ. But given that the words speak of being borne 'into an orchard brown', it was also likely to have been recited or sung at Christmas, certainly during winter. And in Herefordshire, it is among the bare branches of the apple orchards that another brand of mysticism can still be found.

The tradition of wassailing revolves around a torchlight procession that leads the residents out of their homes to the source of the village's life at the deadest, darkest point of the year. Derived from Old Norse and Old English for 'be healthy', wassailing inevitably became associated with drinking and was subsumed, as with so many other traditions, into the Christian feasts. Immediately around Pembridge, the decorations that had been brought in during Advent and Christmas were burned at New Year, normally a ball of hawthorn or mistletoe, which would be taken out to the earliest-sown field and torched, after which cider was poured on the branches. But there were more elaborate ceremonies too:

> Very early in the morning, long before sunrise, the men, boys, tradesmen and dogs of the farm assembled in a corner of a field of autumn-sown wheat; a pole was put upon the ground with a wisp of straw tied to the top of it, and at the foot, straw and brushwood were piled. These were set alight and the men stood in a circle round it with a cake and plentiful supply of cider. The bailiff filled a horn much with the cider and handed it round. He then called for cheers, everyone shouted 'Good old Zider', and as they did so bent slowly towards the fire at each syllable till their backs were horizontal. This was done three times followed by a hearty 'Hip, Hip, Hooray' as they rose again. Cake was eaten and

more cider drunk. Cheers were given for the master and mistress and if there were any very unpopular characters in the neighbour-hood dumb cheers were given as bows were made to the fire. Then the wagoners, taking a wisp of straw, lighted it at the bonfire and tried to run over thirteen teens of wheat before it went out. If he succeeded there would be a good harvest, but if he failed a bad one.

The ritual, recorded by Pembridge resident Mary Langston in the 1930s, would have changed from village to village, but the essentials were always the same: drink, fire and fertility. What was most crucial, however, was the reverencing of the prized field, the prized ox or, in some cases, the oldest tree in the orchard, as gunshot chased away the evil spirits of the previous twelve months and prepared for the arrival of the new. Communing with these ancient plants or the field that would, ultimately, make or break the village, to say nothing of basic mechanisms of survival, has taken on a new power in the face of a worsening environmental situation.

When I was asked by my thoughtful farmer friend Ben and his husband Stevie – the couple who had found the amazing wall paintings – to lead a procession through their orchard, complete with songs and shouts and crowns filled with ivy and hellebores, I was choked by the depth of the ritual, even if I'm a push-over when it comes to such practices. The Wassail Queen sat in the branches of the oldest, most gnarled tree and we processed around its trunk before standing with torches in hand as the Wassail King poured last year's apple juice on the roots. We were all high on cider, but, despite giggling and glugging, couldn't fail to be moved by the words that were sung to the ancient fruit-bearer:

> Old apple tree, we wassail thee
> And hoping thou wilt bear.
> For only god knows where we'll be
> At apple-time next year.
> Oh to blow well and to bear well
> And merry let us be.
> So every man drink up his cup
> And health to the apple tree.

The idea that 'at apple-time next year' we might not know where we would be cut to the core. Once the ritual was over, and I had sung myself hoarse with all the call-and-response of teaching Ben and Stevie's friends the tune and the words, everyone fell silent around the old tree. There isn't a more bitter time to experience that sense of insubstantiality than when standing under apple boughs in the light of a full moon on a clear winter's night. Just for a moment, we imagined that there wasn't a car to drive us home to electric light and gas-powered heating, but instead to a draughty, timber-framed cottage long since plunged into darkness.

The following morning, Alastair and I awoke, a little bleary from the wassail cup, and packed up the oranges and the straw stars. Brushing away the dust and the needles, we went out into the garden with the garlands of bay, box and holly that had gone dry in the house over the festive period, burning them and the mistletoe chandelier in a fire bin. The cloyingly fruity smoke taunted us with its promise of summer fullness. Yet how much more acute must the sense of SAD have been in the 1500s, when all these festivities and more were over and the drudge of January began.

The winters of the late 16th and early 17th centuries were seasons of palpable crisis. In 1593, when Shakespeare began his louring *Tragedy of Richard III* with the memory of a 'winter of discontent', the dramatist was not only writing a description of the time before Richard's brother Edward IV returned to the throne, thanks in part to the Battle of Mortimer's Cross, fought just four miles from Pembridge; he was also commenting on the era's experience of the bleakest of seasons. Denied literal, metaphorical and spiritual light, the people of the age faced both the harshness of nature and the beginning of seismic changes in human philosophy.

The comfort of the gods they had venerated was either revealed as a fallacy or had been removed by the authorities. Failed harvests and increased famine encouraged a shift from local to broader markets, though the promise of expansion proved to be another false idol. Winter perpetuated poverty, harmed livestock and impeded travel. Rather than relying on the market, the Elizabethans had to find more basic doctrines of sufficiency and survival. They could no longer assuage the monarchs that had abandoned them, whether crowned with gold or crowned with thorns. The path to shelter was all that mattered.

VIIII.

Unsprung

THERE'S SOMETHING WRONG WITH the name. Spring speaks of suddenness, though the season never comes quickly – certainly not quickly enough. Born on the second day of March, I know too well how spring is rarely sprung. There has been snow on my birthday, as well as blazing sunshine – and proper warmth with it. Yet the seasons shift not just climatically but also according to how you measure them. The astronomical calendar's idea that winter begins on 21 December and ends three months later seems bizarre, given the freezingness of early December and the balmy February half-term holidays we've enjoyed. Equally static is the meteorological calendar's shift every three months – winter is December, January and February entire – though I prefer its idea that I am a child of spring, not of winter; a sort of less heroic (and less heterosexual) Siegmund from Wagner's *Die Walküre*. 'You are the spring,' his (unknown) twin sister and soon-to-be lover Sieglinde sings in ecstasy, 'that I have yearned for in the frost and ice of winter.' It's a moment from the opera that we often play, volume high, in Stepps House, as if to goad spring on.

In Wagner's original, the season is given as *Lenz*. An older word, poetic in inference, *Lenz* was also used in German as the mark of age – that you had so many springs under your belt.

It's an alternative to *Frühling*, which speaks of dawn and earliness. Both words are, however, more drawn out than the abrupt English. The French *printemps* is similarly (and unsurprisingly) lyrical. Even Dutch, at risk of being as blunt as my own language, differentiates between *voorjaar* and *lente*, with more than a hint of religiosity and poetry in the latter. Immediately, I think of that old adage, *festina lente*, make haste slowly.

The first season of the year deserves this languid libretto. Ornithologists know it. Standing afield for days on end, they wait, like the 'speculating rooks' of one of Edward Thomas's shortest poems, for what most of us below cannot see, not only winter passing but also the arrival of avian life that is seasonal and, in turn, defining of the new season. Beginning at the southern tip of Britain in March and reaching its northern shores by May, there is an almighty procession of birds, each carrying something of the south with them, whether it be the dust of the Sahara or the moisture of the Congolese rainforests. Deep in the slump of winter, I long for their coming and the confirmation of warmth they bring on the wing.

As we drove through Herefordshire on a late-March afternoon, my birthday celebrated, St David's daffodils already 'going over to the other side' (as my mum would say), it wasn't our *eyes* that were thrilled – though the county's golden hours are always blindingly beautiful – but our *ears*. The din was colossal. Even Wagner's Sieglinde would have struggled to crest over the waves of sound emanating from the hedgerows, those ancient partitions, dating back millennia, that were also planted to enclose common land. Now, at least, they were gladdened by robins, wagtails, tits, finches, sparrows and wrens. Eventually, the swallows, swifts, house martins and cuckoos would be added to the commotion. The low feedback of winter-sleepy bees in the garden, ducking into the heads of the last tête-à-têtes and the rusting hellebores, combined with birds barracking in the yew to make for an antiphony not witnessed since the Gabrielis at St Mark's in Venice. On the old drovers' route across Hergest Ridge, at the western edge of the county, another harbinger of life could be found. Here, on winter walks, just a few weeks before, Welsh winds had hurled ice in our path. But as the frost receded, the skylarks dropped their silver chains of sound from miles overhead.

There are skylarks galore around Pembridge too and I've often wondered whether they inspired Vaughan Williams when he first journeyed to the village in 1909. He had come to collect folk songs from agricultural labourers and travellers, though there's every likelihood he would have also noted the village's avian residents. Earlier that year, the novelist and poet George Meredith had died, whose 1881 poem 'The Lark Ascending' Vaughan Williams had cherished since his youth; it may well have been in his thoughts again that summer. The bird's song would have mixed with the sounds of Pembridge, with the modality and cadences of folk song later informing the spiralling, violin-led idyll of the same name that the composer wrote in 1914 but only unveiled after the Great War had wreaked its havoc.

The 'aerial rings' of these larks and other birds jetting from hedgerow to hedgerow delivered the biggest natural high for the recovering SAD victim. Eyes starved of light were finally able to feast and I could almost kid myself that the warmth was real.

I donned shorts and found my sunglasses. Asparagus emerged from plastic tunnels in the Vale of Evesham and around Ross-on-Wye and I bought piles of them at Parry's, the greengrocers in Leominster. Frying the spears in oodles of salted butter and black pepper, I added the sweet greasy stalks to (far too much) pasta, a handful of egg yolks and some shaved Parmesan. To be away from writing and lecturing for a moment, to have Alastair back from his job too, was a thrill, though I knew his fidgetiness would kick in after just two days of drinking on the lawn.

'I THINK I'll varnish those doors,' he said, pointing to the garden room. 'They've needed doing for a while; I'll go to B&Q tomorrow.' It was highly commendable, of course, though Alastair's restlessness often manifested itself in practical tasks. One journey to a hardware shop could turn into many, as, trip by trip, he grasped that we didn't have the necessary equipment, that the varnish purchased is only for indoor use or that the ladder won't quite reach. The job is always done, and done well, but more often than not resembles the painting of the Forth Bridge. I used to resist the plans, finding the whole process too enervating, but I've come to realize that it is a way to a happy home.

After, surprisingly, just two trips, Alastair managed to purchase the requisite sandpapers, masking tape, brushes and varnish to fix the doors. And they needed it. Following months of ice, rain and snow, the flakes from the previous summer had turned to nigh-untreated wood. Water would eventually make its way in. And unlike the Elizabethan timbers in the house, these fifteen-year-old doors didn't promise longevity.

Alastair took great pride in his work. He slowly sanded away, clearing the sawdust with a brush, before tilting the doors in the light to make sure it was even and then announcing, as the sky bled red, that he'd begin varnishing in the morning. Applied like syrup, it soaked in more rapidly than he had expected, indicative of the need for repair. The fumes were a bit much for me, so I opened the windows and met a clear sweetness that I've only really experienced before at Bwlch-y-rhiw. Winter has even longer talons in the valley around my late grandfather's farm, with lambing left until March, even later, whereas the sheep had given birth in Pembridge back in February. It was all part of the season's gradual arrival. But as Alastair finished for the day, that freshness died and the breeze instead brought bitterness. We lit the fire, warned that the warm spell was only brief, but had no idea how furious its rejection would be.

There was an entirely different light creeping behind the curtains at dawn the following morning. The heating had kicked in again, making the floorboards and timbers crack as they expanded, and the wood burner was still warm from the night before. But, outside, snow was falling in great clumps. It was the fourth day of April. The view up to the church and the belfry from our bedroom window was almost entirely impeded by the white. Winter had not done with us. In the short term, it made the job that Alastair had just begun impossible to complete. The varnish had frozen in the pot in the shed and couldn't be used under five degrees in any case. The second coat would have to wait. As would more asparagus. Gorging on spring delights one week, I was back to making broth the next.

Had she been with us, my mum would have sensed the dead season's reappearance. Rubbing her hands with sudden speed, she delivers the Welsh saying with theatrical gusto: *Troy dy dyn a y tân yn dangos fod eira yn agos!* (Turn your arse to the fire, the snow's coming). Like Dadcu, my late grandfather, Mum has the ability to smell snow. Living at the top of the valley, often cut off for weeks, she knew well the violence of winter and its seemingly inexplicable returns, even after the lambs had been skipping up the hillside for days.

As well as reminding me of my mother's meteorological gifts and her lilting Welsh adages, this year's return of wintry weather provided an almost direct re-enactment of one of the 16th-century paintings that had been seizing my imagination, giving a rare Technicolor insight into life 450 years ago. Because Bruegel's villagers, existing in the artist's mind's-eye 'everywhere-land', also experienced spring as a slovenly affair, witnessed in *The Gloomy Day*, the painting he created to represent this time of year.

As in his autumnal picture, *The Return of the Herd*, earthy tones dominate, especially in the foreground, where we're treated to the sequence's most detailed vision of a village. Thatched timber-framed houses fill a maze of rough-surfaced streets, that medieval mix of earth and stones familiar from the ground underneath Pembridge's Market Hall, which recent excavations had dated to the building's origins. There is a diminutive church in the village too, albeit with a much grander apsidal sanctuary at

its east end. Yet the settlement itself is run-down, with a vagrant pissing against the pub – the same pub, we imagine, found in Bruegel's *The Massacre of the Innocents*, with its sign featuring a star. Other houses have been battered by the winter months, moss clings to the roofs and the village's populace is out, in the first gasp of dry, unfreezing weather, to repair the thatch and re-patch the walls.

The main focus of this industry is in the foreground. Bruegel's familiar format of the hillside, with the view sweeping below, allows us to look at one house in particular. A tree has fallen down in a winter storm, luckily missing the building, and men and women are lopping and breaking up the wood, perhaps even using some of it to restore their home or fill the hearth.

Another villager focuses his attentions on a much shorter tree, with switches coming out of the stump. It could be hazel, the straight branches of which were used for the wattle and daub of timber-framed houses, the trees as prevalent around Pembridge today as they were when the panels of our home were first made. Outside Bruegel's village, however, the wood is not hazel but osier, a kind of willow. It is similarly used for stakes, albeit more often in basketwork and fencing, as well as for beanpoles and pea sticks. Yet not everyone in the painting is so conscientious. In the bottom right-hand corner, three characters are enacting carnival games, part of a pre-Lenten ritual which points to the season that will follow.

Industrious or indolent, all the villagers are completely unaware of the scene beyond. Only we, the external viewer, can see what is about to happen. In the mountains above, glaciers are encroaching and look set to swallow a castle whole, not unlike the fortifications in *The Hunters in the Snow* – was this another of Bruegel's moralizing moments? Worse, however, is unfolding in the lowlands and, chiefly, at sea – here, the parallel with the artist's homeland is clear. The spring tide and its waves have breached the dykes, inundating various homes. The farmer's cows, assumed safe in *The Return of the Herd*, are being driven from the water, as he tries to save his livestock and livelihood. Meantime, ships of trade and war are wrecked in great number. For all the brilliance and diligence of human endeavour, nature has to be obeyed. And in the 16th century, she was an increasingly unpredictable taskmistress.

·   ·   ·

UNABLE TO carry on with decorating the outside of the house, Alastair decided that we should go to the pub for lunch. The New Inn was just a snowball's throw from the front door, but we decided to wear wellies for the short traipse through the slush. Inside, the fire was blazing, heat bouncing off its William and Mary iron back, and the girls were chatting and giggling as usual. On the specials board, there was a fish soup made from roasted lobster shells.

'Go through to the back bar,' Jane said, 'I'll bring your pints round,' pulling our favourite beer from the 17th-century Three Tuns Brewery in Bishop's Castle.

Glyn, who runs a translating business, had already nabbed the seat right next to the hearth, so we sat on the settle. He was in a typically garrulous mood.

'I needed a pint. It's bloody freezing at the house.'

Glyn had been doing extensive renovations to a place in one of the hamlets around Pembridge for some time. It was a labour of love, putting back as much of the original structure as possible. It hadn't always been the case, this sense of care for the black-and-white houses of the county, judging by the dilapidated poverty of the village for much of the 20th century, but the tide was certainly turning.

'We had one of those delivered last week,' he said, pointing up at a beam that went right across the bar.

'Huge, aren't they?'

'That's probably a ship's timber,' he said, playfully.

It was a theory, often repeated, that the larger timbers of the wooden structures of the 16th century – and later – had been repurposed from ships, even taken from shipwrecks, like the one in Bruegel's *The Gloomy Day*. But even more sensationally, and as a point of national pride, a whole mythology had evolved around the reuse of material from an event of which Bruegel could have known nothing, one of the natural world's most brutal negations of human endeavour.

In late May 1588, nearly twenty years after the artist's death, 130 galleons set sail from Lisbon via A Coruña to the Low Countries, with the intention of bringing a Habsburg army to fight against the English. This so-called Armada had three aims: to re-establish Catholicism in Britain; to stop English interference in the Netherlands; and to prevent privateering ships from meddling over the Atlantic. The issues of trade, control and sovereignty that have dominated recent arguments between Britain and continental Europe were similarly endemic to 16th-century life.

The Spanish ships that sailed through the Channel, the Canal de la Mancha, that summer were grand vessels, but the English ships they met at Eddystone Rocks south of Plymouth on 20 July, and at Portland three days later, were fleeter by far. Observing the Armada at close range, Francis Drake was able to establish his strategy. He drove the aggressors east and forced them to anchor off Calais, not far from Dunkirk, where the Duke of Parma's army was meant to be waiting. Communication, however, had failed and the Armada was left exposed. On 28 July, Drake sent in eight warships filled with tar and gunpowder. The Spanish may have already had direct experience of such a tactic at the Siege of Antwerp in 1584–5, though Drake still managed to break the crescent at the Armada's core. With a rising wind, the scattered ships were unable to re-form and the English were victorious at the Battle of Gravelines.

Many native mariners then capitulated to typhus, but the Spanish Habsburg navy was to experience an even worse return home. The commander of the fleet, the fantastically named Don Alonso Pérez de Guzmán y de Zúñiga-Sotomayor, decided not to return to Galicia through the Channel and risk further attack. Instead, he chose to round the British Isles during August, customarily a fine month to embark on such a journey. Except that the weather patterns of the late 16th century were far from predictable. Sailing north to Norway, the fleet turned towards Scotland and reached the Orkneys by September. They had traversed the globe and conquered – and subdued – swathes of Central and South America, but nothing could prepare them for the freak hurricane that then struck, likely caused by comparatively warm air reaching the expanding Arctic ice shelves of the Little Ice Age.

Twenty-four of the fleet were wrecked on the Irish coast by the storms and promptly ransacked. While 130 ships had left the Iberian Peninsula in May, only sixty-seven returned to Santander that October. Five thousand Spanish men died in the process, from drowning, starvation or slaughter. And such was the legend of the loss of the Spanish navy that many inhabitants of timber-framed houses across Ireland, even the British Isles as far as Pembridge, began to claim that their homes were built from Spanish rather than native oak.

It was, as I pointed out to Glyn, the most unlikely material, certainly at The New Inn, situated right next to the village saw pit. Given the immense weight of a ship's timbers and, in the case of Herefordshire, the long distance from any coast, to say nothing of more immediate sources of oak, the mythology barely held water. Slightly less far-fetched was the claim that an avenue of chestnuts at Croft Castle, just five miles from Pembridge and home to a thousand-year-old oak, had grown from barrels of edible nuts taken from the captured vessels of the Armada. Brought to Croft, they were planted over the course of a century to represent the plan of the Spanish and English ships at battle, underlining how deep the legends of the skirmish went into the nation's soul and soil, though not the climatic circumstances that brought about the ruin of the Hispanic fleet.

BRUEGEL, LIKE those living and drinking in Pembridge, knew nothing of the Armada; though, unlike landlocked Herefordians, the artist would have witnessed many a grand galleon, Spanish included, leaving Antwerp. In 1561, his colleagues Hieronymus Cock and Cornelis van Dalem published the artist's depiction of a naval battle on the Strait of Messina, which he'd based on scenes witnessed during his trip around Italy and which may, like Cock's volumes of decorative schemes, have come to Britain in printed form.

Ships, like those in *The Gloomy Day*, are frequent occurrences in the work of Bruegel and his contemporaries; they offered a symbol of man's pride, but also of his imprudence and misplaced power. A whole harbour of vessels, small and tall, is called into service for the construction of the hubristic Tower of Babel, painted not once but twice by Bruegel – the larger of the two

images, the one that had been in Jonghelinck's collection, is now in Vienna. But if those ships are lost in the enormity and fruit-lessness of the Mesopotamians' enterprise, a single vessel makes the point even more eloquently in Bruegel's most vaunted paint-ing: *Landscape with the Fall of Icarus*.

Like the 1565 seasons, the image, with its ice-clad mountains, offers another all-encompassing view. Agricultural labourers go about their business, so engrossed in their work that they miss the figure whose waxed wings have been melted by the sun and who is now plummeting into the sea. It is, perhaps, indicative of a much grander folly – or futility – given the proximity of an impressive carrack, sailing out into the sunlight though equally sure to meet storms. And the angle of Bruegel's farmer would have reminded sharp, artistically-minded viewers of another figure: the chilling ploughman in Holbein's *The Dance of Death*, doomed to work until released by the ultimate reaper.

Obliviousness to catastrophe threads through the 16th century as a whole. It even goes to the heartwood of the material from which the homes and galleons of the age were constructed. Fundamentally utilitarian, oak was nonetheless wasted on imprudent projects and there is no doubt that in a colder, more intemperate climate, oak was becoming scarce. Observing the rings in the manifestly simple, chunky timbers of our small market storehouse, we could see how widely spaced they were – the cause of the dendrochronologists' frustrated visit – indicating that they could even predate the coldest snaps of the Little Ice Age and its scarcity of timber, so, perhaps, before 1570, as far back as Bruegel's 1565 paintings.

Elsewhere in the village, builders and carpenters had been quite wasteful, indulging in a practice called close studding, a decorative scheme that features numerous vertical struts between the main timbers, often serving little practical purpose. It didn't stop me coveting the house in question, however – quite the opposite. Other, more elaborate patterns were simply decadent in the circumstances, a show of wealth. Yet so extreme was the felling of oak in England during the 1500s that Elizabeth I had to introduce the first oak plantation in Windsor Great Park, the very land that she and her advisors had plundered for their projects. In a chillier climate, however, the oaks they planted around the great castle would take many years to reach the height and usefulness of their predecessors.

· · ·

WHETHER YOU were the monarch or a middling type, the effects of climate change were obvious, everywhere felt, yet everywhere misunderstood. Frequently, superstition surrounded the failure of harvests, with cries of a god who had abandoned his people. And similarly supernatural schemes are to be found in one of the most captivating dramas of the period. Dating from 1595–6, Shakespeare's *A Midsummer Night's Dream* features a vivid account of the shifting climate. The play was written during a year of particularly violent plunges in temperature, including the freezing of the Thames (as would happen again in 1608, 1621, 1635, 1649, 1655, 1663, 1666, 1677, 1684 and 1695). The effects were felt across Europe, with Bruegel's later and often slavishly copycatting countryman Lucas van Valckenborch capturing the year's frost markets, sledges and blizzards. Glaciers encroached on Swiss and French villages, while Dutch explorers in the Arctic found that the conditions they needed for passage were considerably less favourable than they had been the previous year. By the end of 1595, the access to the Kara Sea, north of Russia, had become so thick with ice that all expeditions had to be abandoned.

In Shakespeare's play, the changes in the world have been caused by 'the forgeries of jealousy' between Titania and Oberon, queen and king of the fairy realm, specifically over the ownership of a changeling child. But as with the climatic vagaries of everyday life at the time of the play's creation, everyone in society is forced to feel the consequences of the couple's struggle: monarch, mechanical and lover alike:

Therefore the winds, piping to us in vain,
As in revenge, have suck'd up from the sea
Contagious fogs; which falling in the land
Have every pelting river made so proud
That they have overborne their continents:
The ox hath therefore stretch'd his yoke in vain,
The ploughman lost his sweat, and the green corn
Hath rotted ere his youth attain'd a beard;
The fold stands empty in the drowned field,
And crows are fatted with the murrion flock;
The nine men's morris is fill'd up with mud,
And the quaint mazes in the wanton green
For lack of tread are undistinguishable:
The human mortals want their winter here;
No night is now with hymn or carol blest:
Therefore the moon, the governess of floods,
Pale in her anger, washes all the air,
That rheumatic diseases do abound:
And thorough this distemperature we see
The seasons alter: hoary-headed frosts
Fall in the fresh lap of the crimson rose,
And on old Hiems' thin and icy crown
An odorous chaplet of sweet summer buds
Is, as in mockery, set: the spring, the summer,
The childing autumn, angry winter, change
Their wonted liveries, and the mazed world,
By their increase, now knows not which is which.

Titania's speech provides a vivid compilation of contemporary thought and experience. The 'pelting river' and its floods are seen in *The Gloomy Day*, as well as in the inappropriately amusing 1607 woodcut I had found of deluges south of Pembridge. Equally familiar are the consequences for the ox and the ploughman, while the latter's arable crops are left to rot in the fields. The ox's life is spared, but flocks of sheep have already fallen foul of a plague and now only provide meat for crows. The roads are impassable and hymns and carols are of little comfort (though, here, Shakespeare's frequently Catholic overtones may suggest a continuing hostility to the Reformation). It's not just the flocks of sheep who have become susceptible to pestilence, as rheumatic diseases are now a recurrent feature in a world in which the accepted characteristics of the seasons have changed entirely, those enshrined in daily life, as well as in cultural expressions such as Spenser's poems, Bruegel's paintings and the Labours of the Months before them.

In such an uncertain world, it was, perhaps, easier to turn to supernature rather than nature itself, to call the squall that broke the Armada the 'Protestant Wind' – an idea furthered by an inscription on the victors' medal, *Flavit Jehovah et Dissipati Sunt* (Jehovah blew with His winds, and they were scattered) – than it was to investigate causes and lasting consequences. And such obliviousness was common to all ranks of society, whether you were fixing your roof and varnishing your doors after the winter storms or commanding flotillas to recapture England for the sake of a derelict deity.

It was one thing to riff and rhyme on such events, but quite another to understand them on a scientific footing. Yet that was precisely what drove one spiritually maladjusted thinker of the age: the alchemist, astrologer and magician Johann Georg Faust. A historical figure, albeit of vague date and, supposedly, German origin, he is now more readily associated with a literary phenomenon: first the *Historia von D. Johann Fausten*, a cheaply produced chapbook from Frankfurt, published the year before the Spanish Armada; and then Shakespeare's contemporary Christopher Marlowe's *The Tragical History of the Life and Death of Doctor Faustus*. Later, Faust's cause would be taken up by Goethe, Berlioz, Gounod, Mahler, Thomas Mann and others.

Based on an English translation of the Frankfurt text, Marlowe's play opens in the title character's study, where two angels, one good and one bad, have appeared to him. The first encourages a life of inner reflection, bidding Faust reject his lust for necromancy, but it is the devil or, in this case, a bad angel, who, of course, has the much better tune:

> Go forward, Faustus, in that famous art
> Wherein all Nature's treasure is contain'd:
> Be thou on earth as Jove is in the sky,
> Lord and commander of these elements.

To know the world, to know the mysterious catalysts for the devastating changes witnessed in Marlowe's time, these are Faustus's calls and so he summons Mephistophilis to aid his ambition. The choice will, of course, be his 'hellish fall', yet the temptation to 'wonder at unlawful things' and become 'commander of these elements' was pervasive across Europe, even as alleged witches were being rounded up for their apparent role in the destruction of harvests. In 1587, the year of the publication of the original 'Faust' chapbook, and again in 1588, such accusations reached a peak in England and France, with Marlowe's play testifying to the tug of war between accusations of sorcery and more rational explanations.

Ninety per cent of those charged under the Act Against Conjurations, Enchantments and Witchcrafts from 1563 onwards were women. Many were hanged, though the authorities also employed other cruel methods to identify and punish the accused. Frequently, they were thrown into a river or pond. If the suspect floated, they were thought to be of the devil's party, having rejected the waters of baptism, while other 'troublesome and angry' women, including supposed witches, were humiliated on a ducking stool. Like a wooden seesaw with only one seat, this appallingly unsubtle device was used to plunge the offender repeatedly into the water, as recorded in many chapbooks. But there is no need to rely on contemporary illustrations, for the priory church in Leominster, just six miles from Pembridge, contains a preserved ducking stool. It was still in use in 1809, when a notorious local 'scold' called Jane Corran, sometimes known as Jenny Pipes, was paraded through the town and ducked into a tributary of the River Lugg. And there are likewise many Pembridge myths of village adversaries being summarily tipped into the River Arrow, even in recent years.

Superstition was yet more widespread during the 1500s, at least according to markings in Stepps House. Cleaning up from

damage caused by a small deluge of rainwater that had breached the outer beams and poured down the inside wall of our dining room, I found a hexafoil etched into one of the timbers (much like the Virgo Virginum motif upstairs). Sometimes known as daisy wheels, these circular designs occur frequently in Gothic art and architecture, including in the windows of St Mary's Church in Pembridge. In our home, however, it was used as a protective symbol, an apotropaic (from the Greek, to ward off evil). The markings have been found in many ancient buildings, from dwellings to barns, and were often placed by doorways and fireplaces to block the entry of the nefarious. Ours was scratched into the timber next to the old front door and may well have been a way to protect the storehouse from ruin – or to guard later occupants, when it was converted into a home. But like the ducking stool in Leominster, it told of the continuing fight between superstition and more methodical systems, even if it was tricky to separate fact from fiction.

RUDOLF II, the great Habsburg patron of the arts and one-time owner of Bruegel's season paintings, was a fervent supporter of science in its shaky infancy. Like Bruegel's art, such pursuits were a way of seeing into how the world operated within a wider cosmic order, though, initially, these interests were more readily associated with turning base metal into gold. Rudolf was not alone in this regard. Philip II of Spain also devoted much of his time, money and energy to chemical experiments aimed at metallic metamorphosis, which derived from the idea of 'principal matter', the so-called philosopher's stone, sitting at the heart of every thing and being. Having spent his teenage years in Spain, Rudolf II continued the Hispanic Habsburg's passion for this brand of nonsense when he moved his seat of government from Vienna to Prague in the 1580s.

Rudolf's interests in alchemy and philosophy weren't necessarily contradictory to the business of running the Habsburg realm and the Holy Roman Empire, but they nonetheless pointed to an inability to make political decisions, to say nothing of a depressive streak. As a result, his throne in Prague was far from being the heart of a militaristic superpower. Instead, it became the centre of an alchemical industry, placed within a suitably ornamented city of totems and temples. To aid his aims, Rudolf

employed the medium (cum charlatan) Sir Edward Kelly, who was travelling throughout Europe in the early 1580s with his more famous colleague John Dee. The two have often been depicted as English equivalents of the figure of Faustus, much like the cover image for an early edition of Marlowe's play.

Both Kelly and Dee had links to the area around Pembridge: Kelly was born in Worcester in 1555, while Dee's family hailed from Pilleth, ten miles north-west of the village. Although he was born in London, Dee retained links with Pilleth, which had been a place of worship since the early Celtic church. It had also been the site of an appalling battle between the English and the Welsh, where, as Shakespeare states in *Henry IV Part I*, a thousand

Herefordshire men were summarily butchered. Driving through Pilleth today is to experience that weightiness and eeriness first-hand. Placed in a dank valley, it may once have been a site of spiritual succour, no doubt instigating the ministry of John Dee, later rector of Upton-upon-Severn, though there is also something of the night about the area, inspiring a man who was equally lured by knowledge of treasures buried in the Marches as he was by a life devoted to Christ.

When the somewhat less scientific Dee left Prague in 1589 – he was more given to conjuring angels through crystal balls than creating sources of gold – Kelly remained and became Rudolf's chief alchemist. He was, in many ways, the model for a crucial but absent character in Karel Čapek's 1922 play *The Makropulos Affair*, adapted as an opera by Leoš Janáček. Čapek's fictional scientist Hieronymus Makropulos was an alchemist who was also commanded to prepare a potion to extend the Emperor's life. When the potion was complete, the Emperor told Makropulos to test it on his daughter, Elina, who promptly fell into a coma. Like Kelly, who failed to produce the requisite gold, Makropulos was sent to prison (even though Elina survived into the 20th century). Fabulous though they seem, such fictions point to the dedication with which early pseudoscientific projects were pursued, and not just in Prague, for when Kelly's colleague Dee returned to England, he was taken into the confidence of Queen Elizabeth.

A comparable scientific transformation was required by common agricultural labourers too, those who, undoubtedly, felt the very worst effects of climate change during the Little Ice Age.

Rather than superstition, a coherent approach was needed, based on observation, cataloguing and lessons learned. Battling against the unknown, villagers sought to reinvent their methods. There was a veritable revolution in agriculture, with many of the new English policies, like the art of landscape painting, learned from the Dutch. With an almost identical climate, the English were able to follow Netherlandish models, including draining their land more efficiently, even in the more undulating soils of Herefordshire. In Bruegel's homeland, windmills aided the process of irrigation, as captured in both his and his sons' paintings. Rotation of produce was also key, instead of leaving fields fallow (every second or third year). The planting of nitrogen-releasing clover and vegetables such as deep-rooted turnips for forage became an essential part of the county's agriculture. Potatoes, however, which had been imported, according to myth, by Walter Raleigh, were not considered good enough for livestock, let alone the family table, and had to wait until much later to be introduced to the area. Nowadays, potatoes thrive in Herefordshire, feeding the great chipping and frying machines at Tyrrell's crisps, three miles from Pembridge, which are then sold around the world in a marked reversal of the vegetable's fortunes.

If science in its infancy was more about power than truth, the emergence of quantifiable philosophies surrounding the laws of nature, including the apple that fell on Isaac Newton's head in the 1660s, powerfully redressed the balance. Something that could be ratified through the plainness of numbers was very different to the necromancy of Faust or the gold-lusting antics of Marches mystics at the Habsburg and Elizabethan courts. Through the raw experience of nature, the position of the human race shifted. We were not, as in Bruegel's paintings, just an aggregate part of the ordered universe, but were given rational thought to understand and interrogate our surroundings, even if we had no power to change them. In the 17th century, instead of being trapped within the image, more and more thinking men and women were granted the position offered by Bruegel to Nicolaes Jonghelinck and his guests, to stand apart from the world and analyse the cycle afresh.

They had also created the tools for that analysis. Working with the printing presses, scientists were able to spread their ideas by the same routes that had allowed the imagery of Bruegel and others to make its way from publishing houses in Antwerp to domestic dwellings in Herefordshire and beyond. With ready access to international reports of experiments, findings and hypotheses, as well as expeditions to the Arctic and the glaciers of the Alps, scientists were able to pool their resources, even finding themselves mimicked by well-meaning if not wholly well-read amateurs. But it would take much longer for a farmer in Pembridge, for instance, to gain access to these records, to say nothing of newfangled contraptions such as the telescope, an early-17th-century invention, or the barometers and thermometers that were becoming ubiquitous in places of learning and exalted homes.

For all the investigations that followed the plummeting temperatures at the end of the 16th century, a lasting understanding of how human endeavour and nature did or didn't work together was more elusive. At the very moment the Little Ice Age and its unpredictable climate began to recede from collective memory, the Industrial Revolution, the peak – or trough – of the market forces triggered by the 16th century's experience of climate change, brought about the beginning of more irrevocable shifts. This time, however, the transformation had not come from without but from within.

At first, industry promised rational, reckonable work for the peasantry and was again based on mathematics and mechanics, far away from the apparent disorder of nature and its arduous work in the field. The culture of production and acquisition that followed prompted a nonetheless seismic shift in working methods and, more crucially, in the environment. Capital rather than survival became key. Emancipating thousands, the Industrial Revolution also killed off the means by which villages such as Pembridge had thrived and instead swelled the populations of nearby towns, including Leominster and Hereford, as well as centres further afield – a pattern repeated across Europe and the colonized globe, as rural to urban migration increased. Villages lost their purpose, identities and residents, when the railways didn't bypass them entirely. Fresh economic models may in part have been born out of the 'failure' of nature and subsistent agriculture, but the revised market in turn came to diminish nature – and humankind's place within it – as plunging temperatures and increased glaciation were put violently into reverse.

Over the last two centuries, even that most epic physical manifestation of the Little Ice Age, the intruding glaciers of Bruegel's painterly imagination, went the other way. In the late 16th and early 17th centuries, Alpine moraine had grown at an alarming rate, recorded by peasants fearing the destruction of their villages and early naturalists alike. Recently, the opposite has been the case. Early one morning in July 2017, two bodies were discovered on the Tsanfleuron glacier, east of Montreux, at an altitude of 2,615 metres. Searching through missing person's reports, it was discovered that the corpses were of a married couple who had left home on 15 August 1942 to milk their cows in the high mountain pastures – like the animals in Bruegel's *The Return of the Herd*, the cattle were subject to transhumance. The couple tragically never returned and ice slowly enveloped their bodies until the rising median temperatures of the early 21st century resulted in the shrinking of the glacier and uncovered their snowy graves.

A happier by-product of the reversal of the trends of the Little Ice Age is a flourishing of viticultural activity across Northern Europe. Even ambitious Swedes have begun planting vines along the country's southern coast. Herefordshire too has seen an increased number of wineries, marking a return to life during the reign of Henry VIII, when there were 139 sizeable vineyards in England and Wales. Eleven of these were under the ownership of the Crown and sixty-seven were run by noble families. The rest were owned by the church and largely monastic, later seized into Crown or aristocratic tenure at the Dissolution. By the time the Little Ice Age arrived in full strength towards the end of the 16th century, however, the winemaking history of England was put on pause until human endeavour and the worst effects of the Industrial Revolution changed all that. So however brilliant the results of local makers, including

lip-smacking bottles of Bacchus from the vineyards at Codding-
ton near the Malvern Hills, there is a symbolic bitterness on the
palate.

Where, four hundred years ago, the loss of national winemaking and the fear of freak accidents could provoke both religious
superstition and scientific revolutions in equal measure, we
now have the power of the latter at our fingertips, with reasonable, computable information about how and why our climate
is changing. Unfortunately, despite the advances, the balance of
truth to power has followed the glaciers' retreating path. Where,
previously, the crowned heads of Europe courted the expertise
of scientists – quacks and geniuses alike – such expertise has
become distrusted by populists who believe that the market, in
part created out of former confusion, will save all, even when the
market has, continually, failed. Furthermore, some have dared to
proclaim that the deity will, once more, intervene – or that the
causes of climate change are theological.

While the idea of human progress quickly becomes fatu-
ous, the narrative continues in the use of terminology such as
the Dark Ages, the Renaissance and the Age of Enlightenment.
According to this sequence, human endeavour has moved from
a lethargic, self-sufficient agriculture, rooted in villages such as
Pembridge, typified by inefficiency and poverty, towards a balanced, freely commercial society, in which science, productivity
and reason hold sway. It is easy to emphasize this chronicle when
you gaze into the eyes of the peasants in Bruegel's world, as
Jonghelinck and his guests were invited to do, or by juxtaposing
their outwardly crude building techniques, like so many cottages

in Pembridge, against the towering skyscrapers of rampant capitalism. Looking at our house, however, it was the 400-year-old sections of the building that needed no hand of repair.

THE SNOW melted and the temperature shot up just as quickly as it had plunged. Alastair was able to finish the varnishing and then, finally, chip off the masking tape, which had turned as hard as plaster in the cold. Captivated by his perseverance, I stood at the other end of the room, underneath one of our house's oldest wall plates. When he came to visit, Duncan James had thought this section showed signs of recycling, though perhaps it was also evidence of an earlier building that had been placed on this important site in the middle of the village. Whatever its origins, the timber was now safely inside our home and protected from the elements, but it continued to announce its history through old peg, saw and axe marks, two empty mortise joints and a sequence of holes for wattle posts, long since gone, as well as an enormous crack through the sapwood, which had been ravaged by Elizabethan, Jacobean, Carolian, Hanoverian, Victorian and 20th-century woodworm. Heavily marked, it was an unassuming piece of wood, yet so handsome in its restraint. It spoke of an ancient building technique that needed no advocate, for there it stood, as it had for over four centuries, keeping our house in its place and telling stories, as well as hiding secrets, down the ages.

The kind of building we had bought, its general type – or, specifically, the material that holds it up – has taught us most about

the Elizabethan period's shifting climate. The dendrochronologists who came to age our house had noted elsewhere the effect
of those crashing temperatures on the growth of trees felled at
the time. But our historical counterparts must have seen that
too, returning to the saw pit with less and less oak from which to
build. Experiencing changes in nature and God's apparent wrath,
they, like Marlowe's Faustus, were driven 'to practice more than
heavenly power permits', to begin a scientific revolution and,
consequently, to speak truth to power.

At first, the villagers in *The Gloomy Day* appear oblivious to
what is happening in the distance and we disparage their ignor-
ance. Yet they can also be seen to have adopted a Voltaire-like
response, *avant la lettre*, to the inconsistencies of the world; they
go about their business, they cultivate their gardens. Certainly,
they are without blame when it comes to the changes and chances
of their climate. And in any event, during the 16th century, the
ability to confirm what they might have observed in the distance
and to understand it through rational scientific means was not
yet available to them. It is, however, available to us.

Looking at *The Gloomy Day* or flicking through the parchment in the archives, we constantly belittle the peasants – the
word itself has changed meaning, become judgemental – yet
we continue to be blind to our own incipient disasters and the
lessons of glaciers growing and shrinking in turn. Unlike our
16th-century reflections, we have now been gifted what Marlowe
calls 'that famous art wherein all Nature's treasure is contain'd'.
If, as Brian Fagan has written, 'the Little Ice Age is the story of
Europeans' struggle against the most fundamental of all human

vulnerabilities', why has it taken — is it taking — us so long to realize that the same is true now as the narrative changes direction? Bruegel's villagers are powerless, but we, varnishing our doors in the hope of warmth, see exactly what we have to do. Titania's 'mazed world' does indeed now know which is which.

X.

The Scent of Hawthorn

WHEN SPRING PROPER COMES to Herefordshire, it comes in riot. Along the county's lanes, the campions, bluebells and cow parsley provide gossamer embroidery against the hedgerows' generous baize. A velvety blue hangs in the sky and for a brief moment the orchards bloom. There is, on the breeze, the softest scent of apple and pear blossom – pink, blushing equivalents of their blowsier citric cousins of the south. Nature's rush is reflected in the rush of human love, 'when merry lads are playing', as Orazio Vecchi's text for Thomas Morley's 1595 Maytime madrigal puts it. And May was when two other lads, my husband and I, got married.

The fifth month of the year has long been associated with love and fecundity, in both the pagan and the Christian worlds. The latter is evinced by the gloriously affected coronation of statues of the Virgin Mary in churches and cathedrals, especially prior to the Reformation, though still at Belmont Abbey, south of Hereford. And there are the similar crownings of May Queens at village fetes, with Pembridge's Cowslip Fair, at one time seeing the county's largest hiring of labourers for the impending harvest, marking the true beginning of spring in the village. The need for such a public platform for temporary contracting may have ceased, with the attendant celebrations and competitions now moved to July, but the superstitions surrounding the Cowslip Fair endure.

Alastair learned that directly when he was planting vegetables in our allotment at the western end of the village. The allotments fill an old farmer's field, with £35 per year guaranteeing us a half plot. It reminded me of common-land policies, before the village's fields were enclosed, or more immediately of the 16th-century rent rolls and glebe terriers detailing the system of burgages and tenements and rent thereon. Regardless of the system in question, however, there was still a hierarchy of expertise and seniority in evidence, even to this day.

Planting our seedling potatoes, peas and beans one afternoon, while I was writing at home, Alastair was chided for his apparent folly by one of the allotment elders.

'You can't plant runner beans before Pembridge Fair,' Rod shouted across two of the plots. Looking at his already burgeoning patch, Alastair realized he was dealing with an expert.

'But the weather's wonderful,' my husband responded, in typically optimistic terms, looking at a sky filled with swallows.

Rod's response didn't even reach the level of a monosyllable. Alastair had been warned and forty-eight hours later, after a stunning, star-spangled night over the village, the spring's final but most vicious frost descended. It burned all the new growth on the box bushes in the garden and, of course, claimed the runner beans in the allotment. It was the morning of 13 May, when our forebears would have begun putting out their bottle stalls and nine-pin quoits to celebrate the Cowslip Fair and what I thought must have been the delightful, A. E. Housman-style task of picking the best lads for the harvest.

Although the burnt and subsequently blanched leaves of the box made me fret about a more rapacious disease claiming our hedges, the clean air of a clear night had boosted all the colour in the garden. It had also encouraged more of spring's arrivals, with the smallest birds fighting against the larger crows and pigeons for supremacy. Fat balls in the feeders were devoured as quickly as they were put out and the ground beneath was strewn with husks of peanuts. The feeding rarely abated. At first light, there was scratching in the eaves, our residents having squeezed under the barge boards and trusses to create their vernal homes for breeding and rearing and first flight. The gap next to the bathroom extractor fan provided a particularly frenzied ingress. And beyond the house, out in the orchards and the village's plantation of poplars, which looked more like Imperial Russia than Elizabethan England, there was the dull marimba of a woodpecker, tapping its way to the main business of sunrise. It was all so gloriously inevitable, this sudden rush of life. But during the year in question, nature's giddiness above went entirely against what was emerging below.

WHEN THE insurance salesman's question first triggered this foray into the lives of those who built our Herefordshire home, when I began to meet those who had worked in the fields around the village or who had first sat in the back bar of The New Inn, over four hundred years before, I could never have imagined that

I would have been afforded a spring in which one of the major experiences of the age would be replicated, to some extent, in my own. As the tulips and alliums erupted from the soil and the delicacy of forget-me-nots and snake's-head fritillaries laughed in the breeze, we were commanded to break all springtime revelry and keep a global disease at bay. It was the plague of the age and had coincided with profusions of hawthorn at the edges of the woods and fields, the scent of which was said to remind many of the smell of pestilence during the 16th century.

But it was not only sickness itself that took us back in time; the parallel insistence on distance – from friends, family and, to a lesser extent, neighbours – also replicated the experience of how life would have been four hundred years ago. We based ourselves in Pembridge, with all institutions closed and my freelance work largely cancelled, and came to know the village better than ever before. We found new paths and bridleways, desperate not to repeat walks, and thereby discovered hamlets more or less untouched by time. Without the endless revving of cars, despite continuing farm work, the buildings, both functional and domestic, seemed frozen in the past. And although the fields saw an energetic profusion of rapeseed, that more modern presence, we were encountering vistas that hadn't changed at all.

We had always appreciated the interconnectedness, as well as the distance, between Pembridge and its outlying hamlets – Bearwood, Broxwood, Hardwick, Luntley, Marston and Weston – but walking between them with Toby allowed us to know more intensely the sense of isolation that the Elizabethans must have felt. And yet the separation also stimulated a more or less complete reliance on the village. Since we'd arrived in Pembridge, we had tried to buy our food from nearby farmers and growers, which the immediate field-to-table exchange of a lockdown only intensified, returning us to a moment when the market in the village was much more crucial than those further afield. Going to Leominster or Hereford for a major shop became a rarity, like a 1500s villager's trip to one of those larger centres, long before ready convenience – and ready waste. It was also possible to see that the localism and dependency enforced by isolation were all too subject to shortage and, more mundanely, fatigue. Recalling one of the lutenist John Dowland's most popular songs, published in 1603 and sung beautifully by our friend Ed on a recent album (one of our lockdown tracks), we were reminded how 'time stands still', seeing the end of one Elizabethan era through another.

The pandemic that had caused this moment of pause was, luckily, something of a rarity thanks to advances in medical science – though they may yet become more common. The 16th century, on the other hand, was a veritable age of illness. The death rate from influenza alone was normally 2.5 per cent and could easily swell to 7.2 per cent, thereby claiming an average of 5 per cent of the population every year. In relation to current numbers in the UK, that would result in over three million annual deaths from influenza. As opposed to now, however, the Elizabethan flu was basically untreatable, though cures such as smashed baby swallows mixed with parts of lavender, strawberry, thyme and rosemary abounded. Herbs and, where they could be found, spices were generally key to treatment, though any knowledge of the causes, to say nothing of lasting remedies, was scant; mortality was a significant part of daily life.

Sanitation was likewise appalling, with bodily filth a major source of ill health. Typhus and plague were often carried and spread among the starving poor of Elizabethan society. Then, as now, deprivation was the engine room of death. Public and personal hygiene was worse in cities – the pervasiveness of our pandemic has revealed similar centres – and it was not uncommon for the two-storey shaft of a household privy, where there was one, to contain up to two hundred gallons of piss and shit at any one time. If such smells, indicative of more problematic filth, were common to urban centres, the countryside was not without its displeasures. In his 1558–9 treatise, *A newe booke entituled the Gouernement of Healthe*, the priest and doctor William Bullein railed against 'plain people in the country [. . .] carters, threshers, colliers and ploughmen, [who] seldom wash their hands, as appeareth by their filthiness, and very few times comb their heads, as is seen by flocks, nits, grease, feathers, straw and such like, which hang in their hairs'. The self-righteousness of Bullein the cleric is perhaps more apparent in his account than any study as a physician, but there is no doubt that Elizabethan England was a generally unsanitary place, hence the almost constant household fires on which old piss-stained floor rushes were burned, alongside more pleasant scents such as lavender and garden herbs.

In this environment, the Elizabethans were doubtless less shocked by outbreaks of illness, particularly influenza and malaria (known as the ague or fever), than the modern world has proved. In an era of violence and regular public executions, the sacrality of life was, arguably (and somewhat ironically), less defended than in our own, increasingly secular age. Yet, even for the Elizabethans, the impact of pestilence was profound. Various approximations are given for the number of plague deaths in England and, taken together, they average an eye-watering quarter of a million victims over the course of Gloriana's reign.

In the 1520s, England had a population of just 2.4 million, much as it had been at the beginning of the 14th century, stagnating as a result of the intervening Black Death. During the 16th century, however, the population expanded and by 1541, according to various records including parish registers, it had grown to approximately 2.8 million. By 1581, around the time our home was built, England contained 3.6 million people. For 250,000 of that population to have died from plague, even when cast over a long reign, made for a chilling number, though it also prompted many to train as medics, with one practitioner being available for every four hundred citizens in the diocese of Canterbury alone, discounting midwives and wet nurses.

In wider society, outside the era's growing medical profession, the response was eerily familiar. Social distancing was a prerequisite. In Henry Petowe's *The Country Ague* of 1625, an acrostic bids readers, specifically 'all your Rope-tard Nose-gay-Bearers', to 'stand father off', ending with a warning that only through repentance of sin will the plague end – a caution recently repeated by one 'official Bible reader'. Towns and cities were worst hit. In 1579–80, Norwich, then the second largest city in England, lost 25 per cent of its population in one extended outbreak – amounting to approximately 7,500 individuals. If the same were applied to the people of Norwich today, there would have been 53,000 deaths.

In Stratford in 1564, the year of Shakespeare's birth, his hometown witnessed the deaths of 13 per cent of the population – 260 mortalities then or 3,500 now. On 11 July, just three months after the bard appeared in the world, *Hic incepit pestis* (Here begins the plague) was written in the burial register of the church where he had been christened. Leaving Stratford and likely staying in his mother's farmhouse in nearby Wilmcote, Shakespeare was lucky to survive. Across England, 50 per cent of all children under the age of one died. And had he been born in London, where he later made his name, there is every chance the young boy would have fallen victim, with the capital outstripping all other cities in the number of its deaths. London's bills of mortality, delivered like evening bulletins, detailed other appalling statistics: 1603 alone

brought 32,257 plague deaths in its wake, or 16 per cent. Were the
same to be true today, 1.5 million Londoners would have died.

It is little wonder that the disease coloured Shakespeare's
language, with a plague cast on both houses in *Romeo and Juliet*,
Iago pouring 'pestilence' into Othello's ear and Beatrice, albeit
more humorously, comparing Benedict's company to the malady.
In 1606, three years after one of the worst plagues witnessed
during Shakespeare's life, the disease returned to London with
vicious haste. It is likely that this was when the poet and play-
wright took the opportunity to focus on new projects, including
King Lear. Six months later, once the disease had again abated and
the theatres reopened, the play appeared on stage for the first
time. Like Ben Jonson's later drama *The Alchemist*, set at a time
of outbreak, pestilence is mentioned by many characters in the
tragedy of the addled king. 'A plague upon your epileptic vis-
age!' Kent rages at Oswald, while Lear describes the 'plagues that
hang in this pendulous air' and, shouting at his daughter Goneril,
references one of the disease's worst symptoms:

> But yet thou art my flesh, my blood, my daughter;
> Or rather a disease that's in my flesh,
> Which I must needs call mine: thou art a boil,
> A plague-sore, an embossed carbuncle,
> In my corrupted blood.

Despite the dystopian nature of Lear's divided kingdom, Shakespeare's play did not reflect contemporary reality, even during
the very worst outbreaks. There was certainly a sense of hiatus,

and deaths were reported minute by minute, excepting those among the undocumented starving poor – recent bulletins have been similarly selective – but Elizabethan principles of good neighbourliness were, generally, not lost.

During such times, Shakespeare was just as able to turn to less political, less fractured thoughts. In 1592, when his career was beginning to take off, having written *The Comedy of Errors*, the three parts of *Henry VI* and, perhaps, *Richard III*, the pestilence culled one in every twelve Londoners. Yet the young Shakespeare showed agility and found himself a patron, Henry Wriothesley, 3rd Earl of Southampton, and penned poetry rather than plays, including *Venus and Adonis*. This long text's pastoral theme points to a fundamental distinction in the burgeoning genre of plague literature between the urban, considered dystopic and pestilen-tial, and the rural, where plague deaths were nowhere near as prevalent, though its symptoms are also recorded by Shakespeare:

> Even as the sun with purple-colour'd face
> Had ta'en his last leave of the weeping morn,
> Rose-cheek'd Adonis tried him to the chase;
> Hunting he lov'd, but love he laugh'd to scorn;
> > Sick-thoughted Venus makes amain unto him,
> > And like a bold-fac'd suitor 'gins to woo him.

The juxtaposition of 'sick-thoughted' Venus and 'rose-cheek'd' Adonis, notably a hunter, a manifestly bucolic pursuit, hints at tropes repeated in another Maytime plague poem, 'The Passionate Shepherd to his Love'. In this, one of Marlowe's most famous ditties, the eponymous swain promises 'beds of roses and a thousand fragrant posies', a traditional panacea, which allows the young girl (or boy, given that it's Marlowe) to enjoy pastoral pleasures freely.

One of the chief perpetuators of the divide between town and country living was John Davies of Hereford. Sometimes linked to Shakespeare's *A Lover's Complaint* on trumped-up evidence, Davies was known in his own time as the author of one of the most extended plague poems: *Humours heau'n on earth; with the ciuile warres of death and fortune. As also the triumph of death: or, the picture of the plague, according to the life; as it was in anno Domini. 1603* (though published, according to surviving editions, in 1609). As the title suggests, it is a rather rambling essay in verse and clearly lays the blame for the illness at the capital's door, due to its residents' iniquity:

> At *London* (sincke of Sin) as at the Fount,
> This all-confounding Pestilence began,
> According to that Plagues most wofull wont,
> From whence it (flowing) all the realme o'reranne.

The distinction between life in the city and that of the country proved largely true, yet, as Davies's cry of 'Witnesse our Citties, Townes and Villages, Which Desolation, day and night, invades' made clear, the countryside was not spared disease.

Badly hit, and on numerous occasions, was the Welsh border settlement of Presteigne. In 1593, the year after Shakespeare had written *Venus and Adonis*, the town, six miles from Pembridge, saw the plague whip through 150 of its small population. While there was a halt in outbreaks at the turn of the century, the plague returned to Presteigne with vehemence in 1610 and 1636–7, the latter proving grave right across Herefordshire, from the county's north-west corner to Ross-on-Wye in the south.

It came much closer to home too. In 1580, the year that Norwich was so badly struck, there was a particularly vicious epidemic in Herefordshire, as well as in Plymouth, Gloucestershire, Bury St Edmunds and Rye. The woodcut of a funeral procession that heralds November in Spenser's *The Shepheardes Calender*, published the previous year, would have been an all-too-familiar sight. Spurred not least by a chilling remark from Alastair one morning that 'there's a fresh grave in the churchyard', I wanted to know how the plague had specifically changed the lives of Pembridge residents, who it had claimed and how many of them had similarly been buried next door.

When I was allowed to return to the archive, I found the records for St Mary's that had previously been stored in a large chest in the church but which were now thankfully transferred to the safety of the building in Hereford. These were thick volumes of parchment, later paper, bound in rough leather and tied with gut. But unlike their covers and the majority of the Elizabethan volumes and documents I had already examined, these lists of village baptisms, marriages and burials had been kept immaculately, despite changes in the parish priest and his handwriting. The records went back to 1564 and until 1770 were kept together, only later being split into separate events. As a result, it allowed you to get a clear picture of village life.

I turned to 1580, a year I knew had been grave for almost all of Britain's population, as well as locally. It was easy to see increases in parish events, not just the rushes of marriages in early spring and summer, but also a rise in the number of burials, with May 1580 bringing tragedy to the lives of Pembridge folk – and to two of its families in particular. That month, there were six burials in all, which was not a staggering number, certainly when compared to Presteigne's 150 deaths over the course of 1593, but enough to mark an upsurge in misfortune.

Thomas Stone was the first to be buried that May, on the sixth day of the month. While other contemporary burial records mark plague fatalities with an ominous P in the margin, no cause of death was given here. There was also joy, with the baptism of Joanna, the daughter of John Bishop and his wife (also called Joanna), on Sunday 11 May 1580, doubtless taking place within a few days of her birth, as was the tradition:

Johanna filia Johannis Bishopp baptizata fuerat xi die mensis.

The same Sunday (and maybe as part of the same service), Elizabeth, the daughter of another villager, Thomas Hunt, was baptized. But on the very next day, according to the next line in the register, both the Bishop and Hunt families had to return to St Mary's:

Johanna filia Johannis Bishopp sepulta fuit xii° die mensis maÿ
Elizabetha filia Thome Hunt sepulta erat eode die

Both newborn girls were buried that Monday, likely evidence of the chilling statistic that half of all babies under the age of one died of the plague. But for John Bishop, the tragedy wasn't over. On Friday 23 May, tucked under the listings for two more baptisms, there is another haunting entry in the register:

Johanna uxor Johannis Bishopp sepulta erat xxiii die eiusdem mensis

Just eleven days after interring his daughter, John Bishop also had to bury his wife, from whom their child had taken her name. The parish records gave no immediate evidence that these appalling events were anything but a terrible blip – John's wife Joanna may well have died, like her daughter, of complications following childbirth – but I decided to look back at the years immediately preceding these misfortunes to see whether there was a pattern. In May 1577, three years before the deaths of Joanna, Joanna and Elizabeth, there were no records of burials at all that month. There was one burial in June, three in July, one in August and one in September – six in all for the late spring and summer of 1577. Seven burials in total were recorded during the same months in 1578 and five in 1579. But 1580 was clearly different, with fourteen burials recorded between May and September that year, equalling an increase of 133 per cent in one village alone.

But if 1580 in Pembridge seemed to reflect a national or at least cross-county epidemic, it wasn't always the case; outbreaks could be relatively contained. In July 1593, the month in which twelve plague victims were buried in Presteigne, there was only one funeral in Pembridge (with, again, no cause of death given).

In 1610, the year after John Davies of Hereford's *Humours heau'n on earth* first appeared in print, when Herefordshire towns such as Ledbury and Bromyard were suffering badly from the plague, burials in Pembridge were few and far between. It wouldn't be until 1636–7, when the parish records were being written in English rather than cod Latin, that Pembridge suffered once more, particularly in February 1637, when seven villagers were buried alongside the remains of John Bishop's wife and daughter in the sizeable plot outside our bedroom window.

DURING THOSE spring days, cheered at least by the bobbing alliums in the garden and a smog of wilder blooms beyond, I kept being drawn back to the graveyard. It now lacked any marker of the plague deaths of the past or the lime pits where victims may well have been thrown, yet even without these signs the sheer scale was impossible to ignore. After all, the church and its burial sites were the first thing I saw when I opened the curtains in the morning and they were the last thing I viewed before turning in for the day.

'What are you looking at?' Alastair said, late one evening, as I leaned out of the bedroom window.

'Someone's in the graveyard.'

'Nonsense. There's no one around. Hasn't been for weeks.'

'Up there, by the west end of the church. There's a car.'

Alastair climbed out of bed and I could make out the distant light of a cigarette, its orange embers glowing and then withdrawing with every puff. The church had been closed for weeks

– not something that had happened during the Elizabethan plague, when fires 'in moveable pans' were burned to keep the building and congregation free from disease – so it was doubly strange for us to see anyone.

'I'm going down to take a look.'

I made my way outside and quietly opened the gate from the garden, walking over the grass towards the smoker in question; they didn't flinch at my presence, though I kept a cautious distance. There were actually two vehicles, both of which had driven up the short maintenance ramp from Buthall Hill onto the church land. By the first, a small three-door thing, the smoker was sitting in what might have been a wheelchair. Nobody else was visible, certainly no one inside the second car, a large black pickup, much like the ones owned by the young rich farmers around Pembridge; it had darkened windows and was raised high on its suspension.

'Something's up,' I said, when I returned to the bedroom.

'It's absolutely fine,' Alastair responded. 'We'll just keep an eye out if we wake during the night.'

As a light sleeper, there was no way I was going to be able to ignore what was going on outside. Nonetheless, I drifted off after most of a bottle of Côtes-du-Rhône, before waking at 00:47, according to the radio on Alastair's side of the bed.

'What now?' he groaned, after I'd leaned over to check the time.

'Just going to the loo.'

Which I was, though I couldn't resist looking through the window.

'They're still there!'

'OK,' he said slowly, sitting up, 'that is a little odd.'

'Quiet village, middle of lockdown . . . there's no better time to steal the communion silver. I told you.'

Alastair now joined me behind the curtain, where we peered through a small gap, so as not to give ourselves away. At that moment, the indicators on the pickup flashed as the doors were locked and a tall though otherwise nondescript man made his way towards the entrance to the church. He had a torch in hand, which flashed along the grass, before turning its beam into the porch and inside the nave.

'This is not good,' I insisted, reaching for my phone.

'Just wait!'

'No, I'm calling the police' – at which the torch flashed at the stained glass.

'Police please,' I said to the 999 operator, watching the heist unfold.

I explained what we had and were witnessing and West Mercia Police promptly dispatched a squad car, telling me that officers were coming to deal with the problem.

'If there are any further developments, please contact us immediately, Mr Plumley,' the operator said.

Twelve minutes later, there was a ring at the front door, when my phone also started to buzz. I answered the latter nervously, as the same operator told me to go downstairs and speak to the officer on the scene. Opening up, I was confronted by a well-built woman around my age with a large Alsatian. We chatted briefly and I pointed the way to the church, up by our old front door.

'Thank you. Please wait inside, while we investigate.'

She made her way up the steps, followed by two other uniformed officers, who had emerged from another police car, parked up the slope. As I returned to our bedroom, admittedly having checked the bolts on the back door, Alastair was at the window.

'They've examined the cars and two of them have walked around the back.'

'They're inside, for goodness' sake!'

I stood where I was, too jumpy to watch.

'She's going in,' Alastair whispered.

'What?' I said, joining him.

We could see the plain-clothes dog handler standing at the porch, the Alsatian straining at its lead. The officer spoke with a raised voice, which ricocheted off the buildings.

'This is the police. Please come out slowly and with your hands visible.'

I was shivering and saw the tall car-locker appear from the door of St Mary's. At that, the conversation reverted to a normal, night-time volume and we were unable to hear anything that was discussed. But after a few minutes, the plain-clothes officer came back down the path and rang our doorbell once more.

'Thank you so much for your concern, Mr Plumley. It was good of you to call us. Luckily, it's only a bat survey. Were you not told?'

I went puce with embarrassment.

'No, I wasn't. I'm so sorry, officer. I really didn't mean to waste your time.'

'Not at all. You couldn't have known. And do phone us whenever things genuinely look suspicious, as they did this evening. Sleep well.'

I closed the door and should have laughed. Upstairs, Alastair was giggling, though he was also too adrenalin-filled to be entirely relaxed. We didn't sleep a wink and the following morning met the mocking ire of Jane from the pub.

'Thirty-five years I've had this place and I have *never* had the police outside. And then you two buggers move in and they're here at one in the morning!'

To add insult to injury, my brother decided to send us a bat box as a present for the garden, a rare dose of absurdity in an otherwise humourless spring, though I was duly congratulated by the churchwardens for being 'so considerate'. So, I continued to keep watch over the graveyard as the weeks of isolation unfolded, relieved that things didn't always become as violent as they first appeared, or as tragic as they were elsewhere.

LIFE WAS fragile. But however much the Elizabethan pestilence spread through the countryside, sometimes taking out entire villages and causing more settlements to be abandoned, as they had been due to the systematic enclosure of common land, the juxtaposition of an urban hell and a rural idyll persisted, deriving in part from the visual language of earlier in the 16th century. It is certainly there in the work of the artist who had come to haunt my journey back in time. Often, Bruegel, like his older compatriot Hieronymus Bosch, depicts illnesses in the grisliest of terms. Bloated gorgons feast on the flesh of corrupt and innocent alike, while fires consume their homes.

Completed around three years before the season paintings, *The Triumph of Death* is one of Bruegel's blackest creations, a response to the *danse macabre* or *Totentanz* images that had become as prevalent within the Books of Hours as the Labours of the Months, including inspiring Holbein's particularly chilling response in 1523–6, which would have been widely disseminated throughout the 16th century. Such schemes were also used in the decoration of ecclesiastical buildings; a cloister attached to St Paul's Cathedral in London included a *danse macabre* until Jane Seymour's eldest brother Edward, the Earl of Somerset, demolished it in 1549. Again, however, the Edwardian Reformation wasn't able to excise all such images and a lone skeleton, perhaps the vestige of a larger arrangement, continues to stare down from the walls of the Welsh church of St Issui at Partrishow, south of Pembridge.

Whether printed or painted, the principal motif of the *Totentanz* was a chillingly gleeful skeleton (or skeletons) who laughs as he commands all walks of life to dance to their graves. Little sense of divine judgement or, indeed, redemption is offered, instead suggesting that such comforts would have to be found elsewhere in the text or building in question. In general, the figure of Death in Bosch, Bruegel and Holbein's pictures, which were copied with varying degrees of quality across Europe, was particularly ireful towards the wealthy.

The plague, on the other hand, was heedless of rank or riches. Among the victims of the age, merchants were, unsurprisingly, susceptible to the disease – a trader, whose clothes and hair are being ripped from him, is seen in another of Holbein's frightening tableaux. Worse was the situation for the unsanitary poor, who, according to one contemporary account, cared 'not for apparel, though the cold stuck so deep into them, that what with diseases and wanting of [changing clothes], their flesh was eaten with vermin, and corrupt disease grew on them so fast and so grievously that they were past remedy'. That sense of poverty is clearly underlined in the last and most unsettling picture in Holbein's sequence. Here, Death takes a young child by the hand, dragging him or her away from their deprived parents and a meagre, timber-framed home – I couldn't help but think of the bitter tragedy of John Bishop in Pembridge in 1580.

In an age of faith, even if hell raged with uncontrollable fury, heaven was also present, in the bounty of Bruegel's harvest – an eclipsed sun notwithstanding – in the rainbow after a storm and the dove descending through the sky on an early-spring day. But for spring itself – the season that, for all its sunny, floral glory, didn't quite feel like it could be embraced during our own invisible but deadly plague – there was a gap in the narrative and the vibrant visual triggers for the age in which our home was built. High spring is, after all, missing from Nicolaes Jonghelinck's series of Bruegel seasons and no record whatsoever of the panel survives. It was an all too typical void in evidence from the 16th century.

The painting has been gone for some time. When the series left Jonghelinck's possession, it was simply recorded as charting the twelve months of the year, though it seems highly unlikely that there are now seven missing panels, given that the surviving five detail the traditional medieval labours for two months each. More likely is that Jonghelinck had sold *Spring*, to give it a most generic title, before the collection passed into the City of Antwerp's care, or that the city did so post facto. The five other paintings then went to the Habsburgs who controlled the port and, via the various branches of that powerful dynasty, to their imperial capital of Vienna.

Despite the absence, it is possible to imagine what kinds of activities Bruegel would have depicted for April and May and, from there, to imagine scenes, however idealized, that played out in villages across Europe, the plague notwithstanding. We can, after all, follow the very same scheme of monthly tasks and pastimes that influenced the other panels. In April, the main focus would have been the planting and picking of flowers, as well as taking to the countryside after the thaw. Within the woodcuts for Edmund Spenser's *The Shepheardes Calender*, April is the month when Queen Elizabeth and her ladies-in-waiting, including four musicians carrying flute, harp, viol and lute, have wandered into Colin and Hobbinoll's bucolic domain.

The model for this kind of scene can be found in the work of Bruegel's Dutch predecessors, the Limbourg brothers, who were famed for their cycle of the year in the early-15th-century manuscript *Très Riches Heures du Duc de Berry*. April presents an engagement, with a couple exchanging rings before two witnesses. To their side, two further followers are picking flowers while, beyond, a walled orchard is coming into bud. Life has returned and it was touching to see the proposal scene, given that April was the month I asked Alastair to marry me, unwittingly following the traditions of medieval life. Thirteen months later, we were wed, albeit with slightly less pomp than the May-time procession to the woods shown in the Limbourg brothers' image for the month (associated with hawking and courtly love) and certainly less fantastical – though gay marriage might have seemed fantastical enough to the Elizabethans – than the winged horses and round dances in the woodcut accompanying Spenser's rural poems.

There is no need to presume that Bruegel would have been slavish in copying these established schemes, though elements from them would doubtless have informed his much larger, more detailed painting – the one that has since slipped through the cracks of history and disappeared. The fate of Bruegel's image therefore leaves us to make an imaginative leap, drawing on knowledge of his other paintings of the season in question. Travel to San Diego and the Timken Museum of Art and you'll find what is considered the earliest possible extant painting by Bruegel, a 1557 *River Landscape with a Sower*, which was signed and dated in the bottom right-hand corner (as discovered during restoration work in the 1920s).

If the truth of any claim to the painting being by Bruegel is dubious, the format is nonetheless familiar. We stand on top of a hill, looking down through the same kind of timber-framed village featured in the season paintings (and in Herefordshire). One of the houses is caught in a pleasingly warm light, grasses are springing up and there are flowers emerging too. It is most definitely an image you could associate with April or May, though people are so sparse that the painting lacks the 1565 series' special focus on humankind's position within nature.

More densely populated is one of Bruegel's last documented images, *The Magpie on the Gallows*. It dates from 1568 and spring is, again, featured in great lusciousness. Offered the same kind of vantage point above a village and river valley, the viewer takes in a manifestly happy scene, with dancing peasants, ticking the box for May, and flowers frothing in great blossoms on the trees. Birds have filled the sky and life is flourishing. But, as ever with Bruegel, there is a sting in the tail, specifically that of a pair of magpies, who hang around the gallows, the implement of torture in *The Return of the Herd*. The birds and the gibbet remind us that death is also present in Arcadia, that the plague runs rampant in the spring. More precisely, Bruegel appears to have been alluding to one of two Dutch sayings: to dance or to shit on the gallows, meaning to tempt fate. Both paintings are tantalizing, but ultimately unhelpful. One might not even be by Bruegel, whereas the magpies are on a wooden panel much smaller than any of the season paintings. And even Bruegel's pen and ink drawing of *Spring* from 1565, the year he completed Jonghelinck's series, with its market gardening and sheep shearing, is in the wrong format (to say nothing of the materials). Instead, we just have to invent what might have been.

THAT IS precisely what Michael Frayn did in his farcical art-history romp *Headlong*, as amateur art historian Martin Clay makes his way to meet a boorish aristocrat called Tony Churt, who lives in freezing splendour in his ancestral home. It's stuffed with he knows not what; 'there were three of these Dutch buggers' is one of Frayn's deathless lines. But he also gives to his protagonist the thrill of discovering one of the art world's greatest losses: Bruegel's missing season painting, at least for a moment.

Reading the text, you sense the elation: of being that person to see something for the first time in over four hundred years; to place the last piece of a puzzle down on the table – and believe me, having attempted and never finished a thousand-piece Bruegel jigsaw during the pandemic, I can only imagine the feeling; to experience the art-historical equivalent of winning the lottery.

I'm looking down from wooded hills into a valley. The valley runs diagonally from near the bottom left of the picture, with a river that meanders through it, past a village, past a castle crowning a bluff, to a distant town at the edge of the sea, close to the high horizon. Running along the left-hand side of the valley are mountains, with jagged crags sticking up like broken teeth, and snow still lying in the high side valleys. It's spring. On the woods below the snowline, and tumbling away in front of me from where I'm standing, there's the first shimmer of April green. The high valley air's still cold, but as you move down into the valley the chill dies away. The colours change, from cool brilliant greens to deeper and deeper blues. The season seems to shift in front of you from April into May as you travel south into the eye of the sun.

Among the trees just below me is a group of clumsy figures, some of them breaking branches of white blossom from the trees, some caught awkwardly in the middle of a heavy clumping dance. A bagpiper sits on a stump; you can almost hear the harsh, pentatonic drone. People are dancing because it's spring again, and they're alive to see it.

Far away in the mountains a herd is being moved up the familiar muddy scars towards its summer pasture.

It's a witty compilation of so many Bruegel tropes. The narrative of transhumance, picked up from *The Return of the Herd*, is put into reverse. The general vista is the one viewed in the 1568 *The Magpie on the Gallows*, the dancing peasants too, though the bagpiper is from one of two other Bruegel paintings: the first, now in the Detroit Institute of Arts, is *The Wedding Dance*, thought to have been painted the year after the seasons; and the second is *The Peasant Dance*, *c*.1568, kept alongside the drearier seasonal landscapes in the Kunsthistorisches Museum in Vienna. But as easy as it is to play 'I spy' with Frayn's prose, it's impossible not to be enthralled by the actuality of it all, the feeling that you too could be holding this missing painting, this document of time and living, and to know how this insightful, glorious scheme of artworks, embracing all European culture and each and every part of the Continent's landscape and traditions at one crucial point in its history, might have been completed. An ellipsis, just for a moment, meets a full stop.

The painful sense of incompleteness that we now feel was, however, perhaps intended from the start: not that there should only have been five paintings, with *Spring* missing, but that the complete cycle of six would together have implied an absence. In choosing six panels, Bruegel may well have been proposing a parallel to the six days of creation described in the Book of Genesis – 'and God saw that it was good' – with the seventh, the Sabbath, being understood by dint of its non-appearance. But as well as beginnings, the paintings also suggest endings, specifically the second coming of Christ on the last day, with the natural cycle of a year – of many years – leading to that event. Perhaps, Jonghelinck hung all eight of his Bruegel paintings in the same room, with *The Tower of Babel* emphasizing human sin and failure at one end and, at the other, *The Procession to Calvary* suggesting the presence, however small or distant within the crowd, of the redeemer who would return to judge us all. Even within the season paintings, the end of times is repeatedly inferred, with the floods of *The Gloomy Day*, including a dove from Ararat, and a rainbow over the vineyards in *The Return of the Herd*, a motif familiar to contemporary viewers from the doom paintings found behind the rood screens of their churches.

Bruegel's worldview would certainly have embraced this level of thinking; his iconography is, by dint of the Labours of the Months, indebted to such a complex mix of lay and religious inference. But the paintings also show how the world was experienced directly by humankind, not as some expression of overriding divinity, in acts of creation and final judgement, but as a source of splendour and ephemerality, terror and timelessness. That the villagers of *The Gloomy Day* could see only the former but will soon be the victims of the latter was underlined by its (presumably) adjacent position to *The Hunters in the Snow*, from which, surely, they would have learned their lessons. But with the (missing) panel of *Spring* on the other side, why look to the past when we and they might imagine vernal bounty was just around the corner? Sadly, we will probably never know what kind of message and which cultural and agricultural traditions were represented by Bruegel. As much as has been preserved and is remembered, so much has been lost and forgotten.

TODAY, WE record almost everything. Vast digital archives are created of even our most mundane actions. In many ways, it's counter-intuitive, given the cliché of the digital age as an era of refuse, of endlessly generating and destroying information. It is often asked how collections of letters and diaries will be published in the future when so little is logged. Photographs, the supposed gold standard of modern documentation, are now rarely transferred to hard copy. Weddings, the first walk of a child, all gone in a virtual rubbish bin, heedless of how precious the information is and, particularly, how invaluable it might prove to the next generation. History, however, is equally destructive.

Looking back at a resolutely non-digital age, it is clear that an absence of evidence is apparent wherever you turn. While there are many documents, wills, court rolls and parish records preserved, much more has fallen by the wayside, making the reconstruction of any period, not least the 1500s, like a trapeze act. Very few documents from Pembridge's past survive and what is legible largely relates to the inhabitants' interactions with the higher and richer echelons of society. Diaries or commonplace books are fascinating but rare, making it almost impossible to determine what the everyday person under the Market Hall thought about their country and where it was going.

It's part of a historiographical construct known as the 'middling sort', a group that is somewhat reflective of today's middle class – and with the same mutability – but partly embracing the wider peasantry below. The middling sort included artisans, tradesmen (for they were, largely, men) and the educated, and was made up of yeomen and gentlemen within the sphere of a village-cum-town like Pembridge. They had an element of control over the processes – mercantile, law keeping, land owning and otherwise – that concerned the locality, rather than wider national structures, though they were certainly above the husbandmen of the village and its poor, whose stories have almost entirely vanished.

It is not a grand story, but it is here that the equivalents of most of the readers of this book and its author are found. Theirs are the lives that tell us how the economy worked and developed on the smallest scale, who people tended to marry, where they came from, what their daily tasks were and what they possessed – or wanted to possess – as well as what they transferred when their time was up, due to plague or otherwise. Their lives also tell us how these people showed loyalty to political and religious causes and, through them, to a sense of patriotic conviction and the national and global narrative of beheadings, Armadas and the hearts and stomachs of kings and queens.

I had learned that it is through observation of these lives, taking one building, one village or one yeoman as a model for others, notwithstanding local differences, that a more intense picture of the age can be constructed. It was, after all, strongly felt that the domestic sphere was in itself a reflection of the wider state, with William Gouge in 1622 likening the home to a hive, 'out of which are sent many swarms of bees, for in families are all sorts of people bred and brought up: and out of families are they lent in the Church and Commonwealth'. It is therefore in the minutiae of village life, more than in the period's buccaneering militaristic endeavours, that a truer sense of a nation can be found – then as now. Approximations of the British people and its supposed will, of speaking for presumed majorities while denigrating and failing to listen to minorities, political or wealth-derived, lead to misunderstandings and misrepresentations of an entire population, certainly to a lack of nuance or fluctuation in their position.

Removed from a period, the act of re-creating such a narrative is even more fraught with pitfalls and forced to rely on guess-work or parallel accounts, not least when the lives of villagers in a place such as Pembridge – which was, all things considered, a comparatively grand settlement within the area, with pubs and trade and major religious foundations – were haphazardly documented, if at all. Much of the population was still illiterate and, even where literacy was on the rise, little was recorded. What was written down can therefore provide only a sliver, a spring-board to investigation, rather than a complete tale, even for one household. And yet there is always something to provide that taste, a detail tantalizing enough to begin the process.

Our home fitted perfectly into such a fragmentary and, con-sequently, frustrating narrative, with no year of construction, no immediate ability to date its timbers and no real inhabitants during the market's prime. The story of Pembridge, as I had found, leafing through the parchment of the past, with its jumble of Latin and English written in highly wrought and deeply coarse hands alike, had more gaps in its plot than it offered ripping yarns. Like the roads that joined Elizabethan villages together, its history had been washed away and left impassable for months. Woodworm had come to nibble around what remained, before it buckled entirely when facing the violence of the elements.

Still, I was left wondering exactly when and how Stepps House had come into existence, even if I was beginning to accept I might never know. I had learned to be glad of the lack of clarity.

Not having an unequivocal date of construction meant being able to live right across a century and era. And our home not having a specific purpose, but many potential purposes, had permitted me to imagine a whole host of different walks of life, as well as the mercantile, religious and political spheres of the turbulent time in which it was built.

With its crucial position in the village, between market and church, it certainly reflected something of the commonwealth that, at best, underpinned the philosophies and principles of the Elizabethan age, before those systems fractured through both necessity and wilful expansion. At worst, our house, the original building, spoke of tithes, tax and control. And it was also a reminder of the paucity of harvests, the rationing of food and the subjugation of the poor that served to create a society as divided as our own. When the plague arrived, or when disastrous weather patterns indicative of broader ecological change loomed over the horizon, the building's immediate milieu and the fabric of the country at large felt apart. Locked within the walls of our home, gazing over the graveyard, I was forced to realize how little life had changed.

XI.

Before the Fall

THE DAWN CHORUS HAD begun to abate. Gone was the reckless din of April and early May. The birds' commencement address now took on a more practised, bel canto lilt. Warmth lingered through the dark hours and the smell of hay hit high in the nose. Summer was upon us. The sparrows in the eaves had lost one egg in the to and fro of nest insurance and scrummaging, but they had also fostered a quarrel of surviving youngsters, who flitted with alacrity. Their wake-up duties performed, there came a second call, as one of the twin sisters, Marguerite or Catherine, living in Rose Cottage opposite, came to unlock the church. Their tread was marked by the jangle of ancient, comically large keys, one of which featured a lavish blade, more like a labyrinth than it was the solution to a puzzle. Climbing the steps next to the house and on across the churchyard, the swallows already skimming the dew, the sisters were the first human signs of the new day. I was set on hearing another.

The sun was shooting through the window, warming the bed and throwing the most honeyed, reflected light back on our two pieces of linenfold panelling. Having made the morning tea, I decided to take Toby for his walkies, to leave Alastair to snooze, and see the best of the day. Bolting through the garden

gate, Toby and I made our way through the first pasture, where sheep were clustered in the corner, and on into the fields of rape and wheat. The latter, still green, was just getting to the perfect height, as rigidity gave way to a pleasing wave, quicksilvering in the sun. I thought of my grandfather, Dadcu, who would often stop his Triumph Dolomite, normally using only the handbrake, wind down the window and watch the breeze roll through an arable crop. And I thought of the Herefordshire priest and poet Thomas Traherne, who, when walking the county's fields, was inspired to similar moments of rapture:

> The corn was orient and immortal wheat, which never should be reaped, nor was ever sown. I thought it had stood from ever-lasting to everlasting. The dust and stones of the street were as precious as gold: the gates were at first the end of the world. The green trees when I saw them first through one of the gates

transported and ravished me, their sweetness and unusual beauty
made my heart to leap, and almost mad with ecstasy, they were
such strange and wonderful things. [. . .] Eternity was manifest
in the Light of the Day, and something infinite behind everything
appeared which talked with my expectation and moved my desire.

My shoes were wet from the grass. I walked through the first
orchard, past the hogweed and the younger fruit trees and on
to where jaundiced mistletoe, overwhelmed by summer's lease,
hung around their senior cousins.

The blossom had blown and the apples and pears were beginning to gain in strength and size, bursting from the flower's bud.
Each tree was having a growth spurt like a teenager, gangly and
muscular in turn, with freshness about their gait, but also a sense
of dash-suredness. These children of summer, full of unbridled
energy and the promise of length and languor, made you forget
all other seasons. I relished the fall of the leaf and our warm
home on a cold day, to say nothing of the grand floral procession
of early spring, the time of my birth – and the birth of our home
– but summer was the best of the year.

Reaching the end of the first row in the orchard, I found the
gate – was this Traherne's 'end of the world'? Toby stamped
on the ground, like a petulant tap dancer, waiting for it to be
opened. We had to go to the top of the second orchard, beyond
the beehives, into the copse that surrounded a sunken pond.
That's where I was sure I would hear the cuckoo's two-note call,
carried on a resinous breeze of brambles and bracken. I pressed
down the latch; but answer came there none. Other life was

obvious – rabbits darted from Toby's path and robins jogged through the lower branches of the poplars that separated one variety of apples from the next – though not a cuckoo was to be heard or seen.

Other areas had been bragging about the call for weeks. Twitter, aptly named in this regard, reported sightings and hearings in Hampshire, on Wicken Fen, in Suffolk, in my old home of Bedfordshire, even on London Fields and in Epping Forest. Our friend Ben had grown so tired of hearing the bird on his farm outside Leominster that he forgot to tell me. And in the hamlets around Pembridge, the cuckoo had been much apparent, according to our neighbour Jean, calling out at Bearwood, Broxwood and beyond and prompting the hearers' pride when they walked back to the silent village. But, for me, the old adage that the bird's call can be heard from the Feast of St Tiburtius on 14 April to that of John the Baptist on Midsummer's Day was untrue. It was such a familiar disappointment.

Every spring, well into June, I go out with the best of intentions, binoculars slung around my neck, to hear my favourite avian voice and maybe, even, see him. Walking to the ends of fields with Toby, at dawn or at dusk, and cursing so many half-heard wood pigeons, I go, well, cuckoo with cuckoos – or rather their lack. Dadcu set huge store by their presence. He insisted if you had money in your pocket when you first heard the cuckoo each year, that you'd live – and live well – for another twelve months. Dadcu's farm was nigh surrounded by the birds, calling to each other across the valley. Like the lambs, they arrived later than in other places in Britain, but they were always greeted warmly.

Sometimes, standing above the farm, on the boggy slopes of Mynydd Mallaen, you could hear six or seven different calls, some close, some distant, like the breath at the beginning of a Mahler symphony.

When last we went to Bwlch-y-rhiw, I was sure that the journey had been wasted, petulant that we had left Pembridge too late, falling between the morning show and the evening cabaret. Cloudy and a bit windy, the valley in which the farm and my grandparents' graves are nestled didn't feel auspicious on that June day. I harangued Alastair for being so slow to wake – just as he was when I went to the orchards with Toby – but I was quickly silenced as I pushed through the gate to the graveyard and, immediately, heard the cuckoo. I'd made sure, before we left home, to put coins in both our pockets. At first, I thought they might jinx the reason for our trip, but as I smiled, eyes a little wet with memory, I realized the coins were talismans. In the midst of a cemetery, the cuckoo was a sign of life.

My grandfather's and, consequently, my family's love of this bird's sound was, to say the least, going against the grain. Fascinating though the cuckoo and its habits may be for ornithologists and ecologists alike, it is a horrible swindler. The male's familiar call doesn't only announce balmier days, it is also foreboding, a harbinger as much of death as it is of life. Every year, it is followed by his mate's more chilling chuckle, having laid her egg in another's nest. And the apple, or rather the bird, doesn't fall far from the tree, though the original inhabitants will, as the cuckoo chick hatches and pushes out his or her host's eggs and young. Having stolen the nest, the chick remains put for the summer, with the bereft parents duped into feeding the bird, before it takes wing and returns to its other home in equatorial Africa.

In response to these grisly antics, writers have long and rightly outed the bird as a bastard. A 'rewtheless glotoun', according to Chaucer, and a symbol of cuckolding in poems by Shakespeare and Keats, the cuckoo was, perhaps, not the best company, yet the musical side of my personality couldn't fail to be wooed by that fall of a major third, often, supposedly, in the key of D major, though some have observed that the interval changes to a more lachrymose minor third over the course of the summer. Truth be told, whenever I actually have the good luck to hear a cuckoo, I am too excited to think of notating its call or working out the bird's chosen key. I immediately phone Mum, glad for the connection with the past and with Bwlch-y-rhiw, safe in the knowledge that, between those Welsh hills, the bird I am hearing has ancestors where I also have ancestors.

The cuckoo's voice stayed with me always, though Toby, running ahead in the morning light, was unaware of it all, as the great rush of spring gave way to the booziness of summer. Elder scented the air and foxgloves had appeared from the detritus of the cow parsley. The seed was growing, the meadows were blooming and, as the rest of 'Sumer is icumen in' details, the ewe bleats for her lambs, the cow lows for her calves and bullocks prance and billy goats fart. You could well imagine past villagers in Pembridge singing that bawdy song. Although it was penned in Wessex dialogue during the 13th century, according to a manuscript from Reading Abbey, the round had likely been written down by the precentor and sub-prior of nearby Leominster (a dependency of Reading), the rather libidinous, music-loving W. de Wycombe – also known as W. de Wyc, Willelmus de Winchecumbe, Willelmo de Winchecumbe and William of Winchcomb. Could the herald of all this urgency 'icumen in', this shooting-up, really be such a bad thing?

HAPPIER, LESS equivocal by far, is that other badge of English pastoralism and the arrival of the nation's summer: the swallow (though one, we are told, is not quite enough). As I walked back towards the village and our house, they were now properly aloft, skipping through the tops of the grasses and whirling through the haze above. They had arrived on Good Friday and hadn't left our skies since, gradually moving up from the outskirts of the village to provide an athletic pageant every evening above Stepps House. They mixed with their silhouetted cousins, the house martins, and their genetically distinct lookalikes, the swifts.

Like the cuckoo, 'this guest of summer', as Shakespeare called it, is a migratory being, though swallows have been migrating less than they used to. The trend has been witnessed across Europe. While my grandparents, as well as previous residents of Stepps House, once saw these acrobats in great numbers, the intensification of farming since the Second World War and the plummeting numbers of insects, as well as wild-flower meadows, due to increased use of pesticides, has meant that English summers have lost one of their defining features. The birds that still arrive nonetheless bring their memories of Africa on the wing. Or could they be thought of as British, and not guests at all, given that they were born and bred above these lands? The division of their year certainly determines more time below the equator than above it, residing as far south as the Cape of Good Hope for six months, before journeying north for six weeks. By the time they have to leave again, around September, they have been in the skies above Pembridge for just over four months, nesting in the eaves of the village's houses and listening to their stories. And they bring with them the warmth of the sub-Sahara, marking their arrival with a burst of celandines – the anglicized form of *chelidon* (Greek for swallow).

As another of these gracious summer wonders sliced an ogee over the fields, I tried to imagine what it had seen and what its young would see when they returned. Coming from the end of Africa, the swallow parents had travelled over the abandoned German diamond towns of the Namibian deserts and skimmed the Congo delta, before rising high above the equator. After the humidity of the central rainforests would have come the sparseness of the Sahara or the Atlas Mountains, with the promise of Europe beyond: first, the Straits of Gibraltar; then the Moorish castles and hill towns of Andalusia, as well as the great aqueduct at Segovia, where many of the Pembridge birds' cousins would have the chance to play all summer.

Our gulp then glided above the Adour, the Garonne and the Loire, onwards to Britain. Like the drovers, albeit on a much grander scale, the swallows slashed the earth and defied boundaries with their flight paths, their tribe lines, like those ancient tracks that mark the matrilineal inheritance of modern humans, right back to their origins on the same continent from which the swallows came. Lucky them to travel in warmth, lucky them never to feel the collapse of autumn or the wrath of winter. Theirs is a time of continual bounty. It was impossible not to envy them, not just that static spring and early summer, but also in general, at a time in British or, more specifically, English history, when such freedoms had been eradicated by enervating sociopolitical debate.

EVEN IN the face of a plague, the biggest exercise in cutting the country adrift from its neighbours was being pursued at all possible cost, though our house and its history had already reminded me that English exceptionalism was nothing new. But where we have an exit from political and economic union, the Elizabethans were divorcing themselves from the spiritual, religious and, through it, political and trading unions of the Catholic Church and its Holy Roman Empire. Some contemporary politicians even used a comparison between the eras as a prop, though they were less keen to underline the xenophobic connotations that came with such a schism.

As England moved away from Europe over the course of the 16th century, especially during Elizabeth's reign, with its repudiation of lingering Marian popery, there was an increased awareness of what it meant to be English, to stand apart and, in so doing, consider people around you as 'other'. It was precisely because of the move away from a God without – specifically, from Rome – towards a God who could seemingly be controlled by the will of the sovereign, to say nothing of the emergence of more atheistical philosophies, that the Elizabethans began to question who they were and how they fitted, like Bruegel's peasants, into a wider system.

The self-assurance of the individual Elizabethan and the era's burgeoning young population, despite all plague and illness, lent contemporary questioning a newly arrogant air. Sovereignty, seemingly the ultimate expression of independence, was as key then as it is vaunted to be now, though power was very much vested in the sovereign himself at the breach with Rome, even if such legislation professed to enshrine the role of parliament and solidify common law. All this provided an odd counterpoint to the rhetoric of expansion and globalization that, with its ships and trade and New World ventures, likewise typified the period, though that was as much due to English failure to control or influence its closest neighbours in Europe, including the loss of the last continental possession in Calais in 1558, as it was a genuine interest in territories further afield. The birth of the Church of England was not only a manifestation of monarchical power in a weakened time, with the head of state as its 'supreme' governor, but also of the nation itself, characterized by a Protestantism that was, despite obvious links to Europe, considered decidedly un-European at home.

Those who came to settle in England from Europe were, nonetheless, predominantly Protestant, refugees from wars fought against the French or the Habsburgs in their many states. Catholic nations and nationals were, contrawise, treated with xenophobic disdain or outright contempt. The migrants who were able to enter and remain in England had to be 'skilled' according to the whims of Elizabeth's advisors. One of the benefits was the influx of French Huguenot lace workers (after the St Bartholomew's Day Massacre of 1572). Others, from Bruegel's homeland, brought knowledge of trade and shipping, as well as printing, already celebrated as close to Pembridge as Wellington, with farmhouse wall paintings that showed the influence of Antwerp and could well have been completed by an artist from the same city. Yet even these 'skilled' workers were rarely welcomed with open arms.

There was a prevailing fear that foreign merchants would steal jobs and trade opportunities and, furthermore, that they were allowed to exist outside local laws and customs. Segregation, linguistic differences and the presence of spies exacerbated concerns, with Walter Raleigh declaring in 1593 that charity should begin at home and not with immigrants. Some 'foreign' groups were driven from the villages where they had settled, while racism, particularly towards those arriving from Africa and the West Indies as part of an ever-expanding slave trade, set another familiar trend.

In general, to be English in the Elizabethan era was to be a nation apart, even from other nations on the same shore, where 'alien' was applied to those beyond Britain and 'foreigner' was reserved for those outside your immediate locale. Wales was incorporated into England during the early 16th century under Henry VIII, thereby stymieing Pembridge's unique position and levying power, yet Wales continued to be thought of as a barbarous place, mired in poverty, fit only for providing meat for

English tables (much like the Scots). Only through adherence to 'English' ways would seemingly peripheral Celtic tribes be civilized. Itinerant groups, such as the drovers and travellers, often met with fear and violence, not least when they came speaking a language other than English. And even though the Welsh tongue and Welsh surnames were – and remain – prevalent in Herefordshire, pronunciations announce the difference between nationals: Gladestry, on the other side of Hergest Ridge is, if a Herefordian, 'Glade-stree'; if Welsh, the village is often called 'Gla-dess-tree'. Rhayader, on the other hand, is 'Raider' to the English and 'Rye-uh-duh' to the Welsh.

Back in the 16th century, it was commercially savvy for drovers and other travelling salesmen to be able to speak English, the better to bargain at market and avoid a backlash. Yet just as there was equivocation over the religious framework of the nation in the 16th century, not least around the borderlands with Wales and the intensely beautiful decoration of its churches – carefully preserved, despite all efforts of the Crown – there was great division about the idea of Britain, which various acts of union throughout the 16th and 17th centuries, to say nothing of bellicose escapades at sea and on land, did little to singularize. A culture of imposing ideas rather than harvesting them from the populace was endemic, though ascertaining what 'ordinary' people actually thought, in comparison with the literate, court-adhering elite, proved tricky, given the lack of literacy and, consequently, written evidence.

Today, proof abounds. The knowledge that Britain is divided, that, as Auden once wrote, while overlooking Herefordshire on the Malvern Hills, 'these years have seen a boom in sorrow', is palpable, though exceptionalism has not only persisted but increased. In the face of grave warnings of an illness killing thousands both far away and among the population of former political partners, the nation's new Henrican head – with just as many sexual partners, though even more surviving children – was deaf to caution. Instead of a watchful 'desire for market segregation', he believed that 'humanity needs some government somewhere that is willing to make the case powerfully for freedom of exchange'. Survival was clearly nothing when compared with 'the right of populations of the Earth to buy and sell freely among each other'.

According to such cuckoo philosophies, Britain – or, given the distribution of the vote, England – could operate alone and, moreover, profit from disaster. The new boom in sorrow could magically be turned into economic boom, despite the fact that many were facing ruin due to a system that had been stripped to the bone and was, consequently, left exposed and unprepared. To put an economy on pause at the very moment the economy in question was facing further impoverishment through isolation from its closest neighbour would surely be catastrophic.

There was, of course, irony to the insistence that the impersonal market would save all in the face of personal loss and confusion. The market had failed, and always would. Isolating in a former storehouse on the edge of England, we were living in its memento mori, with another, the Market Hall, just outside the window. The whole experience of our time in the house, with its revelations about the life of the 16th century and the rhythms of the Elizabethan age, had shown us what we were inhabiting. Our building, our home, was the evidence we needed. And it wasn't connected to the Labours of the Months and their merry order of chores and characters. Instead, the house was the *Totentanz*, the gallows, the gibbet. It underlined the inevitability of an ending: of markets, of empires and much more (and much less) besides.

In a shifting world, with an inconstant climate, where hand-to-mouth self-sufficiency had failed, the entire village had revolved around its market, almost physically screening the influence of the church and any higher purpose from view. It was through the market that Pembridge had hoped to derive its power and primacy. It was through the market that Pembridge had built associations with other centres, both locally and nationally, perhaps even internationally. But it was and continued to be too fragile a system.

When, recently, one of the farmers living and working just outside the village's edge refused access to those who wished to cull the badgers on his land, thereby attempting to prevent the spread of bovine tuberculosis, he found himself at the short end of a purchasing embargo. The corn he had harvested and previously been able to sell to his neighbours as animal feed no longer had purpose (or value). He had, of course, been rightly indignant: while there was evidence that badgers did indeed spread bovine TB, there was no proof that they were the only carriers. Only by purging vulpines, wild deer and other hosts would the disease be eliminated. But his plight pointed to an enduring reality that each person had a role within the market. And our home had likewise been an intrinsic part of it, until such time as it had no purpose at all and the system collapsed.

In its infancy, this narrative of expansion was progressive and triumphant, typified by reciprocation and the wider public good – the hallmarks of Elizabethan living. Unfortunately, however, it only worked when aligned to nurture and welfare and not to capital and profit. When the market economy slipped from being a method of sustaining its society into a consumerist culture, it gave birth to a bastard child who accumulated capital at others' cost, who defended the right of private landowners over the public share, who intensified farming and industry regardless of the impact on health and the environment and who saw the working individual as a commodity. Even before the worst excesses of the late 16th and early 17th centuries, Thomas More had seen the writing on the wall. 'Though they cannot be called a monopoly,' he wrote, 'because they are not engrossed by one person, yet they are in so few hands, and these are so rich, that, as they are not pressed to sell them sooner than they have a mind to it, so they never do it till they have raised the price as high as possible.'

Close to power, close to the oligopoly itself, More saw the beginning of a narrative that would continue right up until the 19th century, when Karl Marx wrote about how the world was and should be run. While the 'moments when great masses of men are suddenly and forcibly torn from their means of subsistence, and hurled as free and "unattached" proletarians on the labour-market' were apparent in various countries and eras, it was most plain to see in what he called the 'classic form' of early modern England and its agrarian centres, including Pembridge. Like the cycle of the seasons, a cycle of stupidity had similarly

become ingrained in human behaviour. The swallows, returning every year, must have seen these repetitions and, above it all, their chuckling song sounded its ridicule.

WALKING BACK from the orchards as the belfry struck eight forty-five, I stood in the churchyard and enjoyed the view. The sun was behind me and our home was kindled by summer light. Inside, Alastair had doubtless drifted off again, the tea cold on the chair next to him. It was from this angle, right by the impressively soaring stained-glass window and huddled, bullet-marked door of the church's west end, that the original form of our home and, perhaps, its function was most apparent. Through the gaps in the other buildings, I could see the Market Hall and The Old Stores, with our place fulfilling the role in trade that Duncan James had deduced when he first visited us to date the structure. But I realized that if I could take away the surviving Victorian gravestones and hedging that divided our garden from the churchyard, that purpose changed.

Now, the building was included in the mechanisms of religion, as either a barn for the collection of parish taxes in kind, an outhouse for the Old Rectory by the churchyard steps to the north or an old chapel or a lychgate. Compared with the other structures from the 16th and 17th centuries around the Market Square, however, Stepps House was clearly diminutive, humble, not the main event. And to me it was therefore self-evident that, without a role of its own, it had to be part and parcel of a larger narrative. Every element of the system had to pull its weight and every element had to be valued and rewarded for its contribution, like the Eastern Europeans who had come back to Herefordshire to pick soft fruit or our friend Ben's Czech employee, the only person, apart from himself, who knew how to drive the tractor for the lettuce harvest.

Such a clear delineation of roles and achievements had been celebrated in the dining room of merchant banker Nicolaes Jonghelinck in 1565 in one of the hubs of the age's own freedom of exchange. The bounty of Jonghelinck's table was the result of scenes witnessed in the very cheeriest of the Bruegel panels on the wall: *Haymaking*. Here, as in the traditional Labours of the Months, was the June of the hay harvest, captured in the most beneficent light of any of the paintings conceived for the villa of

Ter Beke, just outside the walls of Antwerp. The hard landscape of winter has evened out, now gently undulating into a distant river valley – the most familiar geographical feature of the painting. As well as people cutting grass grown for fodder, the wider harvest has begun, with summer fruits and vegetables: the peas and the beans; the strawberries and the cherries. Baskets brim, ready to be carried off and furnish Jonghelinck's feast. In one direction, the harvesters stride to market; in the other, they go through a gate, out into the fields. Rakes are slung over shoulders, promising bounty, just as the hunters' poles in winter showed paucity. The haymaking is well advanced and the wain piled high, the villagers having been blessed with sunny, dry weather. And in the middle of the right-hand side of the painting, the wheat fields of *The Harvesters* are well on their way to ripening.

In the village, the residents are no less fortunate. Their houses are well kept — certainly well repaired after winter — and the church oversees all, as suggested by the wayside shrine in the foreground. Beyond, villagers have gathered on the green to mark midsummer around what may seem like a maypole, though they are likely shooting at a popinjay, also visible in the village in deep winter. The visual links with the other seasons only serve to underline just how collaborative this scene is, with everyone fully absorbed in the joys of summer, whether they be productive or recreational.

Here, again, the kind of scene that Bruegel captured may have derived its model from a monthly cycle, but it also served as a benchmark for various replicas, including among English artists who, as a result of the influx of Northern European Protestants and the sheer applicability of their imagery, were becoming more and more drawn to the landscape. In 2017, a very early portrayal of English rural life came up for sale at Sotheby's in London; in the list of lots, the pen and ink drawing was called *Landscape with Harvesters Returning Home*. The scene is clearly the beginning of the summer's work, with haystacks for drying, like a more detailed, less all-purpose version of the woodcut for June in Spenser's *The Shepheardes Calender*.

Sotheby's experts concluded that the drawing, which I sadly missed at auction, came from the first quarter of the 17th century, basing their guestimate on the clothing worn by the harvesters. Others have suggested it may even date to the end of the 16th century, like our home. Regardless, it was an extraordinary rarity, created, it is thought, by the writer and draughtsman

Henry Peacham. More readily known for his illustrations in early Jacobean volumes, he is from a full generation before native English artists began painting their own landscape. Its survival is indicative of the power and, moreover, relevance of such imagery as a continuing guide to Europe's pastoral practices.

The model for the pen and ink drawing, albeit taken to more lavish ends, was surely Bruegel's *Haymaking* and other works like it, intended as a scene to be relished, both as a picture and for its gleeful subject. The figures within are likewise to be lauded for their labours, with the ever-didactic Bruegel highlighting that Jonghelinck's success as a merchant banker, a role at the apex of 'the history of primitive accumulation' – and of Karl Marx's observation of 'how money is changed into capital; how through

capital surplus-value is made, and from surplus-value more capital' – was derived from the harvesters' hard work. As the world
began to change, Bruegel provided a keen reminder of the utopian
ideal of a mutually beneficial world, even if Marx would go on to
insist that 'the methods of primitive accumulation are anything
but idyllic'. Again, I was reminded of Holbein's ploughman.

It was ironic that Bruegel's *Haymaking* should have had such
a chequered history. Passing through Rudolf II's hands to
Archduke Leopold Wilhelm, the painting was then presumably
gifted to Ferdinand Leopold, the 6th Prince of Lobkowicz, who
displayed it in his family's palace in Vienna, site of the premiere
of Beethoven's 'Eroica' Symphony and, nowadays, the Austrian
Theatre Museum. By 1870, when the Lobkowicz Palace had
become the French embassy, the painting moved with the family
via Bílina to their principal seat in Roudnice nad Labem. It was
from there that the Nazis decided to steal the painting, 'selecting' it for the never-built Führermuseum in Linz, before it was
returned to Czech soil in 1946 to be displayed in the National
Museum in Prague, thanks to a loan from Prince Max Lobkowicz.
His ownership mattered little to the invading Soviet authorities,
however, who promptly confiscated the painting and transferred
it to the state. Now, finally back in the Lobkowicz collection,
it has regained something of its original meaning, as a warning
against taking the proletariat and their 'methods of primitive
accumulation' for granted. Such is the breadth of Bruegel's
vision, from Antwerp to the Alps, from Prague to Pembridge.
The artist understood that the interaction of the individual and
the corporate were central to a civilized society; not just within

the microcosm he paints, sweeping views notwithstanding, but also within the macrocosm it represents.

Viewing the world, hardly unsophisticated as it was in 1565, but manifestly on the cusp of political, scientific and artistic revolutions, he saw the various lines that connected humanity, like the flight paths of the swallows and cuckoos in summer, the branches of the mitochondrial phylogenetic tree, the currents that flow deep in the ocean and dictate the trade routes of grand carracks, the ley lines in the landscapes he painted and the paths of the drovers, herds, flocks and harvesters he witnessed, as well as the inevitable failure of those who rejected nature, favoured exceptionalism and flew too close to the sun. While Bruegel didn't move entirely beyond a religious interpretation of the world in which he lived – like the villagers in Pembridge during the 16th century, he was in hock to a credulous spiritual framework that would take centuries to shift – he was nonetheless attuned to a more objective, scientific view. As well as the natural world and its unfeeling diktat over our lives, Bruegel observed that humankind, for all its sophistication, was helpless in the face of nature.

That view is present too, even on the most seraphic June day, as the poppies and foxgloves bloom on the wayside, birds slice the lazulum above and all looks set to last forever. In the centre and immediate foreground of *Haymaking*, Bruegel places one of his most chilling reminders of the transience of earthly beauty. At closer inspection, the three women about to begin or resume their work in the hayfield are of three different ages, like an abbreviated, gender-balanced form of Jacques' famous speech in *As You Like It*. Closest to us is a strong, redoubtable middle-aged woman, at ease with both the rake in her right hand and the weight of a large urn of refreshments in her left. Also in the group is a more elderly figure, furthest from view, who looks directly ahead, her experience inciting the necessary determination for the task. And then, in the middle, is the youngest of the trio, fresh-faced, perhaps looking at her companions for guidance or looking beyond the image itself – like one of the herd in Bruegel's autumnal painting or the dog in winter – and thereby binding us to her experience.

Each, however, is heedless of what lies in front of them. For as much as the open gate to the field promises plenty, the path also leads to a man repairing and sharpening a collection of scythes. These are, of course, the tools of his trade, linking the image to another of the season paintings, *The Harvesters*, though they also offer a clear and strange premonition of death and 'mere oblivion'. In such a context, the rocky outcrop in the distance, with its instruments of torture providing further echoes across the panels, casts a rare shadow in an image typified by midday sunlight streaming directly from above. Little wonder the youngest of the women looks at us. Perhaps she is aware for whom the bell tolls.

Faced with destruction, humankind is tempted towards the illusion of self-preservation. The attraction of being the outlier and, through it, the victor, may be enormous, but the wings of such a project are held together with wax. Godly or ungodly, Bruegel and the people of his time, faced with staggering levels of mortality, knew the ultimate leveller of death, which neither rank nor wealth nor age could hope to avoid. But there is nonetheless comfort in the networks and interconnectedness of which

Bruegel's work constantly speaks, between Antwerp and the ports of England, the routes the artist took over the Alps to Italy, the customs he observed, reflected in valleys in Wales and in the timber-framed villages of myriad countries, despite individual vernaculars.

While globalization and the world's perennial lust for movement and connectivity have come to be framed as negative forces, they had to remain the goal of any market, more so than the pursuit of capital. Such was the aim of the markets of the early modern era, moving from local, small-scale exchange to centres that became representative of an area, such as Pembridge, that further reflect national and international cooperation. But it was ridiculous to suppose that you could insist on the purely financial aspects of the market without appreciating the benefits of association, the sharing of information and resources, that have become so much easier and could, in the circumstances, be the population of the world's saving grace.

There was no superman riding above nature. It was for all of us in the laboratory to study the cosmos as it was changing before our eyes, humbly understanding our place and fragility within it, as Bruegel had done in, admittedly, less scientific times. As a result of pooling information, the minds that emerged within the shifting world when our home was built were able to see that the procession of seasons and weather patterns, all the climatic predictability that had been enshrined in so many images and prayer books and rituals of the age, was changing – and not for the better.

Their shared modelling allowed them to uncover rational,

logical reasons as to why the world did as it did, the basis for the same kinds of observations that, today, tell us we are on the brink of something much more seismic than the deaths of just a fragment of our population, however tragic they may be. The scythe is there, waiting for us all, if we do not choose the correct path in the hayfield of Bruegel's eschatological view. Faced with the conundrum, then and now, it is little wonder that so many sought external aids, sources of transcendent beauty, many of which have since vanished from our world.

On a June morning, however, there was transcendence aplenty. I crossed the churchyard towards home and descended the steps, past the old front door, set into the building's original core. Reaching the Market Square, I waved to Nick, Bill and Robbie, who were waiting to be picked up to go and play cricket. I went inside but could hear nothing from upstairs, so decided to make Alastair a fresh cup of tea. There was a punnet of strawberries from one of the local farms on the kitchen table, which I washed for breakfast, along with my hands, and then filled the kettle. The house and the village had given us a charmed life, I thought, but as much as the house was a retreat and haven, it was also connected to the world outside, whether I liked it or not. For all its comforts, Stepps House constantly spoke to me of over four centuries of progress, destruction, endeavour, misery, creativity, failure and all the other trappings of life. 'Houses aren't refuges from history,' Bill Bryson wrote; 'they are where history ends up.'

· · ·

IN THE garden that afternoon, Alastair began stripping out the tulip leaves and pulling up alliums that had already gone from green to purple and then to brown. As he worked around me, I fell asleep on the grass and wasted the day. Time was passing, as June vanished and July would too. The cycle would begin again, never identical, but following that same pattern of labours and pictures, the same repeated mistakes and triumphs.

Standing up, I found a cool glass of white wine, next to where I'd abandoned my flip-flops. As I turned around, I saw Alastair retreating into the house with the bottle. The tea-light holders through the beds and borders were lit and I could smell the honeysuckle, warmed by the day, unloading its perfume into the garden. Just beyond the plant in question, the setting sun was catching the arrow of the giant rusty armillary sphere I had bought for Alastair's birthday. It clinched that look of a knot garden, with our mini-orchard of three trees beyond.

On the other side of the hedge, the church was covered in gold. As in the Alps, where the sun does not set at evening but rises through the mountains, casting the valleys into darkness while gilding the summits, so it was in Pembridge. Our little plot turned from aestival abundance to a blackish green within just half an hour, while God's house burned with Pentecostal light – a wonderful trick of nature and siting. The swifts and swallows were above, enjoying the last of the rays. Out in the fields, others were gorging on bugs, while the linnets and goldfinches pecked the fallen florets of wheat, taking what they could before the crop ripened over the coming weeks and the reapers arrived.

I walked back into the house. Inside, Toby, his black muzzle turning grey, was lounging on the sofa, while Alastair was busy lighting more candles. It looked magical. As ever, the house had somehow managed to snuffle away what was glimmering in the garden outside. In the candlelight and the last seam of orange sun, the timbers took on the luxury of chocolate, flaked with time but promising sweetness. All the joints and mortises, the marks, the perforations and the wattle sockets held a history. Not a grand history, not England's palaces and expansive, expensive houses, like the stately homes I'd loved as a child, but the smaller blocks of the narrative that, together, somehow made a nation: the tithe barns, the storehouses and a home for two men between the hills of a heaven-sent county on the edge of England. It was enough.

Looking at the timbers of Stepps House, I moved my hand across sapwood, eroded over the centuries, and found a rough outcrop of bark. Left there over four hundred years ago, it continued to provide us with protection. In other places, the damage had been done. A post in the dining room was covered with a film of dark green gloss and notches had been cut into others to provide supports for shelves, the same post marked with the apotropaic daisy wheel. Similarly plain to see were the carpenters' marks, those runes that had given up at least some of their secrets. Around, the rare bits of heartwood stood proud and I held onto one of the posts marked with a VI. Alastair came to hold my other hand.

'Shall I close up?' he asked, after a pause. Taking his glass, he went to the back of the house to shut the doors to the garden and I went to the front to fasten the windows over the Market

Square. One of the twins, Marguerite or Catherine, I could never tell which, was coming to lock up the church. The light inside the belfry would have already slipped through the arrowslits. The visitors had gone home. 'Anyone in? Anyone in?' she shouted, turning the lock, as the statue of Mary was plunged into a private compline. Down in the square, the cricketers were back from their match and people were dining outside The New Inn and beneath the Market Hall, pints in hand.

The sun, which had earlier reached its apex, fell over the back of the pub, as Bruegel brushed the sky a darker hue. Holding onto the iron casement stay, I saw one of the drinkers in the Market Hall looking directly at the house. He was my age, maybe slightly younger. Smiling, attractive, he drank his beer not from a glass but from a battered pewter tankard, like the ones that hang above the bar. There were other people on his table, but he was sitting alone, at a judicious distance. I took in more of his face, his bearing. He looked slightly careworn. The dust of the day was on his linen shirt. Perhaps he would be going back to the fields. His tousled hair was not the identical short back and sides of now. With his rather severe fringe, he looked a bit like one of the Beatles, maybe older. He nodded, gently raising the tankard, as if he knew me, as if he knew the house – or thought he did.

It had doubtless changed, Stepps House, but it was the same place. He must have known that, looking up the steps towards the churchyard, past the old front door, set into the original structure. It was a frame he had known in another year, a storehouse in and of history, his and mine, mine and ours. I smiled back and closed the window as a tractor rumbled by. Richard, the farmer who had rightly shouted at me during our first week in the village, waved from the cab, his trailer loaded with bales. The first cut was done. We've seen to the very end, and it'll be such a crop of hay as never, I thought, remembering another home, another happy outcome of ownership and deference to history.

High summer held everything in its grasp, fit to choke. The trailer went and, behind, the square was empty; the drinking chap had gone. We will go too. I just hoped we would leave the lightest notch in the timbers, a rune in time. As the tractor turned the corner at the end of the garden and the sound of its engine faded, I caught the cuckoo's final performance. He was out beyond the church, trumpeting an ancient roundelay. All in the end is harvest.

Pembridge — Midsummer, 2021

My and Further Reading

T HE MAJORITY OF THE primary source material cited in the text, including the tithe apportionment maps and lists, the rent rolls and the church records, is held at the Herefordshire Archive and Records Centre (herefordshire.gov.uk/herefordshire-archive-records-centre).

Although some of the wills relating to the locality are also kept in Hereford, a number are to be found at The National Archives (nationalarchives.gov.uk), with some available digitally – a boon during lockdown. Likewise, court records for national interests that nonetheless embrace Herefordshire are stored at Kew. Other records for the history and taxation of Pembridge's environs, what was known as 'Pembridge Foreign' and largely owned by the Devereux family, are at Longleat.

All information concerning Ralph Vaughan Williams and his collection of folk songs around Pembridge is listed on the Vaughan Williams Memorial Library section of the English Folk Dance and Song Society website (vwml.org), as well as in the volumes by Ella Mary Leather and Steve Roud recorded below.

The Transactions of the Woolhope Naturalists' Field Club (woolhopeclub.org.uk) have also been invaluable.

Auden, W. H., *The English Auden* (Faber and Faber)

Behringer, Wolfgang, *A Cultural History of Climate* (Polity)

Blom, Philipp, *Nature's Mutiny* (Picador)

Boym, Svetlana, *The Future of Nostalgia* (Basic Books)

Bray, Alan, *Homosexuality in Renaissance England* (Columbia University Press)

Brogden, Wendy Elizabeth, *Catholicism, Community and Identity in Late Tudor and Early Stuart Herefordshire* (University of Birmingham, PhD Thesis)

Brooks, Alan and Nikolaus Pevsner, *The Buildings of England: Herefordshire* (Yale University Press)

Brunner, Bernd, *Winterlust: Finding Beauty in the Fiercest Season* (Greystone Books)

Brunskill, R. W., *Timber Building in Britain* (Yale University Press)

Bryson, Bill, *At Home* (Black Swan)

Christophers, Brett, *The New Enclosure: The Appropriation of Public Land in Neoliberal Britain* (Verso)

Duffy, Eamon, *A People's Tragedy: Studies in Reformation* (Bloomsbury)

——*The Stripping of the Altars: Traditional Religion in England 1400–1580* (Yale University Press)

——*The Voices of Morebath: Reformation and Rebellion in an English Village* (Yale University Press)

Fagan, Brian, *The Little Ice Age: How Climate Made History 1300–1850* (Basic Books)

Faraday, M. A. (ed.), *The Herefordshire Chantry Valuations of 1547*

Frayn, Michael, *Headlong* (Faber and Faber)

Godwin, Fay and Shirley Toulson, *The Drovers' Roads of Wales* (Whittet Books)

Haag, Sabine (ed.), *Bruegel: The Master* (Thames and Hudson)

Hamling, Tara and Catherine Richardson, *A Day at Home in Early Modern England: Material Culture and Domestic Life, 1500–1700* (Yale University Press)

Hoare, Philip, *Albert and the Whale* (4th Estate)

Holbein, Hans, *The Dance of Death* with a commentary by Ulinka Rublack (Penguin Books)

Honig, Elizabeth Alice, *Pieter Bruegel and the Idea of Human Nature* (Reaktion Books)

Hoppe-Harnoncourt, Alice, Elke Oberthaler, Sabine Pénot, Manfred Sellink and Ron Spronk (eds), *Bruegel – the Hand of the Master: Essays in Context* (Hannibal)

Jenkins, Simon, *Wales: Churches, Houses, Castles* (Allen Lane)

Keates, Jonathan, *The Companion Guide to the Shakespeare Country* (Collins)

Kelly, Henry Ansgar, Louis W. Karlin and Gerard Wegemer (eds), *Thomas More's Trial by Jury: A Procedural and Legal Review with a Collection of Documents* (Boydell Press)

Lane, Rebecca, *Church House Farm, Wellington, Herefordshire: Historic Building Assessment* (Historic England)

Leather, Ella Mary, *The Folk-Lore of Herefordshire* (Logaston Press)

Lewis, Tamsin, *Lord Have Mercy Upon Us: Songs and Hymns in Time of Plague* (Rondo Press)

Lund, Mary Ann, *A User's Guide to Melancholy* (Cambridge University Press)

MacCulloch, Diarmaid, *Thomas Cromwell: A Life* (Allen Lane)

—*Tudor Church Militant: Edward VI and the Protestant Reformation* (Penguin Books)

Macdonald, Benedict and Nicholas Gates, *Orchard: A Year in England's Eden* (William Collins)

Macfarlane, Robert, *The Old Ways: A Journey on Foot* (Penguin Books)

Malvern Museum, *Ancient Hills: A brief guide to the geology and natural history of the Malverns* (Malvern Museum)

Mantel, Hilary, *Wolf Hall* (4th Estate)

—*Bring Up the Bodies* (4th Estate)

—*The Mirror and the Light* (4th Estate)

More, Thomas, trans. and ed. Dominic Baker-Smith, *Utopia* (Penguin Books)

Morris, Jan, *Wales: Epic Views of a Small Country* (Penguin Books)

Mortimer, Ian, *The Time Traveller's Guide to Elizabethan England* (Vintage)

Müller, Jürgen and Thomas Schauerte, *Bruegel: The Complete Works* (Taschen)

Onuf, Alexandra, *The 'Small Landscape' Prints in Early Modern Netherlands* (Routledge)

Orme, Nicholas, *Going to Church in Medieval England* (Yale University Press)

Parker, Peter, *Housman Country: Into the Heart of England* (Little, Brown)

Paterson, Don, *Reading Shakespeare's Sonnets* (Faber and Faber)

Poirier, Agnès, *Notre-Dame: The Soul of France* (One World)

Pye, Michael, *Antwerp: The Glory Years* (Allen Lane)

Rady, Martin, *The Habsburgs: The Rise and Fall of a World Power* (Allen Lane)

Roud, Steve, *Folk Song in England* (Faber and Faber)

—*The English Year: A Month-by-Month Guide to the Nation's Customs and Festivals, from May Day to Mischief Night* (Penguin Books)

Scudamore Stanhope, Berkeley and Harold C. Moffatt, *The Church Plate of the County of Hereford* (Archibald Constable & Co.)

Smith, Wayne, *The Drovers' Roads of the Middle Marches* (Logaston Press)

Spenser, Edmund, ed. Richard A. McCabe, *The Shorter Poems* (Penguin Books)

Sprang, Meganck van, *Bruegel's Winter Scenes* (Yale University Press)

Shrubsole, Guy, *Who Owns England? How We Lost Our Green and Pleasant Land and How to Take It Back* (William Collins)

Sunshine, Paula, *Wattle and Daub* (Shire Publications)

Watkins, Alfred, *The Old Straight Track: Its Mounds, Beacons, Moats, Sites and Mark Stones* (Heritage Hunter)

Weir, Alison, *Henry VIII: King and Court* (Pimlico)

Wilson, Peter H., *Europe's Tragedy: A New History of the Thirty Years War* (Penguin Books)

Woolf, Virginia, *Orlando* (Penguin Books)

Wright, John, *A Natural History of the Hedgerow: and Ditches, Dykes and Dry Stone Walls* (Profile)

Wrightson, Keith, *Earthly Necessities: Economic Lives in Early Modern Britain, 1470–1750* (Penguin Books)

Wrightson, Keith (ed.), *A Social History of England, 1500–1750* (Cambridge University Press)

Yelling, J. A., *Common Field and Enclosure in England 1480–1850* (Macmillan)

Illustrations

T HANK YOU TO THE following people for their help in finding and acquiring illustrations: Bob Anderson; Ben Andrews and John Stevenson; Tom Edwards (Abbott and Holder); Sophie Latimer (Alamy); Sian Phillips (Bridgeman Images); Ilse Jung and Franz Pichorner (Kunsthistorisches Museum); Veronika Graulíková and Petr Slouka (Lobkowicz Collections); and Karolina Koziel (Science and Society Picture Library).

The woodcuts at the beginning of each chapter and on page 85 are from Edmund Spenser's *The Shepheardes Calender*, published in 1579.

Unless otherwise stated below, all photographs are © Gavin Plumley, 2022.

Page 16
Herefordshire
Poster, 1960 – British Railways
(Science Museum Group)

Page 25

ELGAR (aka MONITOR: ELGAR)

Film still, 1962 – directed by Ken Russell

(Everett Collection Inc./Alamy Stock Photo)

Page 82

Elizabethan Street Scene, from 'A Book of Roxburghe Ballads'

Woodcut – English School

(Private Collection/Bridgeman Images)

Page 89

The Harvesters

Oil on wood, 1565 – Pieter Bruegel the Elder

(The Metropolitan Museum of Art, New York – Rogers Fund, 1919 –
www.metmuseum.org)

Page 98

Wall Paintings at Church House Farm, Wellington

Photograph, 2021 – Ben Andrews

(Private Collection)

Page 100

View of Villages in Brabant and Campine: Shepherds with Flock

Etching and engraving, *c.*1559 – after Master of the Small Landscapes

(The Cleveland Museum of Art, Mr. and Mrs. Lewis B. Williams
Collection 1959.86)

Page 121

The Peasant (or Ploughman), from 'The Dance of Death'

Woodcut, *c.*1526, published 1538 – Hans Holbein

(The Metropolitan Museum of Art, New York – Rogers Fund, 1919 –
    www.metmuseum.org)

Page 135

The Return of the Herd

Oil on wood, 1565 – Pieter Bruegel the Elder

(KHM-Museumsverband)

Page 140

Ralph Vaughan Williams and Gustav Holst walking in the Malvern Hills

Photograph, 1921 – William Gillies Whittaker

(British Library)

Page 158

The Hunters in the Snow

Oil on wood, 1565 – Pieter Bruegel the Elder

(KHM-Museumsverband)

Page 173

Portrait of a Man

Watercolour on vellum in a later gilt metal frame, 1590s
    – Nicholas Hilliard

(The Cleveland Museum of Art, The Edward B. Greene Collection
    1941.557)

Page 187

Villagers on Their Way to Church

Tempera colours and gold paint on paper, *c.*1550 – Simon Bening

(The J. Paul Getty Museum, Los Angeles, Ms. 50, recto)

Page 194

The Swan Inn, Pembridge

Photograph – anonymous

(Private Collection)

Page 219

The Gloomy Day

Oil on wood, 1565 – Pieter Bruegel the Elder

(KHM-Museumsverband)

Page 225

Sailing Vessels: Armed Four-Master Putting Out to Sea

Engraving, 1561–5 – after Pieter Bruegel the Elder, engraved by
    Frans Huys

(The Cleveland Museum of Art, Mr. and Mrs. Charles G. Prasse
    Collection 1980.105)

Page 234

The Tragical History of the Life and Death of Doctor Faustus

Woodcut, 1620 – anonymous

(Private Collection)

Page 267

The Child, from 'The Dance of Death'

Woodcut, *c*.1526, published 1538 – Hans Holbein

(The Cleveland Museum of Art, Gift of The Print Club of Cleveland
  1929.169)

Page 296

The Swallow and Other Birds, from 'Aesop's Fable XVIII'

Etching, *c*.1666 – Francis Barlow

(Private Collection/Abbott and Holder)

Page 298

Haymaking

Oil on wood, 1565 – Pieter Bruegel the Elder

(The Lobkowicz Collections, Lobkowicz Palace, Prague Castle,
  Czech Republic)

Page 300

Landscape with Harvesters Returning Home

Pen and brown ink on paper, *c*.1595–1605 – Henry Peacham

(Berger Collection Educational Trust/Bridgeman Images)

Acknowledgements

LIKE ALL BOOKS, *A Home for All Seasons* is the result of hours of lonely work, but it is also the upshot of conversations with others. Some are recorded, particularly those that took place in Pembridge, while others need acknowledging separately, even if such a list can never be complete.

The first two people to read a draft of the book were Philipp Blom and Veronica Buckley. Ever since we met on the station platform in Bamberg, they have been great friends and sounding posts. They have never hesitated to tell me when my ideas are good – and when they are bad. Philipp and Veronica are true mentors and immediately put aside valuable time to read and comment on *A Home for All Seasons*. Subsequent improvements were almost entirely due to their insights.

I am enormously grateful to other early readers too, including my parents, a constant source of strength over the last forty years. Dad's grasp of detail nixed several slips, while Mum's memories of Bwlch-y-rhiw coloured so much of the agricultural life described within. Mum and Dad also listened to me reading draft chapters on FaceTime during lockdown.

My second clutch of readers were equally generous with their time, not least my brother Ian, who read the manuscript in twenty-four hours, as well as Hywel David and William Parry, my North London ambassadors, and Tim Pinchin. And Kirsten Hill's connection with the ending of the book was particularly powerful. Petroc Trelawny and Melinda Patton listened to early chapters on a trip to Cornwall, while Thomas Wynn, Silas Spencer, Alex Hall, Hanh Doan, Catherine Anderson, Patricia Macnaughton and John Gilhooly have been hugely supportive, as have the wider Plumley family (Claire, Ben and George) and the Tighes (Dazzle, John, Charlie, Gillan, Dom, Katherine and Rafferty). I'd also like to pay tribute to Christine Edwards, my husband's right-hand woman, who has printed manuscripts, provided reams of paper and generally been wonderful.

In Herefordshire, John Stevenson was a keen early reader and shared his knowledge of vernacular architecture. Both he and Ben Andrews, a brilliant source of information on local farming, as well as the county in general, have brought much joy to our lives since we met over a pint in The New Inn. I'm likewise grateful for the information about their wall paintings. Garfield Evans was equally giving of his time and knowledge of Pembridge.

The village and its people are, of course, vital to this book, not least Shirley Evans, Jean Heaven, James Duffield, Sarah Bevan, Nicola Jane Chase, Anita and Julian Measey, Marguerite and Catherine Fothergill, Simon Toone and Peter Parker, remembering childhood. The churchwardens, Gill Smith and Jacqui Thomas, have shared their affection for St Mary's, and offered keys to its hidden corners. My initial knowledge of the village was thanks to John Cupper – and the late John Hencher – whose love and warmth remain an inspiration. But Pembridge would be nothing without two more very dear friends: Jane and Rosie Melvin at The New Inn are the heart of the village and have, since day one, made us feel part of its timber-framed fabric.

Professionally, I must thank Duncan James for his report on the structure of the house and Robert Howard and Alison Arnold for making their ultimately abortive trip to Pembridge. In the same spirit, David Rowley has helped with geological details and Caspar Van Vark with the Dutch, while James Murphy introduced me to Michael Frayn's *Headlong* and Jerry and Carolynne Evans to Bill Bryson's *At Home*. I have also relished my chats with Nicholas Jepson-Biddle and Rob James about the Reformation and our shared admiration for Eamon Duffy's work. Tamsin Lewis was a fount of information on the literature, songs and images of the plague. Finally, I'd like to pay tribute to the team at the Herefordshire Archive and Records Centre, especially Rhys Griffith.

As the book eked its way into being, Miranda Pountney was a lifeline of wit and wisdom. Her experience of the publishing industry has been invaluable and her kindness endless. Ed Lyon was, likewise, a great strength, while his singing, not least of songs by John Dowland, provided the soundtrack for much of the writing of this book.

It is Christopher Rogers I must thank for introducing me to my fabulous agent John Ash – as well as Tom Edwards, my oldest friend, who first recommended PEW Literary. John's anarchic wit and his enthusiasm for my writing, as well as his grasp of the book from individual sentences to whole structure, prove just how lucky I was to find such a support. I'm so grateful to him and the entire PEW office.

And, of course, John found me Atlantic Books. This is a story about home, and Karen Duffy, my publisher, immediately made me feel at home with Atlantic thanks to her wholly personal response to the manuscript. She has been accommodating when I've wanted to talk things through and has always carried the project with care. It speaks of the entire team's level of attention and detail, not least from my clear, calm editor Clare Drysdale and from my copy-editor Sarah-Jane Forder, whose punctiliousness is a thing of wonder. I'd also like to thank Atlantic's managing editor Emma Heyworth-Dunn, Carmen Balit for her stunning cover design and Patty Rennie for typesetting what's tucked inside.

If this book is anything, it is a love song – to the landscape, to the people who live within it and to the gifts it gives us every harvest. *A Home for All Seasons* would, however, be nothing without Stepps House. Bricks, timbers and mortar, it has been made a home by my husband, Alastair, and our dog, Toby. The latter will, sadly, never know just how important he is, though the book is dedicated to him nonetheless. But the primary dedicatee is, of course, Alastair, the love of my life. I owe him everything: the happiness, the space and the time that – if I've got it right – are woven into this book. That's all I've wanted: to walk in such a place with you.